My Los Angeles

My Los Angeles

FROM URBAN RESTRUCTURING TO
REGIONAL URBANIZATION

Edward W. Soja

UNIVERSITY OF CALIFORNIA PRESS

BERKELEY LOS ANGELES LONDON

University of California Press, one of the most distinguished university presses in the United States, enriches lives around the world by advancing scholarship in the humanities, social sciences, and natural sciences. Its activities are supported by the UC Press Foundation and by philanthropic contributions from individuals and institutions. For more information, visit www.ucpress.edu.

University of California Press
Berkeley and Los Angeles, California

University of California Press, Ltd.
London, England

Library of Congress Cataloging-in-Publication Data

Soja, Edward W.
    My Los Angeles : from urban restructuring to regional urbanization / Edward W. Soja.
        pages   cm.
    Includes bibliographical references and index.
    ISBN 978-0-520-28172-1 (cloth : alk. paper) — ISBN 978-0-520-28174-5 (pbk. : alk. paper) — ISBN 978-0-520-95763-3 (ebook)
        1. City planning—California—Los Angeles.   2. Sociology, Urban—California—Los Angeles.   3. Regional planning—California—Los Angeles.   I. Title.
    HT168.L6S65 2014
    307.1′2160979494—dc23
                                                                2013040124

Manufactured in the United States of America

23 22 21 20 19 18 17 16 15 14
10 9 8 7 6 5 4 3 2 1

In keeping with a commitment to support environmentally responsible and sustainable printing practices, UC Press has printed this book on Natures Natural, a fiber that contains 30% post-consumer waste and meets the minimum requirements of ANSI/NISO z39.48–1992 (R 1997) (*Permanence of Paper*).

CONTENTS

ILLUSTRATIONS

MAPS

FIGURES

TABLES

ACKNOWLEDGMENTS

My first expression of thanks goes to Stefano Bloch, without whose assistance chapter 9 could not have been written. Stefano is the source for figures 8 to 12, three of which are painted by the mural artist Mear One and are included with his permission. Special thanks also to Eugene Turner and James Allen, Department of Geography, California State University–Northridge, for preparing on short notice maps 1 to 4. Photo-artist Antonis Ricos, my close friend, helped prepare figures 2 to 6 and map 12, which were published originally in *Thirdspace: Journeys to Los Angeles and Other Real-and-Imagined Places* (Blackwell Publishers, 1996). Coordinating the illustrative material, preparing it all for publication, and redrawing figure 7 entirely was Sean Combs, not the rap star but my son-in-law and father of the exceedingly delightful Addison. Thanks, Sean.

Chapters 1 to 8 draw to different degrees on my previously published work. All the major sources are identified for each chapter in appendix 1. Worth mentioning in particular are maps 5 to 11, which are reproduced from *Postmodern Geographies: The Reassertion of Space in Critical Social Theory*, published by Verso Press in 1989 and republished in their Radical Thinkers series in 2011. Sections of chapter 3 are taken directly from "Inside Exopolis: Everyday Life in the Postmodern World," chapter 8 in *Thirdspace*. I would also like to thank University of Minnesota Press for adaptations from *Seeking Spatial Justice* (2010) in chapter 8, and University of California Press for the use of map 13 from the introduction to *The City*, coauthored by Allen Scott and Edward W. Soja. Thanks must go to my coauthors: Goetz Wolff, Rebecca Morales, Allen Scott, and Juan Miguel Kanai.

I completed the first draft of this book while taking advantage of the excellent facilities of the Canadian Centre for Architecture in Montreal as a

Mellon Senior Research Fellow from July 2 to August 10, 2012. My thanks to the Mellon Foundation, and to Phyllis Lambert (Founding Director) and Mirko Zardini (Director and Chief Curator) of the CCA. Helpful from the start and throughout my stay in Montreal was Alexis Sornin, Head of the Study Centre. Thanks also to Catherine Bella, who served as my research assistant. Learning about local and regional politics in Montreal added significantly to the last three chapters.

Introduction

With its incomparable outward reach, Los Angeles vividly screens itself everywhere on earth, evoking images—and strong opinions—from practically everyone, including many who have never been there and depend on the opinions and images of others to shape their impressions. Its iconic imagery provokes exaggeration, fomenting emotionally excessive repulsion as well as unbridled attraction. Real and imagined LA seethes with such paradoxes— provocative intertwinings of utopia and dystopia, brilliant sunshine and noir decadence, opportunity and danger, optimism and despair.

Further complicating any understanding of the actual place, Los Angeles for the past century has been a fountainhead of imaginative fantasy, emitting a mesmerizing force that obscures reality by eroding the difference between the real and the imagined, fact and fiction. As one observer put it, Los Angeles has a "history of forgetting,"[1] swallowing its past and re-creating its own fantastic reality. No other city is shrouded in such an armor of deflective imagery, making it difficult to know whether what one sees is actually there, or whether there is a there there at all, to paraphrase and relocate Gertrude Stein's well-known comment on another part of California.[2]

LA's first major surge of urban development in the late nineteenth century was rooted in creative simulations of an Edenic Los Angeles, from the ersatz romanticism of the Ramona myth, which preached peaceful interracial love in an earthly paradise,[3] to the rampant real estate boosterism that slyly attracted millions of Americans to the life-saving sunshine and other boastful attractions of Iowa's Pacific seaport. What was covered up in this forgetful reimagining, among other embarrassing blemishes, was the jingoistic ardor that accompanied the ethnic cleansing of Spanish-speaking Los Angeles after the war of 1846–48. This great American land grab would, after the war, take the gold of Northern California while bleaching LA non-Hispanic white.

More global in its impact was Hollywood, America's fulsome dream machine, pouring out realistic fakes that entertained nearly everyone on earth. Virtually synonymous with Los Angeles for most of the world, Hollywood became the fountainhead for an epidemic spread of what the cultural critic Jean Baudrillard called hyperreality, confusing our ability to tell the difference between the real and the imagined, fact and fiction. Baudrillard blithely proclaims that when hyperreality, Hollywood generated or otherwise, takes hold of individual and collective behavior, "the map precedes the territory": the real material world (and with it actually existing Los Angeles) seems to melt into its never completely accurate representations, into—pardon the cliché—the reel world.

Blossoming from all these increasingly influential simulations of reality, of course, was Disneyland, established in Orange County in 1956 and mapped out by its professional "imagineers" into its representative continental zones: Tomorrowland, Adventureland, Frontierland, and Fantasyland, all entered through a shrunken version of Main Street USA, the better to fool you into thinking it is all really real. Hyperreality, however, was not confined by the boundaries of the theme park. Spreading out from Disneyland and covering adjacent Orange and Los Angeles counties was a thick blanket of deception that has made it increasingly difficult for everyone involved to tell the difference between what is real and what is purely (or impurely) imagined. The diffusion of this interstitial hyperreality, in between fact and fiction, produced what I describe in chapter 3 as a "scamscape," a constructed geography filled with trickery, misrepresentation, and often innovative forms of fraud, perpetrated, like the savings and loan fiasco of the early 1990s, by people who genuinely believed that what they were doing was not only acceptable but virtuous.

The scamscape and its fantastic extrusions did not stay localized in Southern California, but spread outward and upward in scale through many channels. Politically biased television news broadcasts have emerged promoting national movements of genuine believers, aided by an army of cynical spin doctors sneering at the assumed irrelevance of the "reality-based community." Extending the scamscape even further have been such fabulously successful new media as the computer games of SimCity and its many offshoots, absorbing vast audiences into the simulated wonders of a Second Reality (which is the name of one of the most successful computer games of all time).

No other place has played such a formative and generative role in the diffusion of deceptive hyperreality. But at the same time, the real Los Angeles is even more generatively fantastic. In broadcasting itself nearly everywhere, Los Angeles has become the target of incomparable extremes of attraction and repulsion. Its magnetic force is illustrated by the fact that, over the past hundred years or so, more people (nearly seventeen million and growing) have moved into the urban region of LA than into any other urban region in the United States and probably anywhere else in the Western industrialized world. The global scope of diasporic attraction has been so great that Los Angeles and New York City are today the most ethnically and culturally diverse cities that have ever existed, with schoolchildren speaking over two hundred different languages.

At the same time, and partly perhaps for some of the same reasons, there is no other place that provokes such sneering fear and loathing as does imagined Los Angeles. Matching its magnetism is a dreadful trepidation among perhaps the majority of city dwellers around the world that their city will become "like Los Angeles," that following its prevailing trends will lead to imminent doom and apocalyptic Blade Runner scenarios. When the film *Independence Day* depicted the destruction of New York City, the audience remained quiet and serious. When Los Angeles was blown up, many audiences began cheering in avid appreciation. What a peculiar bundle of emotional extremes are attached to our images of LA: love and hate, attraction and repulsion, uniqueness and ubiquity, brightness and noir. There is nothing like it, yet it is not outrageous to say that everywhere is becoming increasingly like LA.

Becoming "like" LA is more complicated than it seems, however, because the urban reality is always in motion, constantly changing, never slowing down long enough for even the most astute observers to capture it with confidence. How could it be, for example, that what so many described as the most destructively sprawling and wastefully low-density American metropolis is today the densest urbanized area in the country? How can an area once renowned for its antilabor, probusiness environment become the leading edge of the American labor movement? Does it all come together in Los Angeles, or does it all fly apart in disintegrative fragments?

Which of these extremely contrasting LAs will be featured in the following chapters? A quick answer is "both and more," a place where extremes come together in a recombinant whirl. Even when looked at more formally, "Los Angeles" has many different meanings, each distinctive in scale, scope, and point of view. Something similar occurs for other city names, such as *New York,* which can be attached to a city, a state, a multistate region, and the official name of the county/borough of Manhattan. There is no confusion, however, when *New York City* is used. It refers to the five boroughs. Los Angeles as a "city" is more ambiguous, making it necessary to clarify the multiple possibilities that arise when using the name.

DEFINING LOS ANGELES

Substituting the local for a broader view, some use *Los Angeles* to refer specifically to the Central City, the only place deserving to be called "downtown LA." Here the whole of LA is condensed into and represented by its core agglomeration.

The iconic Central City, pivoting around the still striking image of City Hall is truly a central place, the heart of an urbanized area that stretches for sixty miles (one hundred kilometers) in nearly all directions (see map 1). Centrality and agglomeration, two of the defining characteristics of all cities, have always been attached to the Central City, ever since El Pueblo de Nuestra Señora la Reina de los Ángeles de Porciúncula was first established here more than two centuries ago by Spanish missionaries seeking a place for a substantial settlement. Once the site of a native settlement of the Tongva tribe, the Central City has continued to be the primary economic, political, and cultural hub of Los Angeles since 1781. Here today can be found the largest concentration of offices and jobs in Southern California, the largest node of government employment and authority outside Washington, D.C., and one of the world's largest entertainment complexes, serving lovers of opera and classical music as well as fans of basketball and hockey.

The Central City also stands out for its relatively small protuberant island of skyscrapers in a vast low-rise sea of ordinary landscapes. Nevertheless, the skyline, still puny compared to Manhattan or Chicago, now has become a primary postcard symbol for contemporary Los Angeles, as emblematic in popular imagery as the Hollywood sign, even when blanketed in thick green fog.

Despite this fulsome centrality and agglomeration, LA Central City has also been the reference point for a long-standing urban inferiority complex having to do with its size, activity level, and skyline. Now almost entirely

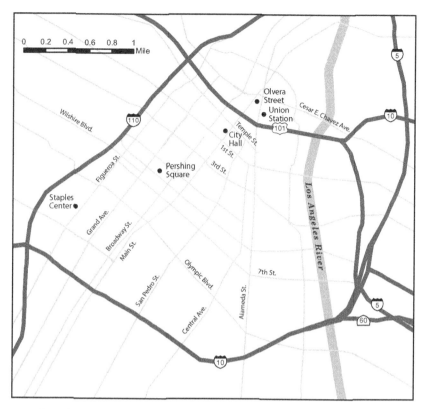

MAP 1 Central City/downtown LA. Cartography by Eugene Turner, Department of Geography, California State University, Northridge.

forgotten, the Central City contained one of the most bustling (and grid-locked) downtowns in the country in the 1920s, when it was the hub of one of the largest public transit networks in any city. Begun earlier but accelerating in the postwar period, however, massive auto-driven suburbanization made LA a representative model of the "new American city," a spread-out metropolitan form consisting of a relatively compacted inner city often filled with large minority populations surrounded by sprawling, low-density, pre-dominantly middle-class and consumerist suburbia.

All downtowns suffered some degree of degradation due to mass suburban growth, LA Central City included. The large government sector stayed put, but most banks, corporate headquarters, department stores, and other "central" activities departed for greener pastures. Ever since the Watts Riots of 1965 and the first round of "urban renewal" in Bunker Hill, dreaming

MAP 2 City of Los Angeles. Cartography by Eugene Turner, Department of Geography, California State University, Northridge.

planners, civic-minded entrepreneurs, and optimistic corporate leaders have periodically proclaimed the imminent emergence of a bustling Manhattan-like, 24/7 downtown core. Some expansion has occurred in nearly all these hopeful cycles, but the decentralized, multinucleated geography of the urban region probably makes it impossible for downtown LA to ever become like Manhattan or the dense downtowns of the larger eastern or European cities.

Nevertheless, the evolving Central City of LA provides an especially revealing window through which to see and understand the urban restructuring process that would dominate urban development in nearly all North American cities in the last half of the twentieth century. Urban restructuring, in one way or another, thematically filters through all the chapters of *My Los Angeles.* To appreciate the scale and scope of this urban restructuring process, however, requires going beyond the space of the Central City, first to the oddly shaped City of Los Angeles (see map 2).

Nearly four million people fill the City of Los Angeles (note the capital *C*, required when referring to the administrative city). In the first half of the twentieth century, the City of Los Angeles grew largely by annexation, absorbing the sprawling suburbs of the San Fernando Valley as well as the established municipality of Hollywood, based largely on control over water supplies. A thin arm of the City, still called the "shoestring," reached southward to San Pedro and the LA half of the enormous Port of Los Angeles–Long Beach, while a western extension touched the Pacific in Venice. Santa Monica resisted annexation, as did Beverly Hills, Culver City, West Hollywood, and up north, San Fernando, each becoming an island enclave surrounded by the City.

Annexation virtually stopped in the second half of the last century, as the metropolitan form, with its constellation of suburbs, took shape, accelerating rapidly after the Second World War. Given its rapid growth and large population, the relative smallness of the urban core made it appear that Los Angeles, usually meaning the City of LA, was merely a congeries of suburbs or, as Dorothy Parker called it, "seventy-two suburbs in search of a city."

Although the terms *City Hall, City Council,* and *Mayor* may refer specifically to the City of Los Angeles, they are often used to refer to a larger urban region, containing dozens of other city halls, city councils, and mayors. The administrative city used to be the unit most widely used to measure city size. Applying this old-fashioned measure, administratively-defined Los Angeles becomes the nation's second largest city, ahead of the City of Chicago but behind the five boroughs that make up New York City. If the boroughs of administrative New York were considered as separate cities, however, Los Angeles would become the largest city in the United States.

Mass suburbanization and, more recently, the increasing urbanization of suburbia make it exceedingly difficult to distinguish what is urban and what is suburban in Los Angeles. The administrative City of Los Angeles, for example, is conventionally classified as "urban" in national comparisons of metropolitan areas, even though much of it consists of classical (if rapidly changing) suburbia. To outsiders, even the Black ghetto of iconic "South Central" and Watts looks almost suburban compared to similar areas "back east." In a bizarre reflection of the ambiguity of the name *Los Angeles,*

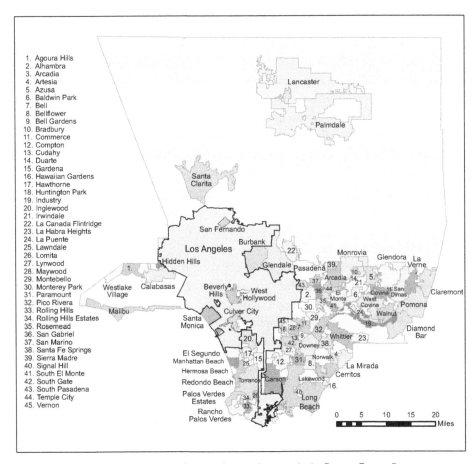

1. Agoura Hills
2. Alhambra
3. Arcadia
4. Artesia
5. Azusa
6. Baldwin Park
7. Bell
8. Bellflower
9. Bell Gardens
10. Bradbury
11. Commerce
12. Compton
13. Cudahy
14. Duarte
15. Gardena
16. Hawaiian Gardens
17. Hawthorne
18. Huntington Park
19. Industry
20. Inglewood
21. Irwindale
22. La Canada Flintridge
23. La Habra Heights
24. La Puente
25. Lawndale
26. Lomita
27. Lynwood
28. Maywood
29. Montebello
30. Monterey Park
31. Paramount
32. Pico Rivera
33. Rolling Hills
34. Rolling Hills Estates
35. Rosemead
36. San Gabriel
37. San Marino
38. Santa Fe Springs
39. Sierra Madre
40. Signal Hill
41. South El Monte
42. South Gate
43. South Pasadena
44. Temple City
45. Vernon

MAP 3 Incorporated places in Los Angeles County. Cartography by Eugene Turner, Department of Geography, California State University, Northridge.

while the suburbs of the San Fernando Valley are part of the City, "suburban" LA often includes Long Beach, with nearly half a million inhabitants and its own downtown, city hall, and police force, as well as literally dozens of other municipalities with populations greater than a hundred thousand.

The City of LA is thus limited as a definition of Los Angeles as a whole, even though it is frequently used as such, in the media and in popular discourse. If looking only at the City of LA is problematic, then what do I mean when I refer to "my Los Angeles"? At the very least, there is the County of Los Angeles (see map 3).

The County of Los Angeles is reputed to be the largest local government unit in the Western world, with a total population of around ten million (9,818,605 in 2010). A regional view of Los Angeles begins here, and this regional perspective will prevail in subsequent chapters. For many decades, the county defined Greater Los Angeles and what the U.S. Census called the Los Angeles–Long Beach Standard Metropolitan Statistical Area (SMSA). Some say regional planning in America began in LA County, with its long-established but not very powerful Regional Planning Commission.[4]

The Los Angeles region, however, only begins with the county. What is now called the Los Angeles–Long Beach–Santa Ana Metropolitan Statistical Area (MSA) has replaced the SMSA, reflecting the degree to which the vast LA "basin" that you see when flying into Los Angeles International Airport (LAX) spreads continuously over two counties, Los Angeles and Orange. The old SMSA category required naming all the larger cities included. As this became ridiculously cumbersome in the LA region, with so many cities surpassing 150,000, the new MSA simply added Santa Ana, the county seat of Orange, to officially combine the two counties into a new "Greater LA" of 12,944,801 inhabitants. For comparative purposes, according to the 2010 census, the New York City MSA has a population of 19,015,900, while Chicago, the old second city, has 9,504,753, followed by the MSAs of Dallas, Houston, Philadelphia, and Washington, D.C.

Some in Orange County protested this absorption of the county into a Greater Los Angeles region, fearing that the distinctiveness of the county would be lost. They argue that Orange County deserves to be an MSA of its own, with a population of around three million, ranking it among the twenty largest MSAs in the country. It was certainly no longer a suburb of Los Angeles, and its population density and cities such as Irvine, the largest planned New Town in the United States and a place where there are probably more jobs than bedrooms, indicate that it is now more urban than suburban.

There are times when my Los Angeles includes Orange County, while at other times OC is treated separately. The expansion of Greater Los Angeles into Orange County is indicative, however, of a broader trend that can be found in many metropolitan regions everywhere in the world. The modern metropolis seems to be breaking out of its old boundaries and becoming larger and larger, one of the defining features of what I describe as *regional urbanization*. The "metropolis unbound," as some have called it, has led to the creation of still another regional definition of the expansive city as a

Fresno County

Inyo County

Tulare County

Kern County

- Los Angeles City
- Associated counties
- Major freeways

Ventura County

Los Angeles County

City of Los Angeles

San Bernardino County

Orange County

Riverside County

San Diego County

Imperial County

0 25 50 75 100 Miles

MAP 4 Los Angeles city region. Cartography by Eugene Turner, Department of Geography, California State University, Northridge.

polynucleated, networked, and globalized *city region* or, less often used until now, *regional city.*[5]

Recognizing the increasing regional scale of the city, the Office of Management and Budget (OMB) now defines Combined Statistical Areas (CSAs), dropping the term *metropolitan* entirely, while the U.S. Census focuses increasing attention on what it defines as the "Urbanized Area," roughly coincident with the CSA. For Los Angeles, the CSA adds the Riverside–San Bernardino MSA and Ventura County to form the five-county *city region of Los Angeles* (see map 4), with a population of 18,081,514 in 2011, compared to 22,214,083 for the twenty-three counties of the New York City CSA, and 9,729,825 for the Chicago-Naperville-Michigan City CSA. The three largest city regions are followed in order by the CSAs for Washington, D.C., Boston, and San Jose (now larger than San Francisco and Oakland).

The city region of LA, still focused around the old downtown, is a vast network of cities, at least forty of which have a population greater than one hundred thousand. The latest count of municipalities in the five-county area is close to 190. Every decade sees the still growing City of Los Angeles's proportion of the total regional population shrink. Similarly, the Central City employment cluster remains the largest, but its domination has decreased relative to others. Densities are increasing almost everywhere, with immigrant areas around the Central City reaching density levels comparable with Manhattan, while large swathes of suburbia are becoming more urban. Rather than spreading ever outward, eating up vast tracts of desert or agricultural land, the old metropolitan area for the most part is being in-filled, an essential part of the regional urbanization process that has been going on for the past thirty years.[6]

The city region or regional city has replaced *Greater* and *Metropolitan* in international comparisons of city size, such as the listing produced each year by the United Nations' Office of the Habitat. Los Angeles stands out on these lists as the only fast-growing city region in the industrialized world outside of Japan. In the national listing of urbanized areas and their population density, Los Angeles stands out even more dramatically, surpassing New York City in 1990 as the *densest urbanized area* in the United States, just one of a long list of startling developments in Los Angeles arising from its forty years of urban restructuring.[7]

"MY" LOS ANGELES

A few words are needed to explain this "possessive" title. I have been writing about Los Angeles for more than thirty years, following an early career focused mainly on the geography of economic development in East Africa. I have never published a book specifically on Los Angeles but have used it mainly as an illustrative case for more general and theoretical arguments.[8] In doing so, I have become fairly widely known in a broadly defined field of urban studies for my "readings" of Los Angeles. Here I try to put these readings together into a coherent whole, while rethinking, updating, and explaining their changing emphasis and point of view. I do not reject other interpretations or alternative viewpoints but focus attention on my own extensive writings on Los Angeles (see appendix 1 for the separate bibliographic listing of my published work on LA).

All my past academic writings have been deeply immersed in advocating an assertive spatial perspective, and the same will be true in *My Los Angeles*. Thinking seriously about space and place is still not comfortable or familiar to most readers, academic or otherwise, even with the so-called spatial turn that has spread some degree of spatial thinking to practically every discipline and subject area over the past ten or fifteen years.[9] Despite the personal theoretical odyssey that is embedded in these pages, however, I try as far as I can to let Los Angeles itself take center stage, on its own, in all its engaging specificity.

I have always thought of myself as more of a regionalist than an urbanist, and my interpretations of Los Angeles reflect this assertive regional perspective. This regionalism has several implications. First, it indicates a "big picture" emphasis. You will be disappointed if you expect a series of stories of individuals or intimate street scenes illustrating larger biographical themes and memories. My regional perspective is intentionally *macro*-geographical, concerned more with the urban region as a whole than with microscopic inspection and empirical detail. I understand the attractions of the so-called view from below, but presenting a large number of such localized viewpoints, especially from the vast metro-sea of Los Angeles, is difficult to comprehend without an overarching conceptual framework—a view from above, so to speak.

Although I may occasionally look at specific areas in greater detail, the major objective is to understand the regional dynamic of urban development in a general way, one that allows if not encourages comparisons with other city regions of the world. Local particularities and uniqueness are interesting only to the extent that they inform a wider general understanding of the movement from urban restructuring to regional urbanization. The same holds for historical detail and analysis. I delve into the history of Los Angeles only when this can shed light onto what has been happening since 1965, not just in LA but elsewhere as well. Stated somewhat differently, I am more interested in learning *from* Los Angeles than *about* Los Angeles.

Second, the regional emphasis creates a special disciplinary connection to the fields of geography and urban-regional planning. I list myself on IRS tax forms as a geographer-planner, and this geographically oriented approach to planning and urban studies features prominently in every chapter of *My Los Angeles,* both in shaping my viewpoint and in my references to the wider literature. This regional-geographical-spatial emphasis is not meant to exclude sociology, anthropology, political science, or any other way of studying the city and urban issues, but emphasis is given to scholarship and scholars that demonstrate a strong spatial perspective.

Guiding my career as a geographer-planner has been a firm belief that whatever your interests may be, they can be advanced and enhanced by adopting a "consequential" spatial perspective, one that sees the spatial organization of society (or the city) as not just an outcome of social processes but also an explanatory or "causal" force in itself, affecting these social processes in significant ways. In this sense, I see space as much more than physical form and look at human geographies as socialized spaces, the product of a mutually formative socio-spatial interaction or "dialectic."[10]

There are many aspects of Los Angeles I do not attempt to cover. For example, although some commentary on national and to a lesser extent global politics and geopolitics runs through the text, I do not discuss local urban politics to any great extent. Nor do I deal in any detail with environmental issues, not because they are unimportant but because I cannot find an effective way to link environmental debates to the crisis-generated restructuring of Los Angeles over the past forty years, except at a most superficial level.[11] The debates calling for sustainable or "smart" urban development, cogent though they may be, do not fit well into the story being told here about urban restructuring since the 1960s.

Some may still be disappointed with what is included in or excluded from my regional interpretations of Los Angeles, but I must emphasize that this is a personal view, a rethinking and reinterpretation of what I have written about LA over the past thirty years. And yes, what follows is not just about Los Angeles but also about my particular and evolving interpretations of its development over time and space, making this somewhat of an intellectual autobiography, at least since my arrival in Los Angeles in 1972.

Whether it is surprising or not I cannot tell, but it is at least a little bit ironic that Los Angeles—virtually neglected in academic urban literature and simplistically stereotyped in popular discourse up to the 1970s—became in the ensuing decades the focal point for the development of new and widely recognized urban theories, abundant empirical studies of urbanism as a way of life, and some of the most innovative urban-based social movements found anywhere in the world. This has given birth, internally in part but just as much due to external attribution, to the idea of a Los Angeles "school" of urban studies. And here too, in this act of academic identification, there are controversial and contradictory extremes of opinion. Aggressive school boosters and blasters abound, reminding one of the old saying that academic politics are so vicious because so little is at stake.

Enjoyable as it may be to read about these academic squabbles, they will not feature prominently in *My Los Angeles*, not because I don't take sides on the key issues but because I want observing and understanding Los Angeles to be my primary focus. In any case, it does not matter whether or not there is an LA School. What does matter, however, is the recognition that an unusually large and influential literature on Los Angeles has emerged over the past thirty years, changing the image of Los Angeles from bizarre exception to one of the most evocative, representative, and trendsetting urban regions in the world.

INSPIRATIONS

Shaping what follows to some degree are three books on Los Angeles that stand out among the best and most popular books ever written about a city. Each combats the distorted imagery so adhesively attached to Los Angeles and uses LA to rekindle our urban imagination about major issues affecting the contemporary world.

The earliest of these eye-opening revisionings of Los Angeles and the larger regional scene was *Southern California Country: An Island on the Land,* written by the journalist, radical lawyer, and progressive activist Carey McWilliams and published in 1946. McWilliams keyed in on the city's insular uniqueness and daunting dynamism, while reflecting on its persistent ethnic tensions and complex cultural identity. Clashing with the establishment's views of tawdry or bizarre Los Angeles, McWilliams saw in Southern California a "league of cities" coming together under "the hegemony of Los Angeles," which he predicted would become "the most fantastic city in the world."

McWilliams never wrote directly about the fantastic city (or was it the city of fantasy?) he was expecting. Soon after the publication of *An Island on the Land,* he moved east to become the very progressive editor of *Nation* magazine for twenty years, achieving particular recognition for breaking the news of the Bay of Pigs invasion of Cuba. What he did, however, was to define a role several other journalist-scholars would occupy in subsequent years: educating the ignorant or oblivious elite of the Eastern Seaboard about the positive qualities of Los Angeles and California in general. LA boosters were penny-a-dozen during the twentieth century but, along with Hollywood's dream machine, they concocted a frivolous and overly romanticized vision of Los Angeles for the world to see. McWilliams was a hard-nosed critical thinker whose writings on such topics as the exploitation of immigrant farmworkers and the injustices of Japanese wartime internment created a more balanced and informed model that would be followed by many other, often more academic, critical thinkers.

As McWilliams's efforts faded, along came another iconoclastic critic enamored with Los Angeles and eager to tell the world about this fascinating and fantastic city. Reyner Banham's *Architecture of the Four Ecologies,* published in 1971, gave us all new insight into the lifestyle geography of Los Angeles. Already well known as an architectural critic in his native England, Banham showed his love for LA in his four ecologies as well as in a rapturous video tour of Los Angeles for the BBC and articles in *New Society* and other journals on such topics as "spontaneity and space" and "the city as scrambled eggs." His delightful wild ride in an exquisitely alfresco convertible made LA more visible and alive, as he dared us to imagine surfing and skiing on the same day, with cocktailed elegance in between.

The boring vastness of what he called the Plains of Id contained most of the people, dwelling, like urban and suburban populations everywhere, in ticky-tacky houses on even less-than-ordinary streets. These normalized landscapes of Californian suburbia were, in his earlier work, idyllized by Banham who, along with the geographer-planner Peter Hall and Paul Barker, editor of *New Society,* concocted in the 1960s what became known in Britain as the "Non-Plan," a kind of celebration of spontaneity trumpeting the "freedoms of suburbia" and the wastefulness of any form of planning that snubbed its nose at suburban life. In the Plains of Id, the psyche of suburbia reached its absorptive climax, and Banham demanded something more than its abject dismissal.[12]

Looking haughtily over the Plains of Id were the privatized Foothills for the rich, nestled into aeries in the Hollywood Hills and signaling what would later become a flood of gated and guarded housing communities. Banham got most of his kicks, however, in two other entertaining ecologies: the fabulously accessible and nearly endless beaches of Surfurbia and, most passionately, the almost erotic excess presented by the freeways of Autopia, which tied it all together. If there was irony or sarcasm in Banham's portrayal of LA, it was joyfully hidden.

Carrying forward the architectural sensitivity of Banham but much more forcefully building on the radical politics and public intellectualism of

McWilliams was *City of Quartz* (1990), written by the meatpacking, truck–driving political journalist and urban scholar, Mike Davis. Davis's apocalyptic blockbuster, as hard-nosed as quartz crystal, tweaked everyone's liberal guilt by presenting LA through the panoptic eyes of a deranged seer in a hovering helicopter. Here the landscape made visible was filled with ecologies of fear and surveillance, or what he aptly described as security-obsessed urbanism. Although he was praised as an urban theoretician, pugnacious Davis actually tried to distance himself from the poststructuralist and postmodern debates swirling around in Los Angeles and the wider realms of urban studies. Unlike McWilliams and Banham, Davis was born and raised in Southern California, and his nativism, rather than any fancy theory, became the foundation for his uncompromising assertiveness.

City of Quartz, in brilliantly crafted prose, introduced the world almost exclusively to the dark (yet always fascinating) side of Los Angeles. Davis prepared himself for this epochal journey as a member of the editorial staff at the *New Left Review* in London and a visitor to the Urban Planning Department at UCLA, where he learned to temper his New Left historicism with some creative geographical thinking. It is almost impossible to know for sure, but my guess is that *City of Quartz* has outsold every other book written specifically about a city, making this geographical history of Los Angeles a standard reference in all branches of urban studies.

Each of these books in its own way exploded the persistently biased (yet not entirely inaccurate) imagery that shrouded Los Angeles from any sensible understanding and opened new ways of looking at and learning from the LA experience. Tying them all together is a heightened geographical imagination, a growing engagement with space and place and the politics that derives from the spatial organization of urban life. In *My Los Angeles,* I push these geographical inspirations and aspirations still further, as I look back on more than thirty years of writing on this always surprising and dynamic metropolis.

EXPECTATIONS

So what can the reader expect in the upcoming chapters? Everything begins in the turbulent aftermath of the Watts Riots of 1965, at a time when LA and the rest of the country were experiencing a devastating deindustrialization. Massive job losses and factory closures were occurring in Los Angeles, but unlike most of the rest of the country, there was also rapid job growth and what would later be called "reindustrialization," the initial stages in the formation of a more flexible, global, and information-based New Economy. Trying to make sense of this combination of growth and decline, deindustrialization and reindustrialization, was the starting point for an extraordinary expansion of academic writing on Los Angeles and on what came to be called crisis-generated urban restructuring.

The first step in writing about urban restructuring was to challenge the theoretical and policy-oriented domination of East Coast urban scholars, who at the time were turning to postindustrialism to explain what was happening to cities and the U.S. economy as a whole. Certain that what we were seeing in Los Angeles was not postindustrial, we focused mainly on industrial restructuring, arguing that the industrial era was not ending but starting a new phase.[13]

It all comes together in Los Angeles, we excitedly proclaimed, referring specifically to the highly varied outcomes of crisis-generated urban restructuring.[14] One could find in LA many of the same conditions found in Frostbelt Detroit and Cleveland as well as Sunbelt Houston, Phoenix, and San Jose. There were also representations of what was happening in Singapore and São Paulo, as well as the rising importance of the Pacific Rim. No other urban region in the industrial world was experiencing such an intensive (and seemingly paradoxical) combination of both extensive industrial decline and rapid industrial growth. Nowhere else was there a clearer exemplification of the emerging post-Fordist, flexible, and globalized New Economy.

Chapter 1 oozes with the confidence and excitement of early discovery. Reflecting the growing influence of Marxist political economy in urban studies at the time, the focus was on crisis formation and the political economy of urban restructuring. Added to this is a more contemporary reinterpretation of urban restructuring as a prolonged search for a "spatial fix"—a reorganization of the urban geography to better meet the needs of the New Economy. There was a conviction that this new Marxian framework of interpretation could explain practically everything that was happening in cities everywhere.

Chapter 2 is decidedly more skeptical and questioning, evoking an effort to break open new ground and alternative ways of understanding Los Angeles and urban change more generally. Rather than looking at how it all comes together in LA, it speaks of taking LA apart, of a process of deconstruction and reconstitution, breaking down and building up again, interpreting Los

Angeles in new and different ways. Experimental in tone and language, the aim was to create a new perspective on the changing worlds of Los Angeles by expanding critical geographical analysis beyond Marxian political economy to a broad-based postmodern critical perspective.

Chapter 2 uncovers and explores a truly "greater" Los Angeles, a big-picture view defined by a sixty-mile circle (one hundred kilometers) drawn from a central point in downtown. As it was for urban restructuring, LA continued to be exemplary and representative not just of postmodern urbanism but of a new kind of emerging modern metropolis. Within these circular limits, a new geography had taken shape by the early 1980s. Stretching out to include the built-up areas of five counties and punctuated by nearly 190 municipalities, this new geography was regionally organized in four outer city complexes (Orange County, the Inland Empire, the Greater San Fernando Valley, and LAX-centered Aerospace Alley) surrounding a bulging new inner city, emptied of more than a million poor white and Black residents and refilled with at least five million migrants from practically every nation on earth.

Especially in its peripheral (outer city) urbanization, Los Angeles became a model for new trends in urban development everywhere. All cities that were experiencing growth, it was claimed, were growing like LA, no longer sprouting centrifugally from a dominant central city or "old downtown" but concentrating in new nodes or "edge cities" scattered across the suburban fringes. Some local observers saw this as a peculiar and transcendent reversal wherein the periphery now was determining the center after centuries of the relationship being the other way around.

But the inner city was also experiencing a radical transformation, a new centrality reflecting the growth of one of the largest and densest agglomerations of immigrant "working poor" (another LA-based term) to be found anywhere. Here again there was a paradoxical pairing of opposites, adding to the interplay of deindustrialization and reindustrialization a geography marked by both decentralization and recentralization of population and economic activities in the restructured inner and outer cities.

The guide for this exploration of Greater Los Angeles was not Karl Marx, who inspired the first round of studies, but rather the great Argentinian storyteller Jorge Luis Borges, whose depiction of the "Aleph" as the "space that contains all other spaces" is the leitmotif for a revisioning of what is contained within the sixty-mile circle. A first and extended look focused on the circumference and led to an astounding discovery: Greater Los Angeles at that time (the late 1980s) was surrounded by an almost evenly spaced series of military installations and a level of armed surveillance that raised the question of what was being protected behind these formidable defenses.

The tempting answer was what could be described as the crown jewels of contemporary capitalism: America's largest arsenal of advanced weaponry built up through a series of Pacific wars, almost surely the largest investment of federal monies not only from the Department of Defense but also mortgage subsidies funding the mass suburbanization of Los Angeles, a globalized urban core containing the largest and most diverse immigrant labor pool found anywhere, the largest industrial metropolis in the United States and certainly one of the fastest-growing industrial growth poles of the twentieth century, and the most influential and diverting site of imaginative fantasies, including what is still described as the happiest place on earth.

Chapter 2 ends with a new look at the debates that have developed around the iconic site and interior spaces of the Bonaventure Hotel, a postmodern microcosm of the larger whole. Noted in the discussion of the Bonaventure is the first of a series of illustrative videos that illuminate the text in this and subsequent chapters, creating a visual story line accompanying *My Los Angeles.* These videos are listed in appendix 2.

Chapter 3 continues the fantastic journeys into the real-and-imagined Los Angeles with a detailed look at the largest and arguably the oldest and most representative outer city complex of them all: Orange County. Rather than Borges, the tour guides here are Jean Baudrillard and Umberto Eco, brilliant observers of postmodern America and experienced travelers to Orange County, described by Baudrillard as the "primitive society of the future" and filled with what Eco called "real fakes" and "cathedrals of iconic reassurance." The OC "exopolis," as I called it, was both an "outer" or exo-city and an ex-city, unlike any traditional city of the past. The exopolis is pinned down in a series of representative "scenes," each building toward the spectacular fraud of the Orange County bankruptcy, when the so-called scamscape erupted in a truly postmodern fiscal crisis of enormous proportions. The trigger was the gambling away of the county's tax receipts on reverse repos, hedge funds, and other expressions of "fictional" capital in the hyperreal stock market, led by a tax collector convinced he was doing the right thing.

Each of the scenes and scenarios in chapter 3 depicts a different aspect of SIM-Orange County, from the tightly specialized Leisure Worlds of the elderly to the hyperplanned peculiarities of Irvine, the largest planned New Town in the United States; from the architectural Disneyland of the University of California-Irvine to the San Onofre Nuclear Generating

Station (SONGS), where imminent dangers are covered up with soothing propaganda and simulated safety symbols, effectively illustrating the meaning of simulation, pretending to have what you do not actually have—versus dissimulation or lying, pretending not to have what you actually have. The illustrative value of SONGS persists even after its closure in 2013.

The chapter revolves around extracts from newspaper cuttings rather than more formal academic references. As such, it attempts to capture the immediacies and idiosyncrasies of the moment. Readers are actively encouraged to laugh out loud at these characterizations, but there is a more ominous edge as well: the likelihood that, if nothing is done about it, whatever is found in this primitive community of tomorrow will be reaching your neighborhood in the not so distant future. And furthermore, you might like it!

Exploring Los Angeles directly shifts in chapter 4 to learning through comparisons. First comes an extensive remembrance of a visit to Amsterdam that led to a comparison between the Centrum—perhaps the largest, most lively, and best-preserved sixteenth-century urban core in Europe—and the Central City area of Los Angeles, where most of the population, some say, is made up of homeless along Skid Row. There may be no greater contrast between two city centers anywhere in the world. After some microspatial flânerie through the streets of Amsterdam and the discovery of an almost secretive world keeping alive the utopian-cum-anarchist democratic spirit of the 1960s, the comparison moves on to a larger regional scale where the Netherlands and Los Angeles become much more comparable through shared processes of urban restructuring and postmodern urbanization.

Our exploration of Amsterdam is followed by an edgier comparative study of Los Angeles and the city where I was born and grew up, New York. Here my Angeleno leanings came into conflict with the postindustrial and "dual city" approaches being applied to New York City by a research group that sponsored my visit and participation. Everything, it seemed to me, came together not just in Manhattan (the far-reaching core to my peripheral Bronx upbringing), but even more so on Wall Street (the secretive world I never visited but always knew was there). I called the exaggerated focus "Manhattanitis" and playfully alluded to the "Vanity of the BonFIREs," to refer to the scholarly obsessions with the finance, insurance, and real estate super-cluster near Manhattan's southern tip. This preoccupation with the umbilical center blinds so many of those studying New York to what is happening, or not happening, in the vast suburban fringes of the metropolitan region, so much more sprawling than the urbanizing periphery of Greater

Los Angeles that New York would lose the position it held for most of the twentieth century as the densest urbanized area in the United States to its West Coast competitor.

Sprawl itself is the subject of another comparative study. Using various measures of urban density, the preferred measure of sprawl, Los Angeles stands out paradoxically as the least sprawling, most "compact" large metropolitan region in the country. Sprawl clearly isn't what it used to be if low density is seen as its primary feature. Recent studies have also shown that density-based measures of sprawl show little or no correlation with social inequality, environmental degradation, or curtailed economic growth. By implication, such related ideas as sustainability and planning for "smart" cities need to be rethought in light of these new urban trends. The chapter of comparisons ends with a series of observations on putative Chicago, Los Angeles, and New York "schools" of urban studies.

Chapter 5 revisions Los Angeles again, from urban restructuring and postmodern urbanization to the postmetropolitan transition, seen as an ongoing transformation of the modern metropolis that is happening in varying degrees to all the world's major cities. I argue that the vast and growing literature on this urban transition can be organized around six distinct but interconnected discourses, collections of writings that highlight various aspects of the ongoing deconstruction and reconstitution of the modern metropolis. I purposefully start with a discussion of industrial restructuring, the formation of a new capitalist economy, and the shift from Fordism to post-Fordism, as the most important force behind the postmetropolitan transition. This is followed by what most would consider the most important influence on the changing urban economy, the globalization of capital, labor, and culture.

Both the urban-industrial and globalization discourses are seen as sustained and facilitated (but not caused) by a revolution in information and communication technology. Both also involve a growing regionalist perspective that views cohesive regional economies as generative forces behind globalization and the new phase of flexible and post-Fordist industrial capitalism.

The chapter continues with a look at the interrelated spatial and social impacts of economic restructuring and globalization, with special attention given to increasing income gaps and pronounced social, economic, and political polarization. I focus here on the multisided debates on the origins and implications of economic inequality and polarization, and I present two case studies illustrating the peculiar new spaces arising from urban restructuring and postmodern urbanization.

The final two discourses look at the hard and soft imposition of social control, the former marked by a fortressing of the city and the spread of what Mike Davis called security-obsessed urbanism, the latter by the diverting psychological and ideological effects of simulated scamscapes, wherein actual urban life is played out as if it were a computer game. Both divert attention away from fundamental political issues and activism, helping to explain why the volatile postmetropolis, with all its inequalities and injustices, does not explode more often.

Chapter 6 diverges from a direct focus on Los Angeles. Giving some depth to the critical spatial perspective in *My Los Angeles* is a discussion of the trilogy of books I have written on space and social theory. This brief theoretical excursion is followed by an extended discussion of urban trends arising from the six intertwined discourses discussed in the previous chapter. These trends are not linked to the unique indicative qualities of Los Angeles, but instead represent general directions likely to be taken across all the world's major urban regions in the twenty-first century. This discussion, in addition to moderating an excessive LA-centrism, provides a useful framework for conducting comparative analyses of the evolving transformations of the modern metropolis in both the developed and developing worlds.

In chapter 7, on regional urbanization, still another revisioning takes us to a clearer and more confident discussion of the specific outcome of the postmetropolitan transition. It also provides a better framework for understanding what has been happening in the Los Angeles urban region over the past twenty years. In essence, what is suggested here is that Los Angeles and other major city regions, at least in the more advanced industrialized countries, are experiencing what is almost like a species change, an enveloping paradigm shift from the familiar metropolitan model of urbanization, often thought to be an end stage in itself, to a new regional urbanization process, one in which the entire metropolitan area is being filled in as the once dominant and sprawling suburbanization process recedes in importance. Even where suburbanization has not been extensive, as in the postcolonial cities of the developing world, peripheral urbanization and changing centralities are creating polycentric and networked city regions or regional cities of enormous size and complexity.

Evidence of this epochal shift from metropolitan to regional urbanization has been accumulating for many years, but almost always the new developments (edge cities, outer cities, boomburbs, metroburbia, suburban cities, in-between cities, urban-suburban hybrids) are seen as changes in the same old metropolitan model, with its monocentric dualism between urban and suburban worlds. What we see in an advanced form in LA and developing rapidly in other major city regions can be described as the urbanization of suburbia, eroding the classical and still persistent popular and academic/theoretical division between urban and suburban ways of life and blending them in new ways.

The differentiation of once homogeneous suburbia into many different typologies, along with the complex changes taking place in urban centrality, can no longer fit into traditional metropolitan models and mentalities. Regional urbanization demands not just a new vocabulary of terms and concepts but a radically different way of looking at and understanding cities and urban life. Stimulating as well as stimulated by economic restructuring and globalization, what were once seen as metropolitan cities are now better described as polycentric city regions or regional cities. These paradigmatic new concepts are likely to dominate the discourse and debates on urban development in the twenty-first century, as mass suburban growth is replaced by mass regional urbanization.

The next to last chapter returns more directly to Los Angeles and to what has been happening since the major urban uprising of 1992, now often referred to as the Justice Riots. Illustrating the general theme of seeking spatial justice, the chapter examines the remarkable resurgence of new sociospatial justice movements in Los Angeles, reacting to the extremely unjust geographies created by urban restructuring. Included are discussions of the successful lawsuit won by the Bus Riders Union and the Labor/Community Strategy Center, the battle against Wal-Mart led by the Los Angeles Alliance for a New Economy, and the formation and growing impact of the Right to the City Alliance, now expanding throughout the United States.

A brief concluding chapter looks at the Occupy movement and its particular expressions in Occupy Los Angeles and Occupy Orange County. Special attention is given, thanks to the work and assistance of Stefano Bloch, to the role of graffiti artists and muralists in the movement. I want to thank Stefano for his contributions to this and other chapters of *My Los Angeles*. Attention is also given to the wider implications of the Occupy and Right to the City movements across the globe and more specifically to the growing political role of social agglomerations in public spaces such as Tahrir Square in Cairo and Puerta del Sol in Madrid.

This discussion builds on a stream of critical political commentary that runs through nearly every chapter of *My Los Angeles,* reflecting the increasing urbanization and spatiality of politics in the contemporary world. The regional urbanization depicted here, for example, is today a primary driving force behind all forms of economic development, technological innovation, and cultural creativity. But we are also realizing that it can also lead to worsening economic inequality, political polarization, and environmental degradation. Maximizing the positive effects of regional urbanization while controlling the associated negative consequences will be one of the greatest political and economic challenges of the twenty-first century.

A good portion of the text presented here consists of selected re-readings from previously published work, but this book is not simply a collection of my writings. The few chosen excerpts are embedded and elaborated in a new explanatory text that, at the very least, clarifies the (changing) intentions behind what I have written and tries to reflect the radical changes that have taken place in Los Angeles over the past forty years. Basically, what follows are my evolving interpretations of Los Angeles, presented with the hope that each viewing will add something new to our accumulated understanding of the urban condition generally. After all, now that most of the world lives in cities, the urban represents more than ever before the human condition. But let's not get too heavy here, for my Los Angeles can also be entertaining, amusing, teeming with trivialities, and often quite meaningless. Always be ready to bounce back and forth between such hyperbolic extremes, for this is the essence of LA.

NOTES

1. See Norman Klein, *The History of Forgetting: Los Angeles and the Erasure of Memory* (London: Verso, 1997).

2. Stein's pithy remark "There is no there there," so often applied to Los Angeles, actually referred to Oakland after she returned to her hometown but could not find the house where she grew up. The comment appears in *Everybody's Autobiography* (Boston: Exact Change Publishers, 2004).

3. *Ramona,* a historical romance novel written by Helen Hunt Jackson and published in 1884, reportedly went through three hundred printings and generated Southern California's first great tourist boom. The story revolved around a mixed Scots and Native American orphan girl who survives rounds of Mexican-Californio racism to find her true love. Fitting in well with the anti-Mexican feelings of the

time, it may be the first example of regional "branding," as many locations advertised themselves as part of the story to attract tourist dollars. A play based on Ramona has been performed annually at Hemet since 1923, the longest-running outdoor play in the United States.

4. Very little has been written about the early days of regional planning in Los Angeles, especially in comparison with the more emphatic emergence of regionalism and regional planning in New York City at about the same time. Regional planning in LA was primarily just county planning, with little sense of regionalism.

5. See Allen Scott, ed., *Global City Regions: Trends, Theory, Policy* (Clarendon: Oxford University Press, 2001). See also Peter Calthorpe and William Fulton, *The Regional City* (Washington, DC: Island Press, 2001). Both books are strongly connected to Los Angeles, the first arising from an international conference held at UCLA in 1999, while Fulton, coauthor of the second book, has had close ties with UCLA and the University of Southern California (USC) and has become a leading commentator of urban planning in Southern California.

6. Regional urbanization as a redefinition or end state of urban restructuring will be discussed in much greater detail in subsequent chapters.

7. This statistic has been controversial, as nearly everyone's urban imagination fails to understand how LA can be denser than New York City, especially when one maintains outdated images of both. The densest census tracts remain concentrated in Manhattan, but the packed-in immigrant districts of LA are catching up rapidly. When the accumulation of the densest census tracts reaches 15 percent, Los Angeles passes New York and remains higher than any other metro region. Another determining factor is that the suburbs of Los Angeles are much denser than those of New York, another indication of LA's advanced form of regional urbanization.

8. I have co-edited a book on LA with Allen Scott called *The City: Los Angeles and Urban Theory at the End of the Twentieth Century* (Berkeley and Los Angeles: University of California Press, 1996).

9. For a discussion of the spatial turn, see Edward Soja, "Taking Space Personally," in *The Spatial Turn: Interdisciplinary Perspectives,* ed. Barney Warf and Santa Arias (New York and London: Routledge, 2008), 11–35.

10. The generative foundation of all my research and writing is "The Socio-Spatial Dialectic," *Annals of the Association of American Geographers* 70 (1980): 207–25, an article in which I criticize emerging forms of Marxist and other postpositivist geography for not being spatial enough due to an overprivileging of historical and social relations. I explain this critique of social historicism in more detail in chapter 6.

11. For an eclectic look at environmental issues from an avowedly historical perspective, see William Deverell and Greg Hise, eds., *Land of Sunshine: An Environmental History of Metropolitan Los Angeles* (Pittsburgh, PA: University of Pittsburgh Press, 2005). For more on the politics of Los Angeles, see Raphael Sonenshine, *Politics in Black and White: Race and Power in Los Angeles* (Princeton, NJ: Princeton University Press, 1993); and *The City at Stake: Secession, Reform, and the Battle for Los Angeles* (Princeton, NJ: Princeton University Press, 2004).

12. Paul Barker, with Reyner Banham, Peter Hall, and Cedric Price, "Non-Plan: An Experiment in Freedom," *New Society* 338 (March 20, 1969); and Paul Barker, "Non-Plan Revisited: Or the Real Way Cities Grow (The Tenth Reyner Banham Memorial Lecture)," *Journal of Design History* 12 (1999).

13. Allen Scott and others see this as a third wave of urban and industrial revolution, the first being the original Industrial Revolution and its accompanying surge of urban growth; the second conventionally named Fordism, an industrial revolution and urban surge that rescued capitalism from the Great Depression and world war; and now the rise of a new industrial economy given many names: post-Fordist, global, information intensive, flexible, and most recently from Scott, cognitive-cultural capitalism, leading to the tipping point advanced largely by China and India, wherein the majority of the world's population now lives in city regions of various sizes.

14. The phrase "it all comes together" came from what was then the masthead motto of the *Los Angeles Times,* now no longer used. It would become closely associated with my writings on Los Angeles, with both positive and negative implications.

ONE

When It First Came Together in Los Angeles (1965–1992)

My geohistory of Los Angeles begins in 1965, in the bewildering aftermath of one of the most violent and costly riots in U.S. history. The Watts Riots burned down the core of African American LA and had an even larger, worldwide impact. As one of the leading edges of global urban unrest in the 1960s, the Watts uprising announced to the world that the postwar economic boom in the United States and elsewhere was not going to continue with business as usual, for too many benefited too little from the boom. There were riots and uprisings around the world before and after Watts, but none were as violent, as destructive, and perhaps as symbolic of the end of an era and the beginning of a new one as the events of 1965 in Los Angeles. *My Los Angeles* is in large part an effort to make sense of what happened to LA in the decades following the Watts uprising.

Virtually everything contained in *My Los Angeles* depends on and extends from this first chapter and its central argument that the Watts Riots marked the end of the long postwar economic boom in the United States and signaled the onset of a period of crisis-generated economic restructuring that would affect to some degree every major metropolis in the industrialized world. The argument goes one step further to claim and demonstrate that very few if any other metropolitan areas in the world were as deeply restructured and radically changed as Los Angeles, giving to those who study it a remarkable panorama of experiences and expressions from which to draw insight.

There is some historical sequencing to this look at the urban restructuring of Los Angeles, but what emerges is certainly not a comprehensive history of LA before or after 1965. Nor is the geography of Los Angeles presented in full and permanent detail. To keep the historical and the geographical developing together, I call what I do "geohistory." This and all the chapters that follow are attempts to capture the fluidity of geohistorical development in this constantly changing urban landscape through multiple layers of interpretation and reinterpretation.

CREATING A NEW LOS ANGELES

At least three pronounced "inversions" took place in the four decades following the Watts Riots, each contributing to the city's remarkable metamorphosis. By inversion I mean a major historical reversal in which the LA that existed in the first three-quarters of the twentieth century was turned upside down and inside out. A new Los Angeles was created that in many ways was opposite to the image of Los Angeles that had developed in the academic literature and popular media up to the 1970s and which, despite its outdatedness, continues to dominate many present-day views of Los Angeles as well. One of the first tasks in looking at Los Angeles is to challenge this persistent inheritance of increasingly anachronistic imagery.

The first of these dramatic inversions had to do with the local labor movement. Once the realm of "sunshine and the open shop," to use Mike Davis's felicitous phrase, the old Los Angeles was renowned for its probusiness, antilabor environment. It stood out as a retrogressive counterfoil to New York City and its ultraliberal western outlier, San Francisco. LA had its moments—a significant flirtation with socialism if not anarchism in the 1910s, a breeding ground for revolutionary movements in Mexico and China, the groundbreaking center for the first wave of federally sponsored public housing in the early 1950s—but the dominance of institutions such as the chamber of commerce, the local manufacturers' association, and the then ultraconservative *LA Times* was clearly established and quite capable of breaking the back of any left-of-center trend or militant labor union activity.

The red-baiting war against public housing and the Hollywood blacklisting that arose from the inquisitions of the House Un-American Activities Committee in the 1950s confirmed and consolidated this dominance. Twenty years later, however, Los Angeles began its unexpected emergence as a leading generative and innovative center of the national labor movement, especially with regard to gender equality, gay rights, and above all, the organization of immigrants.[1] Nowhere in metropolitan America have labor unions grown in membership and local power as they have in LA, and nowhere else have immigrants played as central a role in the labor movement. I will return to these remarkable developments in labor-community coalition building from the Watts Riots to the present in chapter 8.

A similar role reversal and image inversion took place with regard to neighborhood identities, place-based politics, and the activities of community-based organizations. For most of the past century, Los Angeles has been seen as the epitome of automobile-based urbanism, with residents creating far-flung "autopian" networks of contacts and attractions rather than forming "proximate communities"—well-defined neighborhoods where pedestrian life flourished and everyone knew and relied upon their neighbors. Berkeley urban planning professor Melvin Webber famously described LA in the 1970s as a "non-place urban realm," where distances were elastic and the local meant little, where many households had unlisted phone numbers and nestled behind high walls and a sign or two reading "Trespassers Will Be Shot."[2] Since 1985, for many different reasons, just the opposite has been happening to community identity and activism. Perhaps nowhere else in the country today are neighborhood, community, and other place-based organizations as numerous, active, and successful, a topic that will also be explored further in chapter 8.

A third material and reputational inversion has transformed Los Angeles from the least dense and most destructively sprawling major metropolis in America—literally and figuratively seventy-two suburbs in search of a city—into the country's densest urbanized area, surpassing the twenty-three-county New York City urbanized area in 1990 and widening its lead ever since. Several factors contributed to this stunning reversal. One of the largest city-focused migrations in world history (at least BC, before China) added almost five million people (almost all from developing countries) to the population of the inner urban core alone. In all, since 1975, nearly eight million were added to the five-county LA urban region, by far the largest growth spurt among cities in the developed world outside Japan and comparable to the expansion of the great Third World megacities, such as Lagos, Dhaka, and Mexico City.

Also contributing to its overall density has been an extensive urbanization of LA's suburbs. For most of the twentieth century, Los Angeles was seen as the model for the sprawling suburbanizing western cities of North America. Today it is the prototype of what I have called regional urbanization, a new mode of urban growth defined primarily by the densification, if not full-scale urbanization, of suburbia and the replacement of the domestic population in the urban core with large numbers of Third World immigrants. I will discuss what I see as an epochal shift from metropolitan to regional urbanization in LA in later chapters. Mentioning it here serves to reinforce and exemplify further the argument that the Los Angeles city region has changed more substantially since 1975 than almost any other in the world. Its iconic suburbia of the past is fast disappearing, the "seaport of Iowa" is now being called the "capital of the Third World," what were once minorities are now in the majority, and the ultimate WASP city is now predominantly Catholic and Evangelical.

Beyond all doubt, Los Angeles is no longer what it used to be. It remains an exemplar of many contemporary urban trends, but these trends are very different from those exemplified by Los Angeles in the first three-quarters of the twentieth century. To cling to these earlier images can lead only to misunderstanding.

DEFLECTING EASTERN BIASES: AGAINST POSTINDUSTRIALISM

Although it was nearly impossible to tell where LA was going in the 1970s, things were undoubtedly changing very quickly. It soon became abundantly clear to the growing cluster of urban researchers trying to make theoretical and practical sense of what was happening in this period that Los Angeles was moving in directions that differed greatly from other major cities in the United States and that these differing paths demanded new ways of thinking about urban development and change. As the material landscape of LA changed dramatically, so too did the methods and means of studying it, to a degree that was just not as pronounced in New York or Chicago or even Atlanta, Miami, or Houston, at least until very recently.

Making theoretical and practical sense of the social and, more emphatically, the spatial patterns of urban restructuring in Los Angeles became the research focus for a group of critical scholars, led primarily at first by urban and regional planners and geographers at UCLA. The first challenge faced by this emerging research cluster was to make their voices heard over the highly influential interpretations of urban change that had emerged among urban analysts and policy makers east of the Mississippi.

The eastern academic and political establishment had already quite confidently assumed they had the answer to what was happening after the end of the postwar boom. To begin with, the United States was experiencing a kind of role reversal in regions and regional development, a "power shift" between the Frostbelt—the heartland of American industrialization, stretching roughly from Saint Louis to New York City—and the Sunbelt, led by the "New South" from Texas to Florida, with a sunny outlier on the Pacific Rim. Enhancing this interpretation were census statistics for 1970 and 1980, which seemed to indicate, especially through the overall decline in manufacturing employment, the beginning of a postindustrial era, with America the affluent at the forefront of an emerging new kind of capitalism.

In this emerging postindustrial society, it seemed that manufacturing no longer mattered, as jobs and the economy as a whole shifted into various tertiary or service activities, from burger flipping to high finance. The resulting *deindustrialization of America,* as it was called, was painful for many, including nearly all the once thriving communities in the American Manufacturing Belt, as well as African Americans and other members of the new "urban underclass," who were seen as being left stranded in the decaying cores of nearly all Frostbelt cities.[3] Also suffering were the big industrial unions and the unionized workers that had benefited so fulsomely from the postwar boom. Economic restructuring—defined almost entirely as deindustrialization—was destructive but necessary, the theoreticians and policy makers claimed. It was deemed an essential part of any recovery from the widespread urban upheavals of the 1960s and the global economic downturn of 1973–74.

To researchers working in and on Los Angeles, this seemed a rather misleading if not wholly inaccurate picture of what was happening. Almost unknown to the eastern establishment, LA had for decades been the country's largest industrial metropolis. To call LA postindustrial seemed absurd, especially since the manufacturing sector had been booming in the 1970s. Relatively few of the nearly one million African Americans in LA were "stranded" far from suburbanizing jobs through some "spatial mismatch." In this mixed urban-suburban landscape, jobs were relatively close by, although racial barriers made these nearby jobs difficult to obtain. Furthermore, unemployment and welfare dependency were not big issues, as the huge Hispanic immigrant population held multiple jobs, forming what was better called an agglomeration of the working poor rather than a welfare-dependent underclass. Even the term *Hispanic* was locally disdained in favor of the ambitiously inclusive new term *Latino,* referring expectantly to everyone coming from south of the U.S. border.

More than a third of Los Angeles's population, the working poor were unable to bring in enough income to rise above official poverty levels despite holding multiple jobs per household. They certainly were not dependent on public welfare, although many claims arose and many studies were conducted as to whether the working poor contributed more than they took from the local economy. Most studies showed they added much more than the welfare they received, although anti-immigrant elements within the Anglo (non-Hispanic white) population continued to demand more discrimination against the working poor, such as denying resident noncitizens the right to public school education. Similar problems were growing in other major metropolitan areas, but they were contextualized and interpreted very differently than they were in Los Angeles, given the ethnic cleansing or bleaching (into Anglo or non-Hispanic white) that Spanish-speaking Californio LA experienced after the U.S.-Mexico War.

Exploding the myths of postindustrialism further encouraged the LA researchers. After an initial period when the new writings from Los Angeles were dismissed as marginal quirkiness or irrelevant banter, there emerged a national and indeed worldwide expansion of interest in what was happening in Los Angeles, especially with regard to what became known as *industrial restructuring* and the related formation of a new *post-Fordist* metropolitan economy and geography. What was coming to an end was not urban industrial capitalism but a phase in its development that came to be described as Fordism, a phase that began in the interwar years, helped the United States and other countries out of the Great Depression, and led the way to the boom years following the Second World War.

As the Los Angeles experience became more widely known, *post-Fordist* (or *postfordist*) rather than *postindustrial* became the more widely used term for the emerging New Economy, although the *postindustrial* label is still widely used to describe cities such as New York or Detroit. One hopes, however, that it is no longer possible for a referee for the National Science Foundation to dismiss an application for support to study industrial restructuring in Los Angeles by saying, "But there is no industry there." Or for the self-proclaimed capitalist's tool, *Forbes* magazine, to publish a map of the hottest high-technology areas in the United States in the early 1980s and ignore LA and Orange County, then containing more high-tech workers than Silicon Valley or Route 128 around Boston. After years of relative neglect, Los Angeles was finally being put on the national and international map as a model of the new post-Fordist industrial metropolis.[4]

URBAN RESTRUCTURING: ANALYZING SOCIAL AND SPATIAL CHANGE IN LOS ANGELES

One of the main sparks for all this attention to LA was the publication in 1983 of "Urban Restructuring: An Analysis of Social and Spatial Change in Los Angeles," which I coauthored with Rebecca Morales and Goetz Wolff (app. 1, source 1A). Morales, one of the early graduates from the urban planning program at UCLA and then a member of the urban planning faculty was at the time engaged in research focusing on the uses of immigrant labor in the economic restructuring process, especially in the automobile industry.[5] This early research is the source of an anecdote that vividly sets the scene for our analysis and understanding of what was happening in Los Angeles in the early 1980s.

Nose and mouth covered against possibly poisonous dust, Morales entered the back room of a small factory in South LA that produced, if I remember correctly, car hubcaps. As she wandered among the immigrant workers, she saw a pile of the final product against the wall. Getting closer, she saw the last step in the production process: stamping each hubcap with the words *MADE IN BRAZIL*. What in the world was going on? Was this just a minor scam, or did it represent a more widespread phenomenon associated with the emerging New Economy and the particular form it was taking in immigrant-filled Los Angeles? It suggested that wages were so low and immigrant labor so abundant that LA-based manufacturing could, with some transport savings and other conditions, compete with Third World producers—as long as the unions and policy makers did not interfere.

Joining Rebecca Morales and me in this initial venture into the urban restructuring process and what could be called the changing political economy of urbanization was Goetz Wolff, then a doctoral student with a degree in political science from Yale and a deep interest in labor issues. He had coauthored a widely cited article on "the world city hypothesis" with the senior planner John Friedmann. Soon after 1983, Goetz would leave graduate school to create his own labor-oriented consulting firm and later become a key figure in the labor movement in Los Angeles, as well as a lecturer and "practitioner faculty" in the UCLA Urban Planning Department. Together, we were working to introduce a significant labor component into urban planning education, a third force, so to speak, beyond but equal to the public and private sectors.

My LA studies began as part of my transition from teaching in the Geography Department at Northwestern University to working with much more activist and "applied" graduate students in urban planning at UCLA.[6] The immediate trigger, however, was an inquiry from the Coalition to Stop Plant Closings, a new alliance organized to fight deindustrialization and the closure of once prosperous factories, mainly producing automobiles, tires, glass, steel, and many consumer durables—what scholars at the time would label the products of "Fordist industries."

While overall job growth was expanding, Los Angeles in the 1970s and early 1980s was also experiencing a significant loss of Fordist manufacturing jobs, primarily in several older heavy industrial zones, such as the area stretching south of downtown to the port of Los Angeles–Long Beach, then and now the second largest city in the urbanized region. Although the economic geography was poorly understood in 1980, and visions of "industrial Los Angeles" were dominated by Hollywood filmmakers leading what was locally called "the" industry, Los Angeles already hosted the largest concentration of manufacturing employment in the United States. Unusually large areas were zoned for industrial use, and specialized municipalities had formed, such as the bluntly named City of Industry and City of Commerce.

Los Angeles was an industrial behemoth, in startling contrast to how it was viewed by many outsiders at the time. The industrial area south of downtown—centered on such blue-collar cities as South Gate and extending to the twin ports of Los Angeles and Long Beach—had so many factories and workers that it ranked with the Ruhr in Germany as the largest continuous urban industrial zone, and there were other Fordist industrial clusters in the San Fernando Valley and the so-called Inland Empire of San Bernardino County.[7]

While Los Angeles certainly could not be labeled postindustrial, it did experience a significant deindustrialization after the recession of the early 1970s. We estimated that at least seventy-five thousand jobs were lost because of factory closures and job layoffs. This was not surprising, given that LA contained the largest assemblage of vulnerable Fordist industries west of the Mississippi. Significantly, this allowed those studying Los Angeles to investigate the causes and consequences of both Frostbelt deindustrialization and the new industrial expansion of the Sunbelt, which we in Los Angeles called *reindustrialization.* There were very few if any metropolises in the world where one could see and study this dynamic interaction between deindustrialization and reindustrialization more clearly than in Los Angeles.

Even with substantial reindustrialization, industrial labor unions and once thriving blue-collar communities were being decimated as rapidly in LA as anywhere else in the country. Factory closures and job losses focused on Fordist industries and the neighborhoods where they were located, while in many other areas around sprawling Los Angeles new kinds of post-Fordist and information-based industries created rings of much wealthier suburban municipalities. It was as if the Sunbelt and Frostbelt had become oddly mixed together in one place. Under siege and utterly confused by the contradictory boom-bust trends they saw around them, and receiving no relevant help from once powerful national union offices, union locals in Los Angeles, building on the precedent set by the United Farm Workers years earlier, began to create new labor-community coalitions, often with the help of scholar-activists from local universities.

This early growth of labor-community unionism and coalition building led to the creation of the Coalition to Stop Plant Closings (CSPC) and its efforts to stem the tide of deindustrialization. One of the first major test cases for the coalition was the threatened closure of a General Electric flatiron plant in Uplands, San Bernardino County. Concerned about how to organize workers at the factory to oppose the closure, especially when workers were being told that they should not worry about closure given the job boom LA was experiencing, the United Electrical Workers union local turned for help via the CSPC to the new group of local university researchers studying Los Angeles.

The project stimulated by the CSPC became the springboard for a major stream of empirical research, theory building, and planning practice that would swell, over the next three decades, to a level probably unsurpassed in any other city. It would also move well beyond the Geography and Urban Planning Departments at UCLA to other universities and disciplines. The explosion of LA-based research and writing took place after three-quarters of a century in which the solid academic literature on Los Angeles barely filled a bookshelf. While the CSPC would fail in its bold effort to control footloose capital during a time of rapid economic and technological change, it would become the political and experiential seedbed for extraordinary developments over the next thirty years that would make Los Angeles an innovative center for labor-community-university coalition building not just in the United States but in the world.

In essence, the Coalition to Stop Plant Closings asked us to help them understand what was happening to Los Angeles in the late 1970s and early 1980s. The request was specifically connected to the United Electrical Workers union, which was facing the possibility of a shutdown of the GE plant in Uplands. "How can we organize on the shop floor to fight against this threatened closure," they asked us, "when, contrary to what was happening back east in the American Manufacturing Belt, jobs seem to be increasingly plentiful in LA?" The workers were saying, "Why bother protesting? We can easily get new jobs." Little did they know that they might have to get two or three jobs to make the same money they were earning in Uplands.

We then set to work on a two-level project. Our first product was a pamphlet that described early warning signs of plant closure that we hoped could be used to mobilize support at the factory. Illustrated by a union cartoonist, the pamphlet was published in 1980. A sampling from the pamphlet is presented here (figures 1a–e); the entire pamphlet can be read online at www.ucpress.edu/go/mylosangeles. With painful irony, the pamphlet appeared on the day it was announced that the GE plant was closing.

The pamphlet was a tiny primer on economic restructuring, although more elaborate answers to the questions raised about factory closures and footloose capital in Los Angeles were contained in our article, "Urban Restructuring." In our broader explanation, we saw capital—in the form of businesses and corporations—responding to the downturn that was clearly evident by the time of the worldwide economic recession in 1973–74. For the national economy, the postwar boom was over, business as usual could no longer be depended on to be profitable and expansionary, and new ideas and new directions were necessary to restore anything like boom conditions. Thus began a period of experimentation, seeking innovations in technology, labor-management relations, and corporate organization in an effort (not always successful) to stimulate renewed economic expansion and improved forms of social control over destabilizing unrest. For the majority of businesses, however, there was a seemingly easier way, at least in the short run, to increase profits: cut costs. And the easiest cost to cut was labor.

Crisis-generated restructuring and the dilemmas faced by the electricians union in Uplands were triggered and driven initially by various methods of cutting labor costs. Firing or laying off workers and closing down factories, especially in the Fordist industrial sector, which had led the postwar boom but was now experiencing the worst economic decline, seemed the easiest method. Throughout the 1970s and into the 1980s, the major industrialized regions of the world, from New England and the American Manufacturing Belt to lowland Scotland, south Wales, northeast England, Wallonia in Belgium, and the Basque country in Spain, experienced varying degrees of deindustrialization, with the greatest devastation associated with weaker

FIGURE 1A Cover of *Shut Down . . . 15 Early Warning Signs of Plant Closure*, prepared by the Coalition to Stop Plant Closings, 1980.

Introduction

In 1980, dozens of communities in Southern California were hit by unexpected plant closings. Too often the companies gave little or no warning to either the communities or their employees.

While the most publicized plant closings have been in the auto, steel, and rubber industries, shutdowns have hit dozens of other industries in Southern California. This should serve as a warning that no worker, industry, or community is safe from shutdowns.

What can you and members of your community do to fight this threat to your job and your neighborhood? There is no state or federal legislation requiring companies to inform workers or communities of impending shutdowns. Therefore, workers and community leaders must be aware of the *early warning signs* of plant closures.

Why is it important to take notice of the *early warning signs?* Early recognition affords you the time for examination and implementation of alternatives to plant closure and losing your job.

FIGURE 1B *Shut Down* pamphlet, page 1.

FIGURE 1C *Shut Down* pamphlet, page 3.

Your company opens a new plant in another state or country making the same thing you are but paying lower wages...

In January 1981 the Max Factor Company announced that its Los Angeles cosmetic production facility would close in 1982. The Los Angeles plant, under union contract with the ILWU, employs 700 workers. Max Factor is currently constructing a new cosmetic factory in North Carolina. When the Los Angeles plant closes, Max Factor will shift all of its orders to North Carolina.

Often plants are not closed, but new ones are opened, producing the same product. Having parallel production facilities within the country and around the world guarantees that the corporation is not dependent on any one production facility for the smooth flow of its operations. It also allows a corporation to pit different groups of workers against each other.

FIGURE 1D *Shut Down* pamphlet, page 4.

national labor unions and deficient state welfare policies.[8] Continental Europe saw lower levels of deindustrialization, Great Britain somewhat more, and the United States the most.

Even in the United States, such cost cutting was not always easy. The American postwar boom, which was one of the most dramatic and successful in the history of capitalism, especially in Los Angeles, had created the

For example, when Canadian nickel workers at the ENCO plant went on strike the company sent the business to a duplicate plant in Mexico. The Mexican plant proceeded to take up where the striking Canadian workers had left off.

No new machines to replace the old ones...

The Firestone Rubber Company plant was built in Southgate in the 1920's. The machines used by Firestone were designed to build "bias ply" tires. Over the years other tire companies, especially Michelin, captured a greater share of the tire market by selling "radial" tires. A radial tire requires different machines, which Firestone did not have. Rather than invest in the new machinery necessary for constructing the radial tire, Firestone continued with their antiquated technology. In the end, Firestone closed the plant completely.

FIGURE 1E *Shut Down* pamphlet, page 5.

world's largest suburbanized middle class, as unionized workers received huge benefits, ranging from health provision to housing subsidies, in large part by agreeing through collective bargaining to forgo full-scale strikes or not to interrupt production and to increase productivity in other ways in return for increasing wages and benefits. This involved what some called a "social contract" among big labor, big government, and big corporations. Firing workers and closing factories without explanation were within the rights of corporate management in the United States (if inconceivable in, say, Scandinavia), but strong industrial labor unions would make such tactics very difficult.

Deindustrialization expanded at a fast pace through several U-turns in the public and private sectors. Union busting became more acceptable than ever before, as signaled by President Reagan's treatment of the air traffic controllers in the early years of his regime and Margaret Thatcher's similar stance with regard to British miners' unions. To enhance the acceptability of such efforts to the voting public, an extraordinary ideological shift was necessary. The majority of voters had to be convinced that a) the economic problems were caused by big government in cahoots with big labor unions, with workers selfishly gorging themselves on social welfare; b) the social contract and its allied policies, from the New Deal to the War on Poverty, had to be dismantled in response to economic decline; and c) the magic of free enterprise markets was a sufficient substitute for what was being lost. In the churning propaganda mills that rationalized, or "spin-doctored," the restructuring process, neoliberalism was born—and would persist as an ideological smokescreen up to the present day.

These conditions formed the background to the challenges faced by the Coalition to Stop Plant Closings. Deindustrialization and reindustrialization were occurring simultaneously and with almost equal force in LA. An extraordinary job boom was taking place, but the majority of these jobs paid low wages, had few if any benefits, and were typically nonunionized. Workers at the GE plant in Uplands, a large proportion of whom were women and minorities, were earning relatively high salaries with good benefits. If laid off, however, they would need to obtain two or three jobs to maintain the same middle-class lifestyle, a cruel trade-off that we described as being "Kmarted," after a popular department store at the time.[9]

Around the country, there was little that could be done to stop increasingly unregulated and footloose capital from moving to new locations (including overseas) in their search for labor savings. Plant closings did not go forward, however, without some resistance in Los Angeles. While not always successful, the Los Angeles Coalition Against Plant Shutdowns (LACAPS), the new name adopted by the Coalition to Stop Plant Closings, pressured state and local government agencies to create or increase the level of special services for displaced workers and introduced state legislation requiring advance notice of plant closings and compensation to displaced workers and affected local communities. LACAPS's efforts, both locally and nationally, even when unsuccessful, planted the seeds that would grow into the resurgence of labor-community coalition building in LA ten years later.

The 1983 article was one of the first published works to specifically focus on urban restructuring. It also signaled several key characteristics of the research cluster (or "school," if one prefers) that would develop in the 1980s. Particularly important was the use of Los Angeles as a laboratory for developing a more general understanding of contemporary urbanization processes around the world. Less attention was given to the unique and particular qualities of the local scene than to how one might better understand what was happening in other cities from studying Los Angeles. Emphasizing the socio-spatial patterns of change reflected the strong geographical or spatial perspective that was as the heart of the research cluster.

This first round of interpreting the restructuring of Los Angeles began, appropriately enough, given our political leanings at the time and the growing influence in urban studies of neo-Marxist geography and sociology, with a letter from Karl Marx requesting information about California. In his 1880 letter to Friedrich Serge, Marx says that California is important because nowhere else has rapid capitalist centralization caused such terrible upheaval so quickly. Marx was referring mainly to the enormous concentration of wealth following the midcentury gold rush and the rise of what some called the "robber barons."[10]

What we saw in Los Angeles was a contemporary form of what Marx called "capitalist centralization"—the beginnings of what would become an extraordinary polarization of wealth, which was an integral part of the crisis-generated restructuring process. *Centralization,* in Marxist terms, refers to a coming together of different fragments of capital, as in the formation of corporate monopolies in the late nineteenth century or other forms of intercorporate cooperation and amalgamation, such as the formation of large corporate conglomerates. As will be discussed further in chapter 5, many different forces combined to concentrate wealth in fewer hands, creating over the past forty years a greater gap between rich and poor in the United States—with the largest gap found in Los Angeles and New York—than at any other time in its history. Glimmers of this process of concentration and polarization were already evident in LA in the 1970s.

Confident in the exemplariness of Los Angeles, our first working assumption was that urban restructuring did not arise out of thin air but was generated by the series of urban, national, and international crises that marked the 1960s and early 1970s. This made the Watts Riots a significant turning point and explains why we insisted that the term *restructuring* needs to be preceded by *crisis-generated,* lest these origins be forgotten. As urban studies at the

time said little about cities in crisis, preferring tendencies toward peaceful equilibrium, Marxism, in the form of the new urban political economy that forcefully emerged in 1973 with the publication of David Harvey's *Social Justice and the City*, became the logical starting point for understanding crisis-generated urban restructuring.

The first sentence in the text announced one of our most important early discoveries—that the five-county built-up area of LA was one of the world's largest industrial metropolises. Moreover, during the 1970s LA had been experiencing a concentration of industrial production, employment growth, and international corporate finance that was probably unmatched in any other city in the advanced industrial countries (and would never be surpassed in LA in any subsequent decade). "Look at Los Angeles," we virtually shouted to the world. "Everyone needs to take notice of its remarkable metamorphosis to understand the contemporary urban condition, wherever one resides."

We backed up our claims with empirical data. According to U.S. Census Bureau Annual Survey of Manufactures statistics, between 1970 and 1980, when the entire United States had a net addition of less than a million manufacturing jobs, the Los Angeles region added 225,800. In comparison, New York City lost 330,000 jobs, and Detroit, LA's major industrial rival in the previous four decades, lost even more.[11] More astonishing, in the same decade, the total population of the LA region grew by 1,300,000, while the number of nonagricultural wage and salary workers increased by 1,315,000. There seems little doubt that Los Angeles during the 1970s was the developed world's most generative job machine, even if the majority of the jobs were not well paid.

We were also quick to point out that this economic boom was not spreading joy and prosperity everywhere. Accompanying the boom (and in part causing it) were extensive job layoffs and plant closures, deepening poverty and unemployment, the appearance of industrial sweatshops reminiscent of Dickensian London, the intensification of ethnic and racial segregation, and increasing rates of urban violence and homelessness. In this juxtaposition of substantial aggregate economic growth with widespread indications of recession and decline, the Los Angeles region appeared to be combining the contrasting dynamics of both Sunbelt and Frostbelt cities, adding to this mix some of the features associated with Third World export-processing zones.

We described Los Angeles as a "peculiar composite metropolis," an "articulated assemblage" of many different patterns of contemporary urbanization—a Houston, a Detroit, a Lower Manhattan, a Singapore, and a

São Paulo rolled into one. This depiction illustrated the title of the chapter in my *Postmodern Geographies* (1989) that presented a revised version of source 1A: "It All Comes Together in Los Angeles" (app. 1, source 1B), a phrase adapted from what was then the banner of the local newspaper ("It All Comes Together in the *Times*").[12] This composite picture of urban restructuring opened up many new directions to investigate. Underlying it all, however, was a view of Los Angeles as a revealing site and situation for understanding the changing political economy of contemporary urbanism everywhere. Many different terms were used to capture this revealing quality without suggesting that every city would follow the LA model. LA was described as representative, indicative, exemplary, symptomatic, paradigmatic.

The findings of our empirical analyses of urban restructuring in Los Angeles can be summarized in a series of maps that originally appeared in sources 1A and 1B (app. 1). Many of these maps were the first of their kind and called for similar mappings in other urban regions.

During the 1970s, the aerospace/electronics cluster of industries grew by 50 percent, with 110,000 jobs added, making it the core manufacturing sector of the LA region and creating one of the largest such concentrations in the world. This "high-tech" sector combined civilian and military-related production, which had become difficult to separate given their shared dependence upon technology arising out of Department of Defense and NASA research and development activities and a heavy reliance on military and defense contracts. Geographically, what could be called a new Silicon Valley developed in Orange County, with smaller clusters in the area around Los Angeles International Airport and in the West San Fernando Valley (see map 5).

Associated with these developments was a marked reduction in unionization rates. Following national trends, California workers in unions declined from 30.9 percent in 1971 to 23.5 percent in 1979, percentages very close to those for LA County. The change in industrialized Orange County, however, was even more pronounced, dropping nearly ten percentage points over the same period, to 13.8 percent. In Orange County manufacturing, there was almost total collapse, with the unionized workforce moving from 26.4 to 10.5 percent, representing an absolute decline of over one-quarter of the union membership in 1971.

The rise of high-tech industries was associated with accelerating decline in older, established manufacturing activities. Since 1978, for example, Los Angeles automobile production, once second only to Detroit, virtually

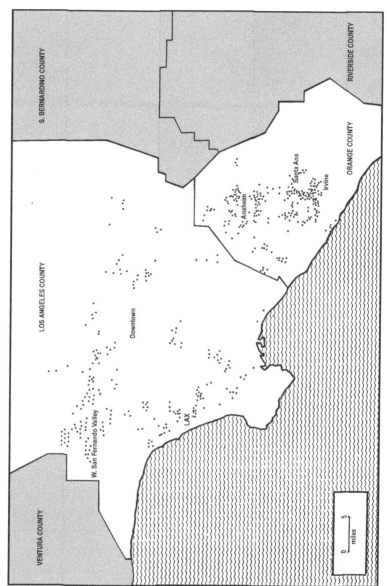

MAP 5 Location of electronics components plants, 1981. From *Postmodern Geographies*, 1989.

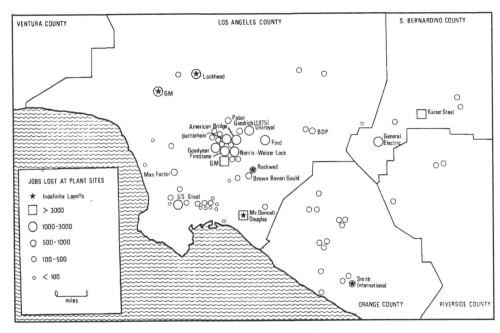

MAP 6 Plant closings and major layoffs, 1978–1982. From *Postmodern Geographies*, 1989.

disappeared, as did the entire rubber tire industry (Goodrich, Firestone, Goodyear, and Uniroyal all closed their factories) and a major portion of the auto-related glass, steel, and steel products sector. Counting a few major "indefinite" layoffs, over seventy-five thousand workers lost their jobs due to plant closings. Map 6, almost an inversion of map 5, shows the geographical distribution of these factory closures. It is no coincidence that actual and threatened plant closures were concentrated in areas and industries that were the most highly unionized, paid relatively high blue-collar wages (with benefits), and employed relatively large numbers of minorities and women. The devastation caused by factory closures made certain areas of Los Angeles resemble parts of Detroit or the South Bronx in the early 1980s, at least in terms of selective deindustrialization, population decline, rising unemployment rates, increasing crime, and general urban decay.[13]

The polarized geography of social class in LA is represented in map 7. The almost complete absence of touching or overlap between blue-collar and executive-managerial residential areas is quite stunning and indicative of the unusually high degree of class polarization. Note also the size of the blue-collar concentration in Long Beach, the region's "second city."

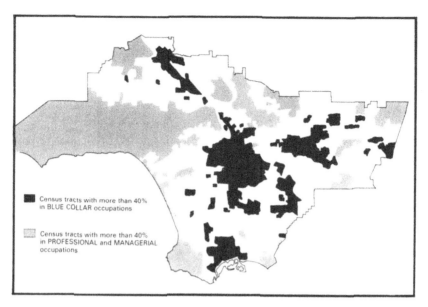

MAP 7 Blue collar and executive-managerial occupations, 1981. From *Postmodern Geographies,* 1989.

Comparing maps 6 and 7 is also quite revealing. The predominantly blue-collar urban core is almost entirely African American and Latino, while the Anglo managers and executives live on the slopes of the Santa Monica and San Gabriel Mountains or on the Palos Verdes Peninsula, far from the teeming center. Urban restructuring in Los Angeles has been closely associated with an enormous influx of immigrants, primarily from countries along the Pacific Rim. The magnitude and diversity of immigration since the Immigration and Nationality Act of 1965 can be compared only with the wave of European migrants to New York City in the late nineteenth and early twentieth centuries. In 1960, Los Angeles County was over 85 percent Anglo. By 1980, Latinos, Blacks, and Asians together accounted for over 50 percent of the population, with the Latino segment growing into the majority in the 1990s (see map 8).

Greatly underestimated in the ethnic map of Los Angeles is the large "undocumented" or "illegal" immigrant population, estimated at somewhere between 400,000 and 1.1 million in 1980. Mexicans made up the largest portion of this group, but there were representatives from almost every country in the world. Together with the majority of the new "legal" immigrants, the "undocumented" population provided the Los Angeles economy with perhaps

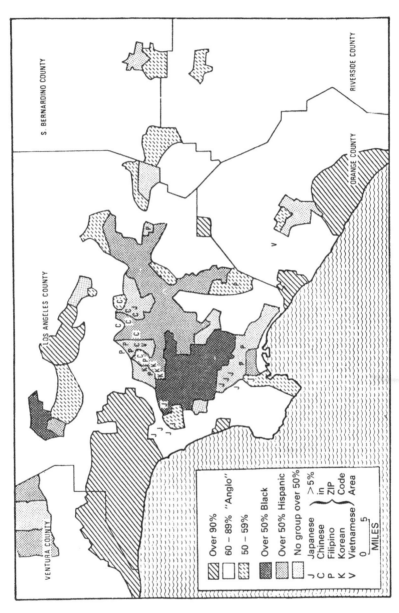

MAP 8 Ethnic distributions, 1981. From *Postmodern Geographies*, 1989.

the largest pool of cheap, manipulable, and easily dischargeable labor of any advanced capitalist city during this boom period. This pool of immigrants, documented or otherwise, were thought to be unorganizable by traditional labor unions in 1980, but by the 1990s they had become the primary force behind the growth of Los Angeles as an innovative center of the national labor movement.

Immigrant labor formed a key part of the restructuring process in Los Angeles, affecting virtually all sectors of the regional economy. Undocumented workers, in particular, were concentrated in small, highly competitive firms in garment and other forms of light manufacturing, including electronics, as well as in hotel, office, and restaurant services. These firms, either too small or too fixed in location to move abroad, typically depend on low-skilled, often transient laborers who can be paid extremely low wages, especially in comparison with unionized blue-collar workers.

In the years between 1965 and 1980, Los Angeles drew ahead of San Francisco and consolidated its position as the financial hub of the western United States and the primary gateway to the Pacific Basin. A reflection of this concentration of the FIRE sector (finance, insurance, real estate) appears in map 9. As one might expect, this financial expansion was accompanied by a major office-building boom, with over thirty million square feet of high-rise office space added between 1972 and 1982, representing more than a 50 percent increase.

With these developments, downtown Los Angeles became the anchor of a control-headquarters complex that stretched westward along Wilshire Boulevard almost twenty miles to the Pacific in Santa Monica. This extended "linear" downtown contained such major nodes as Beverly Hills, Century City, and Westwood. In this almost unbroken ribbon of office development were nearly fifty major corporate headquarters and an additional one-third of the region's hundred million square feet of high-rise office space. Downtown Los Angeles was intensely globalized during this period, with Japanese, Canadian, and British capital playing important roles in a sky-scraper boom that peaked in the late 1980s.

By 1990, the FIRE boom—and so much else—began to decline significantly, as many corporations and banks closed their headquarters in Los Angeles. This economic turnaround would reach a boiling point in the 1992 riots, which exposed the occasionally excessive claims about Los Angeles's relative positioning among the world's major global cities that characterized the first round of writings about the urban restructuring in Los Angeles.

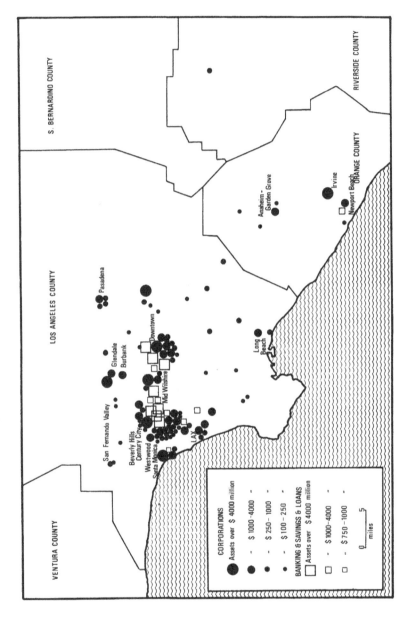

MAP 9 Corporate and banking headquarters, 1981. From *Postmodern Geographies*, 1989.

VENTURA COUNTY

LOS ANGELES COUNTY

S. BERNARDINO COUNTY

RIVERSIDE COUNTY

ORANGE COUNTY

San Fernando Valley

Glendale
Burbank

Pasadena

Beverly Hills
Century City
Westwood
Santa Monica

Downtown

Mid Wilshire

LAX

Long
Beach

Anaheim -
Garden Grove

Irvine

Newport Beach

CORPORATIONS

Assets over $ 4000 million

 - - $1000 - 4000 -

 - - $ 250 - 1000 -

 - - $ 100 - 250 -

BANKING & SAVINGS & LOANS

Assets over $ 4000 million

 - - $1000 - 4000 -

 - - $ 750 - 1000 -

0   5
    miles

What are now called the Justice Riots of 1992 destroyed much of the optimism of the early LA research cluster and stimulated several efforts at reinterpretation, utilizing different ways of looking at urban restructuring.

REINTERPRETATION: URBAN RESTRUCTURING AS AN ATTEMPTED SPATIAL FIX

During the period between the two violent riots of 1965 and 1992, a New Economy took shape nationally and in Los Angeles. It was described in various ways: post-Fordist, information-intensive, flexible, global, neoliberal, and outside Los Angeles, postindustrial. However it may be described, the restructured political economy had significant geographical or spatial repercussions that were only partially described in the first round of writing on urban restructuring. Although we did not use the term in the 1983 article, what we were describing through a spatial analysis of urban restructuring in Los Angeles can be reinterpreted as an example of what David Harvey, in his book *Limits to Capital,* called an attempted "spatial fix," an almost habitual effort by capitalist interests, usually assisted by the state, to shape material geographies to suit their needs, especially and most urgently in times of crisis.[14]

Seeing urban restructuring as an attempted spatial fix can be better understood with reference to a series of related ideas formulated by Harvey. He argued that the social process of capitalist development shaped urban geography and the built environment to fit its needs at a particular moment. But as the needs of capitalist development change over time, becoming especially challenged during periods of crisis, the existing geography and built environment become, to an increasing extent, outdated and dysfunctional, a straitjacket of sorts. A new and different geography is required to meet the changed needs of capital (for instance, the New Economy).[15] But there is a certain fixity to the urban geography. Unlike most institutional structures and unconcretized social relations, one cannot just change the built environment and well-established geographies at will.

For example, the Empire State Building may have been perfectly located when it was built in the 1930s, but by the 1960s it would probably have been more profitable if located somewhere else. But the building cannot simply be picked up and relocated. This dilemma triggers complex reactions, some "stakeholders" wanting to maintain the status quo, others calling for major repair and reconstruction, still others wanting to tear down the building entirely and rebuild something else on the site. This competition over city-space and the built environment is reminiscent of the dilemmas of urban renewal in many U.S. cities, where many different stakeholders had often conflicting plans of what should be done with the city center, typically leading to the poor suffering the most, with urban renewal not so jokingly becoming urban removal of the poor.

Competition and conflicting strategies are built into the attempted spatial fix. So too is what the economist Joseph Schumpeter called "creative destruction." Whereas the new geography of Los Angeles can be said to reflect the needs of the New Economy, the fit and the fix are far from perfect. Not only is capitalism not the only force shaping the new geography, but even its influence is not predestined to be successful. While it is important to recognize that urban restructuring is associated with an attempted spatial fix, there is no reason to assume the fix will effectively bring the crisis to an end.

As noted, there are many other forces shaping—and being shaped by—urban and regional geographies. For example, race and ethnicity powerfully influence the "spatiality" of urban life, as do gender and sexual preference. Ever since the nineteenth-century emergence of the distinctively industrial capitalist city, however, the needs of capital in conjunction with the largely supportive role of the state have almost surely been the most powerful force shaping urban geographies and guiding the processes of crisis-generated restructuring. Hence the emphasis on capital, labor, and their relations in this first round of studying the political economy of urban restructuring.

The notion of a spatial fix fits well into a long-wave rhythm of capitalist development, illustrated earlier in the boom-bust cycle begun in the early 1940s, interrupted by the crises of the 1960s and 1970s, and followed until today by far-reaching economic and urban restructuring. Although most scholars would agree with a broad view of the expansion-crisis-restructuring cycle that began after World War II, not many are comfortable with extending this view into three fifty- to sixty-year cycles, the first from 1848–49 to the end of the nineteenth century, then from the 1890s through the Great Depression and the World War, and finally the long wave that began after the war and probably still exists today.[16]

One does not have to be an advocate of any long-wave theory to realize that there have been three long periods of crisis-generated restructuring since the origins of urban industrial capitalism. Each would generate a New Economy, a modified mode of capitalist development, and most relevant to the present discussion, different geographies extending from the global to the local level. Looking specifically at the industrial capitalist city, the first significant restructuring took place in the last three decades of the nineteenth century, when a New Economy emerged around the formation of huge corporate monopolies and, for the leading industrial countries, highly profitable forays into the peripheries of the capitalist world, during what Eric Hobsbawm called "the Age of Empire."[17]

During the same period, the highly centralized and decidedly competitive industrial capitalist city, due probably in large part to urban unrest in and around the city centers, began to sprout suburbs as well as satellite cities, such as Gary near Chicago, East Saint Louis close by Saint Louis, and Wayne and other automobile satellites surrounding Detroit. This was the beginning of the metropolitan form of urbanization and what can be called the Metropolis Era.

The modern metropolis would boom in the early decades of the twentieth century, much of which was called the Progressive Era in the United States, only to crash in 1929 and further decline during the Great Depression of the 1930s. The 1930s, capped by the human and environmental destruction of the world war, was another period of economic restructuring, creative destruction, and purposeful spatial reorganization. Two names defined the emergent New Economy that would survive depression and war. Fordism, named after the innovative car maker, defined the turn toward assembly-line mass production and automobile-led mass suburbanization and consumerism. Suburbanization and the metropolitan form were also vital parts of Keynesianism, named after the famous British economist whose ideas about crisis management, demand-driven development, and the role of state-provided social welfare in not only driving a profitable and booming economy but also maintaining social control and keeping the peace were equally important in recovery from economic depression and preparation for a costly war.

The third period of economic restructuring and changing urban geographies brings us back to Los Angeles and the focus of this first chapter. Looking back, Los Angeles's geography has evolved through three periods of restructuring. As it began its major growth spurt in the last decades of the nineteenth century, it did not experience much of the dense centralization of the early industrial capitalist city, so vividly modeled by the Chicago School.[18] Although founded in 1781, the city of Los Angeles remained a small peripheral outpost until a century later, when the urbanization process had become more decentralized, extensive residential suburbanization had begun, and clusters of separately incorporated municipalities started to rim the central metropolitan city.

Between 1880 and 1920, the population of Los Angeles grew rapidly from thirty-five thousand to nearly a million inhabitants, but this growth was shaped by the social and spatial relations of the "metropolitan" mode of urbanization rather than that of the earlier centralized industrial capitalist city. As industrialization advanced in the twentieth century, downtown LA did become the largest industrial concentration, but from the start urban industrial growth was polycentric and dispersed in a wider metropolitan network of settlements that seemed to combine urban and suburban characteristics. Los Angeles's greatest growth spurt, however, occurred between 1920 and 1970, the leading period of what can be called the era of the modern metropolis.

The prevailing pattern of residential and industrial location in LA was thus already polynucleated and decentralized, with relatively low overall densities, by 1920, when the city reached one million inhabitants. While the tiny downtown was gridlocked with automobile traffic, the whole region was enmeshed in one of the most extensive and busiest public transit networks of any city, the Pacific red car system. Even with aggressive annexation policies that increased the size of the City of Los Angeles from 85 to 362 square miles in the decade 1910–20, the population of the incorporated areas of the county grew more rapidly than the administrative city itself.

From 1920 to 1940, covering the years of the Great Depression, Los Angeles County added nearly two million inhabitants, roughly evenly divided between city and suburbs. Petroleum refining and the aircraft industry were solidly established, and during the depression four major auto manufacturers opened assembly plants, attracting rubber tire and other auto-related Fordist industries to the area. Los Angeles remained, however, an economic center of relatively small firms engaged in food processing, garment manufacturing, furniture production, tourism, and motion pictures. Despite a history of vigorous workers' struggles, Los Angeles also remained a preeminent center of effective labor control, an area where the open shop was virtually a law in the fifty years following the 1890s depression. Few cities in the country faced more powerful and organized antilabor organizations than LA.

Los Angeles and Detroit presented exemplary representations of the new metropolitan model of urban industrialization, but while Detroit was absorbed into the dynamics of the American Manufacturing Belt, Los Angeles became the widely accepted prototype of the new Western cities: sprawling, low-density, decentralized, seemingly (at least from an eastern viewpoint) almost entirely suburban, not really like cities east of the Mississippi or in Western Europe.

LA suffered relatively little from the Great Depression and, given the sequence of Pacific wars from 1941 through Korea and Vietnam, boomed to an extraordinary degree as "America's arsenal," with its "state-managed" economy pumped up with billions of demand-driving Defense Department dollars. During the Korean War period, 1950–53, total employment reportedly increased by 415,000 jobs, 95,000 in the aircraft industry (by then reoriented from an emphasis on aircraft frames to a more diversified aerospace-electronics–guided missile manufacturing).

By the early 1960s, the City of Los Angeles contained two and a half million people, while Los Angeles County's population reached over six million, more than doubling its size since 1940. Rapid growth would continue at least until the 1990s, making Los Angeles one of the few First World cities to grow significantly in population over the past forty years. As the City of Los Angeles reached a population of more than four million and the entire city region grew to around eighteen million today, the urban geography changed in dramatically new ways, creating a very different urban condition that demanded new methods and modes of analysis and interpretation.

ENDINGS

Sources 1A and 1B, the 1983 article and the 1989 chapter, end in very different ways, the first explicitly political and confident of its radical positioning, the second more questioning and doubtful, en route to new directions of inquiry that sidestep the high modernism of the Marxist discourse for the more open and subtle tones of critical postmodernism. While both noticed the great urban upheaval taking shape after the Watts Riots, the 1983 version continued to focus on the old Los Angeles, with its intensely antilabor environment, weak sense of locality, community, or place-based identity, and uncontrolled low-density sprawl. The magnitude of change and the need this stimulated for new ways of studying Los Angeles are more evident in the conclusion to "It All Comes Together in LA." As a transition to the next chapters, I present a brief excerpt from the 1989 conclusion:

The informed regional description that has been presented thus far, however, depicts only some of the broad vistas visible from the vantage point of Los Angeles. The seen/scene is that of a new geography of (post)modernization, an emerging postfordist urban landscape filled with more flexible systems of production, consumption, exploitation, spatialization, and social control than have hitherto marked the historical geography of capitalism. Having put together this interpreted regional landscape, *I will attempt to take it apart again to see if there are other spaces to be explored, other vistas to be opened to view.*

NOTES

1. See Ruth Milkman, *L.A. Story: Immigrant Workers and the Future of the U.S. Labor Movement* (New York: Russell Sage Foundation, 2006); and Ruth Milkman and Kent Wong, "Organizing Immigrant Workers: Case Studies from Southern California," in *Rekindling the Labor Movement: Labor's Quest for Relevance in the Twenty-First Century,* ed. Lowell Turner, Harry Katz, and Richard Hurd (Ithaca, NY: Cornell University Press, 2001), 99–128. Milkman, a labor sociologist, was director of the UCLA Institute for Industrial Research on Labor and Education (IRLE, formerly the Institute for Industrial Relations) from 2001 to 2008. Wong, a longtime labor activist, is currently director of the UCLA Center for Labor Research and Education. There are no better observers and analysts of the LA labor movement than Milkman and Wong.

2. Melvin Webber, "The Place and the Non-Place Urban Realm," in *Explorations into Urban Structure* (Philadelphia: University of Pennsylvania Press, 1964); see also "Culture, Territoriality, and the Elastic Mile," *Papers in Regional Science* 13, no. 1 (1964): 59–69. Although based in Berkeley, Webber was a keen observer of Los Angeles, which he saw at the time (the 1960s) as epitomizing his notion of "communities without propinquity."

3. See Barry Bluestone and Bennett Harrison, *The Deindustrialization of America* (New York: Basic Books, 1982). For the urban underclass, see William Julius Wilson, *The Truly Disadvantaged: The Inner City, the Underclass, and Public Policy* (Chicago: University of Chicago Press, 1987).

4. Perhaps the greatest beneficiary of the postindustrial myth and its effect on U.S. national policy was China, which would absorb large portions of the Western industrial world's productive capacity to surpass all other countries, including the United States, in overall industrial production. Nowhere else has the complementary interplay between urbanization and industrialization processes been so fully realized.

5. As an independent scholar, Morales has continued her interest in the automobile industry. She has written a novel, *Proving Ground,* about the international auto industry and, with John Heltmann, has recently published *Stealing Cars: Technology*

and Society from the Model T to Today (Baltimore, MD: Johns Hopkins University Press, 2012).

6. I believe to this day that the pressure to apply in some way my theoretical and other ideas made my work sharper and more cogent than would have been the case had I taught in a geography department or outside UCLA, with its activist-oriented Urban Planning Department. Anyone wishing to read more about the UCLA Urban Planning Department and my identity as a geographer-planner may consult my "Translating Theory into Practice: Urban Planning at UCLA," chapter 5 in *Seeking Spatial Justice* (2010), 157–78.

7. The Inland Empire received its name when Kaiser Steel chose to locate a major steel-making factory far inland from the coast during the Second World War. Some say this was done in fear of possible coastal bombing.

8. In some cases, deindustrialization began before 1970, but nearly everywhere it accelerated in the 1970s.

9. Given its reputation for exploitative labor relations, *Wal-Marting* would have been a more appropriate name. At the time, however, Wal-Mart had not penetrated far into urban America, preferring smaller towns and well-populated rural areas.

10. Matthew Josephson, *The Robber Barons: The Great American Capitalists, 1861–1901* (New York: Harcourt Brace, 1934).

11. We also discovered in the manufacturing censuses that in every decade after 1930 (when Detroit was first), Los Angeles led the nation in added manufacturing employment.

12. The 1983 article would have a long life. In 1984, the UCLA Urban Planning Department prepared and published a small pamphlet based on the article (cowritten with Allan Heskin and Marco Cenzatti), and the pamphlet was translated into Italian for the journal *Urbanistica* (1985). There was a French translation in *Revue d'Economie Regionale et Urbaine* (1985); reprintings in Richard Peet's *International Capitalism and Industrial Restructuring* (1987) and Robert Beauregard's *Atop the Urban Hierarchy* (1988); and a German translation in a book on new urban theory coedited by Margit Meyer (1990). A modified version, "Economic Restructuring and the Internationalization of the Los Angeles Region" (app. 1, source 1C), was published in *The Capitalist City*, edited by the sociologists M.P. Smith and J. Feagin (1987), and excerpts from this were reprinted in Anthony Giddens in *Human Societies: A Reader* (1992). Still another version became the centerpiece for source 1B, chapter 8 in *Postmodern Geographies* (1989). The original article and the book chapter would continue to be resurrected as an urban classic in several more recent collections.

13. Parts of south-central Los Angeles, including Watts, for example, were worse off in 1980 than they were at the time of the Watts Riots in 1965. During the "booming" 1970s, the area experienced the greatest deterioration of any community in the region. Population fell by 40,000, the labor force decreased by 20,000, unemployment rates reached at least 12 percent, and median family income dropped to $8,000 below the citywide median and $2,500 below that for local African Americans. Data taken from the *Los Angeles Times*, April 3, 1980.

14. David Harvey, *Limits to Capital* (Oxford: Blackwell, 1982); see also "The Spatial Fix: Hegel, von Thunen, and Marx," *Antipode* 13 (1981): 1–12.

15. This attempted spatial fix does not just apply to the urban scale. At the national scale, spatial restructuring in the United States relates to the pronounced Frostbelt to Sunbelt regional shift; globally the rise of newly industrialized countries, the expansive urban industrialization of China, and other developments are indicative of a new global geography or, as it is more commonly called, a new international division of labor.

16. I say probably since the present period of restructuring, if begun after 1973, has lasted much longer than the previous two. The riots in Los Angeles in the spring of 1992 could have been the start of another worldwide urban crisis but were not. Were 9/11, the Iraq War, and the Great Recession of 2008–9 indications of the end of a long cycle of restructuring? Or was the long-wave cycle disrupted entirely by other unexpected events? These questions cannot be answered here or now.

17. Eric Hobsbawm's periodization of capitalist development begins with *The Age of Revolution 1789–1848* (New York: New American Library, 1962); followed by *The Age of Capital 1848–1875* (New York: Charles Scribner's, 1975); *The Age of Empire 1875–1914* (New York: Pantheon, 1987); and most recently, *The Age of Extremes 1914–1991* (New York: Pantheon, 1994). Hobsbawm died in 2012.

18. It is worth noting that Chicago School models of urban form did not contain extensive suburbs, even though the actual city of Chicago at the time was experiencing significant suburbanization.

TWO

Taking Los Angeles Apart
(1985–1995)

The early work of the Los Angeles research cluster reached a peak of sorts with the publication in 1986 of a special issue on Los Angeles by the influential journal *Society and Space (Environment and Planning D)*. Michael Dear, then professor of geography at the University of Southern California and also a geographer-planner, was a founding editor of the journal and promoted the special issue. He would later refer to it as the symbolic beginning of his version and vision of the so-called Los Angeles School of Urbanism.[1] Basking somewhat in the rapidly growing interest in Los Angeles–based research, Allen Scott and I wrote a highly enthusiastic editorial introduction to the issue (app. 1, source 2A), boldly proclaiming, with late nineteenth-century Paris in mind, that Los Angeles had become the "capital of the late twentieth century" and the "paradigmatic industrial metropolis of the modern world."

We also added, somewhat presciently given what was to happen in LA in 1992, that even with continued economic growth, the widening gap between rich and poor had the potential to trigger "turbulent struggle and confrontation." This darker view of Los Angeles was part of a growing realization that the study of urban restructuring needed to move in new directions. The booming job machine of the 1970s was no longer flourishing, the aerospace industry was shrinking, federal funds no longer flowed as easily into the region, and many of the trends so confidently identified in the first round of urban restructuring studies were coming under attack.

Also coming into question was the Neo-Marxist framework that had guided the early research so effectively and insightfully. Given the new cultural and postmodern critiques that were emerging at the time, modernist forms of Marxism as well as positivist science seemed to have left unexamined too many vital aspects of contemporary society and, in particular, the growing transformation of Los Angeles. The brilliant Marxist analyses of the origins of the urban crises of the 1960s seemed to be increasingly less relevant and less effective in explaining the rapid changes taking place in the modern metropolis in the wake of these crises.

While Marxism's diagnostic power remained strong, its almost smug assurance that it could explain everything through some form of capitalist logic covered over too much, in my view, creating significant silences and omissions that required new and different approaches. The need to create new ground for interpreting the urban restructuring of Los Angeles led me to selectively combine Marxist and postmodern perspectives, a combination that would provoke heated reactions from nearly everyone paying attention to my work. For some, I remained too Marxist to be a postmodernist; to others, it was just the reverse, with postmodernism almost inevitably compromising my Marxism, making it politically impossible to combine the two. Finding both these reactions unacceptably absolutist and unwilling to forgo my combinatorial stance, I adopted a "both-and-also" approach to understanding what was happening in Los Angeles during this period, seeking to go beyond the limitations of both conventional Marxist and fashionable postmodernist approaches, to go in new directions without rejecting either Marxism or postmodernism entirely.

The first product of this alternative approach was a deliberately provocative essay that appeared in the same issue of *Society and Space,* entitled "Taking Los Angeles Apart: Some Fragments of a Critical Human Geography" (app. 1, source 2B), an intentional play on the earlier "It All Comes Together in Los Angeles." The new title pointed to a critical dismantling of earlier approaches to understanding Los Angeles and a search for new ways of looking at this kaleidoscopic metropolis. Everything I would write about Los Angeles after 1986 reflected this endless search for new incremental insights, new discoveries, adding to rather than reinforcing or defending what we had already learned.

This distinction between adding and reinforcing or defending is important for understanding this and subsequent chapters. Making theoretical and practical sense of the crisis-generated restructuring of Los Angeles and its associated search for a spatial fix continues to be the underlying focus, but as LA changes over time, so too does the interpretive perspective. This does not mean that the older interpretations were wrong, but rather that the changing conditions required a different way of looking at urban restructuring and spatial change.

TAKING LOS ANGELES APART: TOWARD A
POSTMODERN GEOGRAPHY

Significantly, "Taking Los Angeles Apart" opens not with a request from Karl Marx for news about California but with a quizzical and querulous Jorge Luis Borges, the great Argentinean short-story writer and cultural critic, trying to make sense of what he called the "Aleph," the place where all places are (where it all comes together?).[2] Borges provides a foundation and springboard for describing the postmodernization of Los Angeles. Building on Borges also encourages more creative language and literary references than ever was the case in the first round of restructuring studies.

In "The Aleph," set in Borges's Buenos Aires, the lead character (Borges himself?) stumbles onto a remarkable site in a friend's cellar, a space that appears to contain all other spaces, the only place on earth where all places exist together. Seeing the Aleph, Borges writes, is the beginning of his despair as a writer, for how can this infinite space, the place where all places are, be captured in written language, which is always linear and restrictively sequential. Simultaneities and synchronicities are much more difficult to convey in a strict temporal narrative.[3]

Quotations from Borges's "The Aleph" are used throughout "Taking Los Angeles Apart" to express the near impossibility of completely capturing the essence of a place like Los Angeles, where seemingly all places are combined simultaneously, each separate and distinct while also intertwined and connected. Like the Aleph, Los Angeles is exceedingly tough to track, peculiarly resistant to conventional description. It does not fit easily into a temporal narrative, for it generates so many conflicting images, confounding historicization, always seeming to stretch laterally instead of unfolding sequentially. At the same time, its spatiality challenges orthodox analysis and interpretation, for it too seems limitless and constantly in motion, never still enough to encompass, too filled with "other spaces" to be informatively described.

"What is this place?" one might ask. Where to focus, to find a starting point, is not obvious, for to some degree Los Angeles is everywhere. It is global in the fullest sense of the word, screening its imagery so widely that probably more people have seen this place—or at least fragments of it—than any other on the planet. Everywhere seems also to be in Los Angeles. Once dubbed Iowa's seaport, Los Angeles today has become entrepôt to the world, a true pivot of the four quarters, a congeries of east and west, north and south. And from every quarter's teeming shores have poured a pool of cultures so diverse that contemporary Los Angeles represents (re-presents) the world in connected urban microcosms, reproducing in situ the customary colors and confrontations of more than a hundred different homelands.

No wonder Borges claimed that describing the Aleph was virtually impossible. "What my eyes beheld was simultaneous," he laments, "but what I shall now write down will be successive, because language is successive. Nonetheless, I will try to recollect what I can. " In the remainder of this chapter, I too will try to recollect what I can, knowing well that any totalizing description of the "LAleph" is impossible. All that can be presented is a succession of fragmentary glimpses, a free association of reflective and interpretive field notes aimed at constructing a postmodern geography of the Los Angeles urban region. What follows can be seen, literally and figuratively, as a voyage of discovery to spaces and places unseen in the first round of restructuring studies.

A ROUND AROUND THE OUTER SPACES OF LOS ANGELES

Finding a place to start was a challenge in itself. Wanting to see LA in all its scales and scope, I chose a mapping of Los Angeles defined by an embracing circle drawn sixty miles (about a hundred kilometers) out from a central point located in the downtown core of the City of Los Angeles. Presenting itself most obviously as the central point was (and is) the monumental twenty-eight-story City Hall, up to the 1920s the only building allowed to surpass the allegedly earthquake-proof 150-foot height limit. Iconically etched in the American popular imagination through the opening images of the TV crime drama *Dragnet,* City Hall is an impressive punctuation point for postmodern Los Angeles. It is capped by a replica of the Mausoleum of Halicarnassus atop a Byzantine rotunda that is etched with an infatuating inscription for all to read: THE CITY CAME INTO BEING TO PRESERVE LIFE, IT EXISTS FOR THE GOOD LIFE. A similar inscription, adapted from Aristotle, exists in one of the tower rooms inside.

The Sixty-Mile Circle mapping was taken from a pamphlet issued by the Security Pacific National Bank to celebrate LA's bicentennial in 1981. The pamphlet was reissued at least seven more times, as the Circle was adopted as a convenient definition of the five-county built-up area of the regional metropolis. Security Pacific was the largest bank headquartered in LA at the time, its name potently connecting two definitive but opposing pillars of the localized economy. *Security* was redolent of the lethal arsenal emanating from LA, then the most powerful assemblage of weapon-making expertise ever established in one place; while *Pacific* signaled tranquility, moderation, amity, peace, concord. Here was another of the many simultaneous contraries, juxtaposed opposites that epitomize Los Angeles. Security Pacific National Bank was absorbed into the Bank of America in 1992.

Securing the Pacific Rim has been the manifest destiny of Los Angeles from its inception in 1781, through its heated competition with San Francisco for commercial and financial hegemony for a century after the gold rush, to the unfolding sequence of Pacific wars that started with the bombing of Pearl Harbor and continued with the wars in Korea and Vietnam, vaulting LA into national and international prominence. To see how this imperial history embeds itself in the material landscape, in almost invisible military geographies, I take you on an imaginative cruise above the circumference of the Sixty-Mile Circle. Map 10, my creative rendition of Greater Los Angeles, will help you find your way. I ask you to suspend disbelief for the moment and imagine that you are flying like a bird (a condor would be appropriate, as you will see) directly above the outer edges of the Los Angeles urbanized area. What you will see is a protective wall like no other in urban history.

Rampart 1. The Circle cuts the south coast almost exactly at the border between Orange and San Diego Counties, near one of the key traffic checkpoints regularly set up to intercept the northward flow of undocumented migrants. Close by are what was once Richard Nixon's San Clemente "White House" and the tension-filled San Onofre Nuclear Generating Station, while directly below are the often photographed road signs showing migrant women and their children crossing the dangerous freeway. But the first rampart to watch is Camp Pendleton Marine Corps Base, the largest military base in California in terms of personnel. Founded in 1942 and covering more than five hundred square miles, Camp Pendleton trained more than two hundred thousand Marines to fight in the Korean and Vietnam Wars. Since 1954, in addition to preparing thousands of marines for war, Camp Pendleton has offered specialized "basic training" services to civilian young men and women called Devil Pups, instilling love of country and the Marine Corps. One can still see rifle targets from the freeway.

Rampart 2. After cruising inland over the extensive and deceptively empty moors of Camp Pendleton, Cleveland National Forest, and the vital Colorado River Aqueduct draining in from the east, we can land

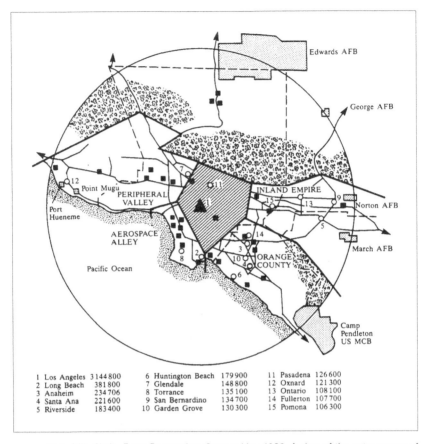

1	Los Angeles	3 144 800	6	Huntington Beach	179 900	11	Pasadena 126 600
2	Long Beach	381 800	7	Glendale	148 800	12	Oxnard 121 300
3	Anaheim	234 706	8	Torrance	135 100	13	Ontario 108 100
4	Santa Ana	221 600	9	San Bernardino	134 700	14	Fullerton 107 700
5	Riverside	183 400	10	Garden Grove	130 300	15	Pomona 106 300

MAP 10 Sixty-Mile Circle. From *Postmodern Geographies,* 1989. A view of the outer spaces of Los Angeles. The urban core is a shaded pentagon; the Central City is shown as a black pyramid. The major military bases are identified; the black squares show the location of the largest defense contractors, and the small open circles represent cities of more than 100,000 inhabitants, listed by name below.

directly on Rampart 2, March Air Force Base, between the city of Riverside and the geographically and socially stranded "off-the-edge" city of Moreno Valley, where thousands wait for new jobs while traveling more than two and a half hours each way to their old ones. More on Moreno Valley in chapter 5. The insides of March were a ready outpost for the roaming Strategic Air Command in 1986. Containing one of the oldest military-operated airports in the country at the time, March would become the major training center for the U.S. Army Air Corps. The shrinking, now almost closed-down base, with barely a thousand remaining inhabitants, continues to hold a popular air show each year called Thunder over the Empire, attracting more than a hundred thousand people in 2010.

Rampart 3. Another quick hop over Sunnymead, the Box Spring Mountains, and the city of Redlands takes us to Rampart 3, Norton Air Force Base, next to the city of San Bernardino. The guidebooks tell us that at the time of our cruise the primary mission of Norton was emergency airlifts, just in case. The base would close entirely in 1994, its squadrons transferred to nearby March and its facilities transformed into San Bernardino International Airport, an ambitiously named facility in that until recently there were no scheduled airlines using it. Like March, there are ongoing efforts to generate private sector jobs at the abandoned Norton, aimed at serving the acute need of the fast-growing population in the relatively jobless Inland Empire, as this part of Riverside and San Bernardino Counties is called.[4]

Rampart 4. To move on, we must rise still higher to pass over the ski-sloped peaks of the San Bernardino Mountains and National Forest, through the Cajon Pass and over the old Santa Fe Trail, into the picturesque Mojave Desert. Near Victorville, one of several boom towns on the fringes of metropolitan Los Angeles, is/was George Air Force Base, closed in 1992. Part of the old base today contains the Southern California Logistics Airport (Victorville's largest employer), a federal penitentiary, a ghost town where the military residences once were, and a site used in 2007 for the DARPA Urban Challenge, a six-hour autonomous robot driving contest sponsored by the Defense Advanced Research Projects Agency, with a first prize of $2 million. DARPA's projects, like the potential ground-drone driverless car aimed at assisting flying drones, devotedly blur the boundary between public and military use.

Rampart 5. About the same distance away is the giant Edwards Air Force Base, Rampart 5, site of NASA and USAF research and development activities and until very recently the primary landing field for unex-ploded space shuttles. Looking back, our stops seem remarkably evenly spaced thus far, almost as if the Central Place theorist Walter Christaller had been secretly plotting them out. Stretching off to the south of Edwards is an important aerospace corridor through Lancaster and Palmdale, two more fringe boom towns, and Air Force Plant 42, which serves Edwards's key historical function as a testing ground for advanced fighters and bombers. To the north of the base is a sprawling network of typically top-secret testing sites, such as China Lake Naval Air Weapons Station. Edwards has been one of the few military bases to grow significantly after the end of the Cold War, continuing what it had been doing since the 1950s—testing almost every new and experimental aircraft created in the United States. It was named a National Historic Landmark in 1985, but its future is unsettled as a result of the end of the manned shuttle program.

Rampart 6. The next leg is longer and more serene, first soaring over the Antelope Valley and Los Angeles Aqueduct, bringing in life-giving water from the rapidly dying Owens River Valley two hundred miles to the north; across Interstate 5 and a long stretch of the Los Padres National Forest, with its Wild Condor Refuge (perhaps a few are soaring with you) to the idyllized town of Ojai, site of Shangri-La in the film *Lost Horizon;* and then to the Pacific again at the Mission of San Buenaventura, on the western edge of the Sixty-Mile Circle where it cuts the border between Ventura and Santa Barbara Counties. A few miles away (the Circle actually cut right through all the other sites) is Rampart 6, a complex consisting of a now inactive air force base at Oxnard; the Naval Construction Battalion Center of Port Hueneme, the only deepwater port between Los Angeles and San Francisco and the only navy-controlled port between San Diego and Seattle; and far above all, the long-sighted Naval Air Missile Center at Point Mugu, now the center of an ordnance testing network that includes Port Hueneme and the navy-owned island of San Nicolas in the Channel Islands, picked up if one extends the Sixty-Mile Circle into the Pacific Ocean, a fitting if secret last leg of our journey.

It is startling how much of the fortified circumference was owned and preserved by the federal government in the 1980s. Premeditation is unlikely to explain this ramparted wall around LA, but certainly some postmeditation on the circumscriptive federal presence—from military installations and testing grounds of all sorts to national forests, parks, and landmarks—is in order.

ENCLOSURES

Our circular journey raises the question of what in the world lies inside these Herculean walls, this fortified circumference of military might? What seems to need such formidable protection? In essence, we return to the same question with which we began: *What is this place?* Is it the "Dream Machines" of

Hollywood that are being protected? Unlikely, I would say, although there may be much more that is hidden behind Hollywood images of Los Angeles, left unscreened and clandestine. Is it the world's largest weapons arsenal that deserves such protection? Surely there must be something more to this place than missiles and bombs?

If anything has emerged in the recent flourish of academic writings on Los Angeles that can help us answer these questions, it is the discovery of extraordinary industrial production, a eureka so contrary to popular perceptions of LA that its explorers have been prone to exaggerate at times to keep their lines of vision sufficiently open and clear against persistent external skepticism and bias. Maybe Los Angeles is not the capital of the twentieth century in the same way that belle époque Paris epitomized the nineteenth century. Yet it is no exaggeration to claim that the Sixty-Mile Circle around Los Angeles contains one of the world's premier industrial growth poles, some of the most valuable "crown jewels" of advanced industrial capitalism.

From 1930 to 1990, Los Angeles led all other metropolitan areas in the United States (including Detroit after 1950) decade by decade in the net addition of manufacturing employment and was close to the top in overall population growth. During the same sixty-year period, no other area has been so pumped with federal money as Los Angeles, the biggest direct chunk coming from the Department of Defense, though other pipelines have fueled industrial growth through numerous federal programs subsidizing suburban consumption and home ownership (suburbsidizing?) and sustaining the development of housing, transportation, and water delivery systems. Add to this federal immigration policies, and it can be easily argued that virtually every segment of the LA economy has some connection to federal inputs.

From the Great Depression to at least 1985, Los Angeles has been the prototypical Keynesian state-city, a federalized metro-sea of state-rescued capitalism, enjoying its place in the Sunbelt. And the federal flow did not drop significantly with the Reagan administration. Nearly two trillion dollars were aimed at LA to foster Reagan's Strategic Defense Initiative, feeding among other targets Hughes Aircraft's attempt to create a giant infrared sensor capable of picking up the warmth of a human body at a distance of a thousand miles in space, and the highly competitive search for more powerful lasers able to incinerate whole cities if necessary. It is not only the space of the Pacific that is being watched over from inside the Sixty-Mile Circle. LA's reach is almost universal. Is it any wonder that it has been so strategically protected? More interesting today is why so much of this fortified rim is being deactivated and abandoned.

On solid ground again, we can begin exploring the intrametropolitan geography that was formed within the Sixty-Mile Circle by the forces of urban restructuring and globalization. Up to 1985, the social and spatial impact of restructuring was unsettled and unpredictable. As Borges intimated for the Aleph, all one could do was to find and list different ways of describing Los Angeles and the perplexing changes that were taking place. After this date, however, reflecting the power of accelerated globalization and economic restructuring, the formation of a new post-Fordist economy, and the neoliberal policies instigated by Reagan and Thatcher, the emerging new "postmodern" geography of Los Angeles became more clearly defined and comprehensible. This reorganized intrametropolitan geography of inner and outer cities is summarized and synthesized in map 10.

By the mid-1980s, four very different outer cities had formed around the inner urban core, which I have chosen to depict, with obvious symbolism, as a pentagon in map 10. The most ephemeral of the four was the effulgent Star Wars colony of weapons manufacturers and aerospace factories that bloomed around Los Angeles International Airport and stretched from Santa Monica on the north (site of the old Douglas Field, where the first DC-3 took off to begin a career of military accomplishment in war after war after war) to the growing conglomerate of guarded and gated communities covering the Palos Verdes Peninsula in the south. Aerospace Alley, as some called this area at the time, was a high-technology super-cluster with an intricate tracery of local links to federal defense- and space-related funding agencies, research and development centers such as the Rand Corporation, all backed by an ancillary network of suppliers and demanders of specialized goods and services.

More than half a million people lived in Aerospace Alley in 1985, with at least three hundred thousand more added during the average working day to sustain the global preeminence of America's main arsenal, flagship of the national security state. At this time, it was reported that nearly half the manufacturing jobs in LA, the country's largest industrial metropolis, were related directly or indirectly to the aerospace industry. Fringed with the beaches that Rayner Banham (1971) called "Surfurbia," Aerospace Alley was

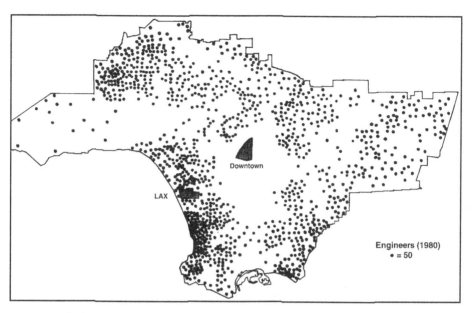

MAP 11 Residential distribution of engineers. From *Postmodern Geographies,* 1989.

also reputed to contain the largest and most homogeneous enclave of scientists, mathematicians, and engineers in the world.

All the accoutrements of the blossoming outer city complex were there: a busy international airport; corridors filled with new office buildings, hotels, and global shopping malls; neatly packaged playgrounds and leisure villages; specialized, master-planned communities for the high technocracy; armed and guarded housing estates for top professionals and executives; and sustaining it all, residual communities of low-wage service workers living in overpriced homes and the accessible enclaves and barrios that provided dependable flows of the cheapest labor power from the bottom bulge of the bimodal labor market. Map 11 shows the extraordinary residential concentration of engineers in this area, and figure 2 illustrates how residential developers used this concentration to focus their advertising. Note how the view from the housing estate eliminates all that is extraneous to an aerospace engineer.

Indicative of the dramatic changes that would reshape Los Angeles after 1985, however, Aerospace Alley has virtually disappeared as such. Hundreds of thousands of aerospace jobs were lost in the subsequent decades, although the area continues to contain large numbers of scientists, engineers, and computer specialists, as well as many of the few remaining census tracts with

FIGURE 2 Specialized housing for engineers and scientists. From *Postmodern Geographies*, 1989.

nearly 100 percent white populations. Much more successful and longer lasting is the outer city of Orange County, perhaps the oldest, largest, and fastest-growing outer city complex found anywhere. If listed as a city in itself (which the U.S. Census Office has trouble doing), OC with its more than three million inhabitants would be one of the ten largest in the country. As richly revealed in the rigorous work of Allen Scott, the development of Orange County illustrates the restructured interplay between urbanization and industrialization that is giving birth to a new kind of "metropolis."[5] My more playful take on OC will be presented in the next chapter, a look "inside exopolis."

There are two other outer cities fringing the pentagonal urban core outlined in map 10. What I have called the Peripheral Valley stretches westward from older industrial centers, such as Van Nuys, through the San Fernando Valley to Chatsworth and Canoga Park, and then to the newer establishments of Thousand Oaks, Camarillo, and other parts of Ventura County. In addition to aerospace, electronics, and other industries, "the Valley," as it is colloquially called, is the world center of the multibillion-dollar pornography industry, the "other" Hollywood. Much of this stretch of classic suburbia is actually within the administrative boundaries of the City of Los Angeles but separated from the "LA Basin" by the Santa Monica Mountains. Feelings of isolation and neglect, as well as the urbanization of suburbia and the influx of immigrant communities, led the San Fernando Valley to attempt—unsuccessfully—to secede from the City of LA in 2002, seeking to split in two one of the world's major urban centers.

Finally, there is the so-called Inland Empire, a wannabe outer city that has to this day not quite achieved its ambitions to be like Orange County. As an anticipatory outer city, the Inland Empire, extending from Pomona on the eastern edge of LA County to the fast-growing county seats of San Bernardino and Riverside, is cruelly packed with new housing estates that automaniacally lure families ever farther from their places of work in Los Angeles and Orange Counties, forcing large numbers of workers to travel more than two hours each way to work and inducing serious socio-pathological problems, such as unusually high rates of suicide and spouse abuse. I will return to these stranded "off-the-edge cities" in chapter 5.

The outer cities of Los Angeles, in 1985 and today, contain well over half the total population of the Los Angeles urbanized region (roughly equivalent to the Sixty-Mile Circle). In the 1980s, suburbia had clearly begun to change into something else, as densities increased and new cities began to form. In the decade or so after 1985, a galaxy of boom towns (boomburbs some called them) emerged on the fringes of Los Angeles. Places like Moreno Valley, Lancaster, Palmdale, Irvine, Rancho Cucamonga, Santa Clarita, and Victorville surged in population, often quadrupling in size. More than three-quarters of the new cities growing past a hundred thousand inhabitants that were identified in the 1990 national census were located in the five-county Los Angeles urbanized region, which amazingly enough in the same census passed the twenty-three-county New York urbanized area as the densest in the country. This densification of Los Angeles was a harbinger of what I would later describe as a dramatic shift from a metropolitan model of urban growth, with its dual urban and suburban worlds, to a new regional urbanization process, mainly infilling rather than spilling over the Sixty-Mile Circle.

Back to the Center

While this growing, seemingly oxymoronic, "urbanization of suburbia" was turning the old metropolis inside out, so to speak, there was also a process of turning the city outside in, as literally millions of immigrants from nearly every country on earth poured into the inner city of Los Angeles, creating population densities as high as Manhattan. Just as one needs to see both deindustrialization and reindustrialization when looking at the changing economy of Los Angeles, it is also necessary to recognize a complex combination of decentralization and recentralization processes, the latter referring not just to the emergence of outer cities, or edge cities, as they are more popularly called, but also to the repopulation of the inner urban core by the immigrant working poor.

To see more of Los Angeles and open up new discoveries, it is necessary to move away from the riveting periphery and return to the central agglomeration, to the still adhesive core of the urbanized landscape. In Los Angeles as in every city, *centrality* defines and gives substance to the specificity of the urban, its social and spatial meaning. Centrality can change in form and function, but urbanization always revolves around a socially constructed agglomeration and the power of occupied centers to cluster and disperse, to centralize and decentralize, to structure spatially all that is social and socially produced. Only with a persistent centrality can there be outer cities and peripheral urbanization. Otherwise, there is no urban at all.

The downtown core of the City of Los Angeles, which the signs call "Central City," is the agglomerative and symbolic nucleus of the Sixty-Mile

Circle. Given what is contained within the Circle, the physical size and appearance of downtown Los Angeles seems almost modest, even after its most recent period of significant expansion. As usual in LA, however, appearances can be deceiving. There is much more in the city center than initially meets the eye.

Downtown serves in ways no other place can as a strategic vantage point, a kind of urban panopticon counterposed to the encirclement of watchful military ramparts and defensive outer cities. Like the central well in Bentham's eminently utilitarian design for a circular prison, the original panopticon, the new skyscrapered downtown can be seen (when smog levels permit) by every separate individual, from all the territorial cells in its orbit. At the same time, only from the advantageous outlook of the center can the surveillant eye see everyone collectively, disembedded but interconnected. Not surprisingly, from its origin, the central city has been an aggregation of overseers, a primary locale for social control, political administration, cultural codification, ideological surveillance, and the incumbent spatial organization of its adherent hinterland.

Looking down and out from City Hall, the site is especially impressive. One can see the largest concentration of government offices and bureaucracy in the country outside Washington, D.C. Nearby stood, before its recent replacement, the imposing police administration building, Parker Center, hallowing the name of a former police chief. Branching off to the northeast is a wedge containing 25 percent of California's overflowing prison population, the teeming core of what would later be called the Prison Industrial Complex.[6] Huddling around the center in 1986 but in other places today were the State Department of Transportation, where wall maps monitor all the freeways of the region; the monumental Times-Mirror building complex, which many claim to have housed the unofficial governing power of Los Angeles; and Saint Vibiana's Cathedral, mother church to one of the largest Catholic archdioceses in the world, today replaced by a new cathedral atop Bunker Hill. Every powerful estate was represented there in the 1980s, right in front of you.

Looking westward, toward the Pacific and the smog-hued sunsets that brilliantly paint the nightfalls of Los Angeles, are the Criminal Courts Building, the Hall of Records and Law Library, the huge Los Angeles County Courthouse and Hall of Administration, major seats of power for what is by far the country's largest county in population, over eight million in 1985 and nearly eleven million today. Across Grand Avenue is the most prominent cultural center of Los Angeles, described on tourist maps as the "cultural crown of Southern California, reigning over orchestral music, vocal performance, opera, theater, and dance," with the Music Center and today the Gehry-designed Walt Disney Concert Hall and the new cathedral sitting atop this cultural acropolis. Just beyond are the City-owned Department of Water and Power (surrounded by usually waterless fountains) and a multilevel extravaganza of freeway interchanges connecting with every corner of the Sixty-Mile Circle, thus symbolically defining LA's swirling centrality.

Along the northern flank of the Central City are the Hall of Justice, the U.S. Federal Courthouse, and the Federal Building, completing the ring of local, city, county, state, and federal government authority that constitutes the Civic Center. Sitting more tranquilly just beyond, cut off by a swathe of freeway, is the preserved remains of the old Spanish and Mexican civic center, now part of El Pueblo de Los Angeles State Historical Park, additional testimony to the lasting power of the central place. Since the origins of Los Angeles in 1781, the downtown sites just described have served as the political *citadel,* the fortressed "little city," designed like other citadels to command, protect, socialize, and dominate the surrounding urban population.

Lest we forget, there is a federal enclave of offices on the east side, near the old police center. It contains the federally run Metropolitan Detention Center, which features on the cover of Mike Davis's *City of Quartz.* I visited this place with Mike and the photographer Robert Morrow just after it opened, when we could wave to the prisoners stretching their arms out through the external bars on the windows overlooking the fern-filled atrium-entrance—a postmodern prison if there ever was one. The site became so popular, especially for academic tourists, that it is now difficult to get close to the entrance because of very active armed guards.

Around the corner is another controversial and attractive "public" space in the federal complex, now virtually closed to the curious visitor (see figures 3 and 4). It contains Jonathan Borofsky's thirty-foot-high *Molecule Man,* a burnished steel sculpture of two interconnected figures shot through with holes (locals call it the "drive-by"), and a remarkable colonnaded plaza rimmed by a neoclassical frieze in which the artist Tom Otterness portrays a radical anarchic vision of toppling governments and rabble-rousing crowds. In the plaza are sculptures of a naked woman breaking her chains and shaking her fist at the world and a naked female baby holding up a giant globe. Together they are called *The New World.*[7]

There is still another part of the citadel that needs to be recognized, the newest acknowledged symbol of LA's urbanity: the bunched castles and cathedrals of corporate power standing clear in the gleaming new "central business district" (CBD). Here too, the LAleph's unending eyes are kept open and reflective, reaching out to and mirroring global spheres of influence, localizing (glocalizing?) the world that is within its reach. Nearly all the corporate landmarks of the new LA CBD have been built since 1970, mainly by international capital (mostly Canadian and Japanese). Logos atop the towers, most announcing a financial presence, were the beacons and attachment points for silvery webs of financial and commercial transactions extending practically everywhere on earth.[8]

Embedded in and around the citadel-LA is a dazzling array of specialized enclaves that play key roles, somewhat noisily at times, in the redevelopment and internationalization of Los Angeles. Let me take you on an ambulatory tour of multicultural downtown, a tour that I have given many visiting scholars curious to find out more about Los Angeles.

We start in the old Chinatown, relocated from a former site near the old plaza by what was called the Chinese Massacre of 1871, the first time Los Angeles broke into the world's news headlines. Most of the shops and restaurants are now owned by Vietnamese Chinese, and a certain decay is setting in as the first suburban Chinatown, predominantly Taiwanese, grows far to the east in the San Gabriel Valley. Close by is El Pueblo Historic Monument, claimed to be the birthplace of Los Angeles, now a major tourist attraction centered on Cal-Mexified Olvera Street, created in the early 1930s as an imitation Latin American marketplace and considered by some to be one of the earliest urban theme parks. Worth a visit today is the América Tropical Interpretive Center, where the famous painting by the radical Mexican muralist David Alfaro Siqueiros, whitewashed after its initial appearance in 1932, became visible again in 2012.[9]

Farther south is Little Tokyo, financed and built by Japanese capital to welcome businessmen from Big Tokyo, but still preserving the activism and resistance of poorer Japanese Americans. Not far away is an induced pseudo-SoHo of artists' lofts and galleries in the old railway yards east of the city center, now housing the avant-garde Southern California Institute of Architecture (Sci-Arc) and other fashionable facilities. Sprinkled around are the strangely anachronistic old wholesale markets (they have disappeared from the centers of most large cities) for produce, flowers, and jewelry. Just to the south, acting as a kind of buffer zone for Little Tokyo and protecting it

FIGURE 3 Jonathon
Borofsky, *Molecule Man*.
From *Thirdspace*, 1996.
Photograph by the
author.

from encroachment by the homeless of Skid Row, is the collection of Asian-owned warehouses known as Toy Town, where perhaps the majority of toys sold in the United States are imported (mainly from China and Thailand) and distributed across the country.

Immediately to the south is Skid Row, "home" to reputedly the largest concentration of homeless people in the country. Their presence induces peculiar street environments, with spiked benches to prevent prone sleepers, barbed-wire-protected garbage bins, and the doorway sprinkler systems in Toy Town warehouses that only operate at night. Next in line are the fetid sweatshops and bustling merchandise marts of the booming garment district, now one of the largest in the United States. Busloads of wealthy shoppers from all over Los Angeles come daily looking for bargain clothing. One can also get here via pedestrian-packed Broadway, another preserved zone and inch-for-inch probably the most profitable shopping street in

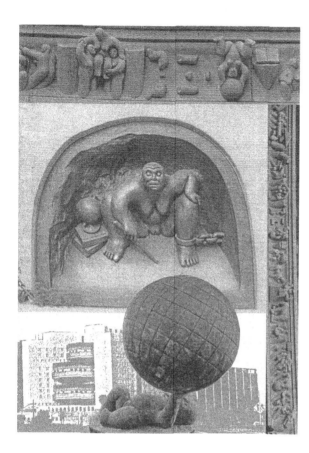

FIGURE 4 Tom Otterness, frieze and *New World* sculptures. From *Thirdspace*, 1996. Photomontage by the author and Antonis Ricos.

the region. Broadway provides a kind of dividing line in the Central City between the Latino worlds and Skid Row homeless to the east and the soaring towers of the central business district and cultural monuments to the west.

All this is within the officially defined Downtown District and can be explored on foot in a day or two, a rarity in car-dependent LA. Farther out are more densely populated new worlds, a teeming corona of ethni-cities that form the densest agglomeration of the immigrant working poor in the United States, close to five million strong today, a million or so less in 1985. Stretching eastward is the enormous and mainly Mexican-American barrio with still unincorporated East Los Angeles at its core. If one adds the surrounding communities, which are more than 85 percent Spanish speaking, such as Boyle Heights and Lincoln Park (both in the City of LA) and a few adjacent municipalities, the total population of the "Greater East-Los" barrio would probably surpass half a million and become the second largest city in the region. Many efforts have been made to incorporate East Los Angeles as its own municipality, but for various reasons every one has failed, leaving the area under the control of a county supervisor.

To the immediate south of downtown is the deindustrializing and virtually unpopulated City of Vernon, densely filled with chickens and pigs awaiting slaughter. Vernon, with perhaps one hundred residents, is one of many specialized industrial municipalities that grew around Los Angeles, such as the bluntly named City of Industry. Recently, Vernon was the focus of the first campaign to disincorporate a city in LA history, following a flood of scandals and corruption claims involving self-aggrandizing local government officials. Vernon is only one part of a contemporary "corruption corridor" that now extends into the wedge of municipalities making up most of the southeastern section of LA County, including the now infamous city of Bell, where a long-standing mayor and other city councillors allegedly siphoned off millions of dollars from the city treasury for their use.

This quadrant of municipalities in southeastern LA County formed a new barrio in the 1980s, created in of one of the most rapid demographic transformations in U.S. urban history. Up until the late 1960s, communities such as South Gate, Bell, Bell Gardens, Cudahy, and Huntington Park contained the largest concentration of formerly poor but then comfortably middle-class southern urban whites in the country. In less than twenty years, the population became more than 90 percent Latino. This wedge contains upward of a million people, making one wonder if anything of this scale and speed of "reverse" gentrification can be found in other American cities. Such rapid change made the area ripe for political corruption, as surviving mainly Anglo members of local city councils, facing Latinoization and voter apathy, took huge amounts of public money to maintain their power and privilege.

Latinos were spreading to the northeast as well, mixed with various Asian populations creating, in places such as Monterey Park, a zone of extraordinary cultural diversity. At one time, the Chinese presence in Monterey Park was so great that street names and shop signs were written only in Chinese, provoking an atypical alliance between Anglo and Latino residents to force through legislation to make English the official municipal language. Faced with pressures against them in Monterey Park, Chinese mainly from Taiwan have spread eastward over the past ten years to create a huge new suburban Chinatown stretching across many municipalities in the San Gabriel Valley.

To the west of downtown, one first encounters the largely Central American barrios of Temple-Beaudry, with its obtrusive backyard oil wells left over from the first boom years in the late nineteenth century; the always crowded shopping streets along and around Alvarado in Echo Park; and the politically active Pico-Union, which would become the center of Latino protest in the Justice Riots of 1992. Some have estimated that around 10 percent of the entire population of El Salvador moved to Los Angeles after 1975, by far the most to this area, which is still the burgeoning center of Central American Los Angeles.

Farther west is the huge and growing Koreatown, wedging itself in between Black LA to the south and the predominantly white Hollywood Hills to the north, creating a volatile racial frontier that would explode in the riots following the verdict in the Rodney King case in 1992. Ever since the early 1980s, the center of the African American community in Los Angeles has been moving westward from its former base in Watts and South Central, most of which has become predominantly Latino. The future of Los Angeles will be deeply affected by the relations among the Korean, Latino, and African American communities.

What stands out from a hard look at the inner city seems almost like an obverse (and perverse) reflection of the outer city, an agglomerative complex of dilapidated and overcrowded housing, low-technology workshops, relics and residuals of an older urbanization, a sprinkling of niches for recentered professionals and supervisors, and above all, the largest concentration of cheap, culturally splintered and occupationally manipulable Third World immigrant labor to be found so tangibly available in any First World urban region. Here in this imperial corona of ethni-cities is another of the crown jewels of Los Angeles, carefully watched over, artfully maintained, and reproduced to service the continued development of the manufactured regional economy.

THE EPICENTER OF THE POSTMODERN CITY

Concluding our tour of the downtown citadel-LA is the Bonaventure Hotel, the iconic landmark for heated debates on postmodern urbanism and, more generally, the efficacy of postmodernist perspectives. Screaming for attention, with its shining circular turrets of bronzed glass, the amazingly storied Bonaventure reflects the splintered labyrinth that stretches for sixty miles around it.[10] Some have argued that the Bonaventure has become a concentrated representation of the restructured spatiality of the late capitalist city: fragmented and fragmenting, homogeneous and homogenizing, divertingly packaged yet curiously incomprehensible, seemingly open in presenting itself to view but constantly pressing to enclose, to compartmentalize, to circumscribe, to incarcerate.

From this postmodern viewpoint, everything imaginable appears to be available inside the Bonaventure, but real places are difficult to find, for its confusing layout makes it difficult to comprehend; its pastiche of superficial reflections bewilders coordination and encourages submission instead. Entry by land is forbidding given its brutal concrete façade, but entrance is nevertheless encouraged at many different levels, from the truly pedestrian skyways above to the bunkered inlets below. Once inside, however, it becomes daunting to get out again without bureaucratic assistance. In so many ways, its architecture recapitulates and reflects the sprawling manufactured and incarcerating geography of Los Angeles.

There has been no conspiracy of design behind the building of the Bonaventure or the socially constructed spatiality of New World cities. Both designs have been conjunctural, reflecting the specifications of the time and place, of period and region. The Bonaventure both simulates the restructured landscape of Los Angeles and is simultaneously simulated by it. From this interpretive interplay of micro- and macro-simulations there emerges an alternative way of looking critically at the human geography of contemporary Los Angeles, of seeing it as a regional mesocosm of postmodernity, in between the micro and macro, the local and the global. A brief Facebook video captures some of these arguments as I am interviewed on the balcony of the Bonaventure (see app. 2, video 1).

This description of the Bonaventure as epitomizing postmodern urbanism is partly inspired by the widely cited remarks of the leading American cultural critic Fredric Jameson in his wildly creative treatment of the Bonaventure in "Postmodernism, or the Cultural Logic of Late Capitalism," first an article in the *New Left Review* (1984) and later a book with the same title published by Verso Press in 1992. It was Jameson who first spoke of getting hopelessly lost in the labyrinthine Bonaventure while attending an academic conference there. He spoke of this "populist insertion into the city fabric" as a "hyperspace" that exposed the archetypal conditions of postmodernity: depthlessness, fragmentation, the reduction of history to nostalgia, and underlying it all, the insistent unsettling of the subordinated subject, unable to find his/her location and being forced into submission to authority.

Complementing Jameson's depiction, there were stories of shops being forced to close because they were located at levels of the four almost identical circular towers that no customers could find. Public complaints abounded about the concrete bunkers that blocked the hotel at ground level, forcing entry via floating skywalks to nowhere. The Bonaventure became a sounding board for all that was wrong—yet provocative—with Los Angeles.

Jameson was particularly ambiguous in his evocation of Bonaventure-based postmodernism, but the critical response to his avowedly spatial interpretation was decidedly prismatic, flying off in so many different directions that it spanned the entire critical spectrum, from delighted appreciation and acclaim to angry dismissal and derision. With the spatial turn not yet in full flow, many scholars were unable to accept or understand such an assertive spatial perspective, even from so prominent a cultural critic as Jameson. To these scholars, postmodernism was connected somehow with what they saw as an overemphasis on space and spatial interpretation. For many architects and geographers, however, it was inspiring to have a prominent critical scholar like Jameson, who at the time of the original 1984 publication was hosting Henri Lefebvre on his only extensive tour of the United States, give such attention to "their" spatial point of view.

Jameson's take on the Bonaventure (which he initially called the Bonaventura, casually locating it on Beacon rather than Bunker Hill) was only a small part of his critical dissection of the "cultural logic of late capitalism," but it had a disproportionate impact on the emerging literature on Los Angeles and especially on the conceptualization of postmodern urbanism. For the growing LA research cluster, Jameson's work had a certain positive attraction, and several meetings were held to explore its wider implications. Outside these local boundaries, reactions depended primarily on established and often wildly disparate personal opinions on postmodernism itself. Given that Jameson seemed at times to be celebrating as well as finding deep faults in postmodern urbanism as it was emerging in Los Angeles and elsewhere, the scope and political passion of the critical response was exceedingly wide, reflecting not just one's position on postmodernism but also one's attitude toward the growing scholarly emphasis on Los Angeles.

The response, then, was truly eclectic. The leading figure of postmodern architecture, Charles Jencks, dismissed the debate entirely by snippily saying that the actual architecture of the Bonaventure was certainly not postmodernist and so did not deserve all the fuss being made of it. Mike Davis, in a *New Left Review* article (1985) still ensconced in Marxist historicism, slammed

FIGURE 5 *The Bastaventure* by Ali Barar and James Kaylor. From *Thirdspace*, 1996. Photograph by Antonis Ricos.

Jameson for his "decadent tropes" and for not seeing the deeper history of labor exploitation in the urban renewal areas of downtown LA. The art historian Donald Preziosi attacked Jameson for being too Marxist, too dependent on historicist master narratives. The critical human geographer Derek Gregory read into the debates a powerful personal-and-political view, opening up questions of gender, sexuality, postcolonial resistance, and the urbanization of the human body. It was as if the Bonaventure had become a crystal ball through which to see postmodern urbanism in all its fantasies and fault lines.

I summarized and commented further on these Bonaventure dialogues in a 1990 article (app. 1, source 5C) marking UCLA's celebration of the bicentennial of the French Revolution (with Jean Baudrillard in attendance).[11] Specially constructed for an exhibition in the Graduate School of Architecture and Urban Planning was the *Bastaventure,* a brilliantly achieved large-scale model constructed by two architecture students, Ali Barar and James Kaylor, in which the turrets of the Bastille fortress transform into the glass towers of the Bonaventure Hotel (see figure 5). As noted above, I was interviewed on the balcony of the Westin Bonaventure Hotel—then threatened with closure—where I suggested that perhaps the abandoned building could become a museum of postmodernism. Worth it or not, the Westin Bonaventure, still surviving as a hotel, has become better known than almost any other site in downtown Los Angeles.[12]

NOTES

1. Michael Dear, "The Los Angeles School of Urbanism: An Intellectual History," *Urban Geography* 24 (2003): 493–509.

2. Borges's "The Aleph" appears in *The Aleph and Other Stories, 1933–1969,* published by Bantam Books in 1972.

3. These observations tap into a larger discussion of social historicism and how the privileging of time and history tends to block critical spatial thinking, the subject of many of my more theoretical writings (to be discussed in more detail in chapter 6).

4. In recent years, the old Norton Air Force Base has become the hub of a fast-growing logistics industry in the Inland Empire, reversing past failures but still not generating a large number of well-paying jobs. More on this in chapter 5.

5. Allen J. Scott, *Metropolis: From the Division of Labor to Urban Form* (Berkeley and Los Angeles: University of California Press, 1988); and *Technopolis: High-Technology Industry and Regional Development in Southern California* (Berkeley and Los Angeles, University of California Press, 1993).

6. Ruth Wilson Gilmore, *Golden Gulag: Prison, Surplus, Crisis and Opposition in Globalizing California* (Berkeley and Los Angeles, University of California Press, 2007).

7. The opening of the Otterness plaza caused a great stir when a federal judge demanded that the bronze statue of a naked and very obviously female baby be hidden from view. Less visible to such prudish judgment were the bold statue of a woman in chains aggressively putting her clenched fist forward and the frieze with its chubby also naked men and women converging to wreck government buildings and dismember the king. The area remains one of the most interesting if rarely visited sites in Los Angeles.

8. In the past five or so years, downtown has been extending southward, toward the old Convention Center and the spanking new Staples Center sports complex, spark of a localized minirevival led by L.A. Live, a $2.5 billion project that opened its first phase in 2007.

9. Siqueiros was a pivotal figure in the development of art and the graffiti-muralist tradition in Los Angeles, New York, and around the world. Some reports say he taught Jackson Pollack drip painting, was the first to use spray cans in painting, and invented the bulbous alphabet used by graffiti artists everywhere. An avowed communist, Siqueiros was always politically controversial, never more so than with his LA mural *América Tropical*. Its restoration by the Getty Foundation was accompanied by many local protests.

10. I am reminded here of Stephen Graham and Simon Marvin, *Splintering Urbanism: Network Infrastructures, Technological Mobility, and the Urban Condition* (London: Routledge, 2001).

11. A revised version of this article appeared in 1996, under the title "Remembrances: A Heterotopology of the Citadel-LA," as chapter 7 in *Thirdspace: Journeys to Los Angeles and Other Real-and-Imagined Places*.

12. The YouTube clip in video 2 (see appendix 2) is taken from the first half of the Open University video, which was shown numerous times in the United Kingdom as well as the United States. The second half of the video focuses primarily on Orange County and forms a good introduction to the next chapter.

THREE

Inside Exopolis

VIEWS OF ORANGE COUNTY (1990–1996)

After "Taking Los Angeles Apart," I could not go back to traditional academic writing and turned instead to the county next door to take another unconventional look at the Los Angeles urbanized area. Orange County was itself both a parody and paradigm of the New American City, an outer city that had grown into a peculiar "postsuburban" metropolis that demanded global attention and not a little scorn. Rather than sixty suburbs in search of a city, as the old Los Angeles was described, OC became a conglomeration of thirty-four cities desperately searching for some sense of centrality—for where the "downtown" might be. Here was an example of amorphous postmodern urbanism just begging to be described in a style appropriate to its main features.

I saw Orange County as a representative part of what I called an *exopolis,* the product of combined processes of decentralization and recentralization. Rather than simple suburbanization, which characterized Orange County up to the 1960s, decentralization took the form of peripheral urbanization, creating cities in what was once sprawling low-density suburbia. Recentralization involved both the growth of these "suburban cities" (some called them edge cities or boomburbs) and filling in of the urban core by mass immigration, as in Los Angeles and many other large world cities.

The term *exopolis* has a double meaning, reminiscent of the Greek *utopia* or *eu-topia,* translated as either "no place" or "good place." The prefix *exo-* connotes both being "outside," as with the growth of the outer city, and "formerly but no longer," as in *ex-wife* or *ex-husband.* This second meaning is intended to suggest that Orange County urbanism is unlike traditional forms of urban development—including, I might add, what we have described for Los Angeles.

"Inside Exopolis" (app. 1, source 3A), my peripatetic tour of Orange County, first appeared in *Variations on a Theme Park: The New American City and the End of Public Space,* edited by the architectural critic Michael Sorkin and published in 1992. It was my most experimental, intentionally amusing, and decidedly postmodern writing. At the time, *exopolis* was my entry into the frenzied competition to find words to describe what was happening in cities outside the urban core, a new urban glossary that includes *outer cities, edge cities, peripheral urbanization, technopoles, technoburbs, silicon landscapes, metroplex, postsuburbia, metroburbia, boomburbs,* and so on. I will return to this explosion of new terms in chapter 7, where I absorb the term *exopolis* into the larger concept of regional urbanization.

Orange County urbanism was drenched with distinctive features demanding serious attention, nothing more so than the artful suspension of factual reality that seemed to pour out of its recreative spaces. Scholars and cultural critics from all over the world saw in OC the most vivid expressions of what Jean Baudrillard, keen observer of Orange County in his *America* (1988), called the production of "hyperreality" and the "precession of simulacra," whereby simulations of the real were rapidly replacing (preceding) reality itself. The map (representing the real in always slightly inaccurate, projected form), for example, now takes precedence over the actual territory it was supposed to represent. As Baudrillard asserted, drawing on biblical symbolism, "The simulacrum is never that which conceals the truth—it is the truth which conceals that there is none. The simulacrum is true." In his own *Travels in Hyperreality* (1986), also touching down in Orange County, Umberto Eco, the Italian philosopher and author of *The Name of the Rose,* would concur, calling what he saw an assemblage of "real fakes."

Reflecting this growing inability to distinguish what is real from what is imaginatively simulated (now an endemic feature of American politics and Fox news broadcasts), I described Orange County as a *scamscape,* where fraudulent behavior has become part of everyday life. Here outward appearances not only deceive but divert us from the possibility that everything real has disappeared. What one sees are thick layers of simulations and simulacra—exact copies of things that may no longer exist, if they ever did in the first place.

The origins and development of the scamscape go back to the mid-nineteenth-century formation of the Anglo city and county of Los Angeles, which included what is now Orange County until its separation in 1889. The

U.S.-Mexican War of 1846–48 prepared the way for two major developments in what was once called Alta California, both rich with pro-American "spin" and imperial power. First and foremost for the American economy and the ability to fight a civil war was the discovery of gold in 1849; the second was the repression of the Californios, descendants of the original settlers of Los Angeles who provided the strongest armed resistance to the occupation of California. Every effort was made to anglicize or Americanize Los Angeles, to bleach it non-Hispanic white by finding ways to weaken the influence of the Spanish-speaking population and the distinctive Californio culture.[1]

The scamscape may have started with full effect in Orange County urbanism, but over the years it has spread to many other arenas, perhaps none more deeply affected than contemporary American politics. In an essay I wrote more recently for *Urban Politics Now* (2008), I spoke of a psychological disorder—a psychasthenia—associated with postmodern urbanism.[2] This psychological disorder induces a kind of anesthetic effect, a dulling diversion and displacement of political awareness and activism caused by the constant availability of enchanting pleasures. Such distraction is typically accompanied by a willing subordination to authority (remember the discussion of the Bonaventure Hotel) as the self becomes lost in city-space, with once sturdy rudders removed and easily followable directions no longer dependable. Sucked into the precession of simulacra, as Baudrillard called it, we become simcitizens living in simcities ruled by simgovernments. What we wear, where we live, who we vote for or against are shaped by images, simulations of the real rather than reality itself.

Vividly illustrating this precession of simulacra was a meeting between influential academic and media critics of the Bush presidency and some spin doctors associated with Karl Rove, then described as "Bush's brain." In response to a barrage of factual attacks on the many and nefarious lies (dissimulations) accumulating around the Iraq war and national economic policy, Rove's representative smugly responded: "You are members of the *reality-based community*. . . . You believe that solutions emerge from your judicious study of discernible reality. . . . That's not the way the world works anymore. . . . When we act, we create our own reality. . . . You are left just to study what we do." In other words, faith replaces factuality; power defines what is real; critics are little more than chroniclers.[3]

In my attempt to do more than chronicle what was happening in Orange County in the late 1980s and early 1990s, I turned to my then bulging file of newspaper clippings. The *Los Angeles Times,* well before it was bought by the Tribune Company and began reporting on Los Angeles as if it were being viewed from clueless Chicago, had excellent local reporters, and nearly every day something interesting appeared, worthy of being cut out and saved. The local free newspaper, the *LA Weekly,* was at the time another source of well-written political and economic commentary on LA (it is now little more than a pansexual dating service and entertainment listing). It seemed entirely appropriate to use these immediate journalistic observations as my reference base for an article on the new American city, the end of public space, and the emergent scamscape. The information was certainly up to date, spontaneously informative, and directly evocative of the new, even if purist academics find such referencing unacceptable.

The original subtitle of "Inside Exopolis: Scenes from Orange County" (app. 1, source 3A) was changed to "Everyday Life in the Postmodern World" in chapter 8 of *Thirdspace* (source 3B), the version I refer to, abridge, and update here. As far as I can tell, neither version was ever reprinted, perhaps because it was more entertaining than conventionally academic. I was told that some used it as a guidebook for touring OC. I hope you will enjoy the read, perhaps laugh out loud occasionally, and possibly learn something too about the new American city and how public as well as private space is being (fraudulently?) redefined.

TOTO, I'VE GOT A FEELING WE'RE NOT IN KANSAS ANYMORE

It's a theme park—a seven hundred and eighty-six square mile theme park—and the theme is "you can have anything you want."

It is the most California-looking of all the Californias: the most like the movies, the most like the stories, the most like the dream.

Orange County is Tomorrowland and Frontierland, merged and inseparable. 18th century mission. 1930s art colony. 1980s corporate headquarters.

There's history everywhere: navigators, conquistadors, padres, rancheros, prospectors, wildcatters. But there's so much Now, the Then is hard to find. The houses are new. The cars are new. The stores, the streets, the schools, the city halls—even the land and the ocean themselves look new.

The temperature today will be in the low 80s. There's a slight offshore breeze. Another just-like-yesterday day in paradise.

Come to Orange County. It's no place like home.[4]

As the spin-doctoring wizards of the California Office of Tourism proclaim, you can have *anything* you want in Orange County, where every day seems just like yesterday but the ever-present Now-ness of Tomorrowland makes the Then hard to find; where every place is slightly off center, breathlessly on the edge but always right in the middle of things, smack on the frontier, nowhere yet now/here like home. To its avid promoters, Orange County is a theme park–themed paradise where the American Dream is repetitively renewed and made infinitely available. This resplendent bazaar of repackaged times and spaces allows all that is contemporary (including histories and geographies) to be encountered and consumed with an almost Edenic simultaneity.

Orange County represents itself as a foretaste of the future, a genuine phenomenological *re-creation* of would-be everyday life in a brilliantly recombinant postmodern world, beyond Oz, beyond even the utopic late modernisms of Disney. The most "California-looking" of all the advertised Californias, Orange County leads the way in the very contemporary competition to identify the Happiest Place on Earth. If any other place is still in the running, it is purely through faithful simulations of the original. And every day more simulations of Orange County are springing up— around Boston, New York, San Francisco, Chicago, Washington, Dallas– Fort Worth, Miami, Atlanta—and most recently Beijing and Shanghai, where Orange County master builders were chosen to create Chinese postsuburbia.

It is almost as if the urban is being reinvented in places like Orange County to celebrate the end of the millennium. And *you are there* whether you like it or not, looking at the coming attractions being screened well beyond modernity's urban fringe. Suspend disbelief for the moment, control the cynical sneers, and enjoy the strangely familiar ride into paradigmatic postmodernity. It may soon be coming to your neighborhood, wherever you are . . .

SCENES FROM ORANGE COUNTY AND A LITTLE BEYOND

The following twelve abbreviated scenes from Orange County are wrapped around newspaper clippings and a few more academic references from other travelers in and through its hyperrealities. To guide you, here is a map of the territory, designed just for this purpose (map 12).

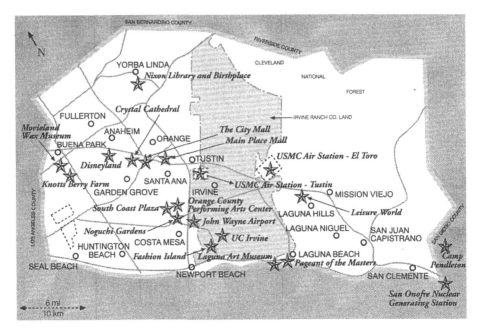

MAP 12 Orange County sites. From *Thirdspace*, 1996.

A VH1 video describing Orange County's global leadership in punk music provides contemporary background for your journey. The makers of the video were shocked to find that Swiss punks in Zurich, Argentine youth in Buenos Aires, and their Korean versions in Seoul all looked to Orange County for their music, clothing, and lifestyle choices. While punk music had died in other originating sites, such as London, New York, and Los Angeles, it was thriving in OC. Hoping to explain how this could occur in a boring suburb of LA, they came to interview me in Irvine and outside Disneyland (app. 2, video 3).

I told them OC was no longer traditional suburbia and had been urbanizing for forty years, creating a new urban form where arch-conservative new wealth made everything available to young men and women, expecting them to excel at least in the world of sports. A youthful mix took shape connecting skateboarding, surfing, water and mountain skiing, and other extreme sports (said to have been invented in OC). Teenage rebellion was difficult with such enticing surroundings, but when it broke through, it often flipped to extreme forms to ensure escape from the smothering local culture.

Punk developed early in OC, almost as if it were a grounding force in the infectious scamscape, a way for spoiled youth to fight further absorption into the enveloping hyperrealities of postsuburbia. If, as I have been arguing, the emergent scamscape represents, among many other effects, a means of social control and discipline, it becomes less surprising to discover in Orange County an especially rich seedbed of punk rebellion. It is also not surprising that this locally freewheeling rebelliousness is heavily commercialized and globally controlled in its external outreach.

Scene 1: A Mythology of Origins

The economic geographer Allen Scott called Orange County "a paradigmatic example of the new patterns of industrialization and urbanization that are now being laid down on the American economic landscape."[5] A quiet agricultural backwater in the 1950s, Orange County began to industrialize in the 1960s, and by the early 1970s a tightly organized high-technology industrial complex had formed to compete with Silicon Valley as a newly industrialized suburban region, a localized version of the NICs—newly industrialized countries, such as Korea and Taiwan.

The exopolis here is depicted first of all as industrial and industrious, a transactional tapestry efficiently knotted into a series of flexible manufacturing and service complexes, great swarms of businesses tied up in hive-like clusters to capture the new "scope" economies of post-Fordist technology. No longer bound by the rigid hierarchical demands of Fordist mass production and assembly lines, a new kind of industrialization was begetting a new kind of "peripheral" urbanization, an offset urban form. The tightly manufactured landscape of flexible economic specialization backed by hyperconservative local politics—the John Birch Society began in overwhelmingly Republican Orange County—is the bedrock of exopolis, not only in Orange County but also around many other large American cities.

To call this densely knit assemblage of manufacturers and their subcontracted servants "postindustrial" is surely to miss the point. And just as surely the area is no longer "sub" urban. Orange County may have no dominant city in the traditional sense, no easily identified center or skyscrapered downtown, but it is a metropolis nonetheless, an industrial capitalist city of a new kind. In places like Irvine, jobs outnumber bedrooms, and it is alleged that as much traffic flows into OC from LA County as in the other direction. We are not in suburbia any more.

Scene 2: Cathedrals of Iconic Reassurance

Spiraling outward from the industrial nucleations of postsuburbia is a remarkable galaxy of locales. Place by place, they too provide paradigmatic reflections of the orbital exopolis. To begin, Umberto Eco in his *Travels in Hyperreality*, takes us to several "absolute fakes, cities that imitate a city": first to the Movieland Wax Museum (a localized but now closed version of Madame Tussaud's) and Knott's Berry Farm (the first of OC's major theme parks), and ultimately to Disneyland, which Eco described as

> a degenerate utopia . . . an ideology realized in the form of a myth . . . presented as at once absolutely realistic and absolutely fantastic . . . a disguised supermarket where you buy obsessively, thinking that you are still playing. . . . Disneyland makes it clear that within its magic enclosure it is fantasy that is being absolutely reproduced . . . but the "total fake" to be enjoyed must seem totally real. . . . Here, in these cathedrals of iconic reassurance, we can not only enjoy a perfect imitation, we can also enjoy the conviction that imitation has reached its apex and afterwards reality will always be inferior to it.[6]

Today the artful simulations of Disneyland seem almost folkloric, crusty residuals of a passing era. Now you do not just choose to visit these hyperreality factories at your leisure; *hyperreality visits you* every day, wherever you choose to be, via various virtual venues.

Scene 3: The Diversions of Yorba Linda

> There are engines and anchors in every country, and they change over time. When I was born in Yorba Linda, the area [Orange County] was an anchor—an agricultural region and something of a playland. It is now the engine of progress in America, an area where entrepreneurs are gathering to drive the American dream forward. Look at the educational infrastructure, the corporate infrastructure, the political leadership, and you see America's future. . . . Its peoples and products are changing America . . . its political leaders are responsible for the peaceful revolution of the East Bloc. Some of my old friends . . . will remain stalwarts of freedom. We owe them a great deal of thanks for their patient support of a sound defense that helped bring about global change. Others are new and shining stars . . . among the most talented additions to the United States Congress in the last twenty-five years. In time . . . they too will become superstars.

Thus spake Richard Milhous Nixon, as reported in the glossy magazine *Orange Coast* in July 1990, just before the grand opening of the Nixon Library and Birthplace in the first of his hometowns, Yorba Linda, once a Quaker settlement and now a large-lot, zoned-for-horses, almost lily-white municipality, tucked away in the northern reaches of Orange County.

The difficult-to-find, subterranean Nixon Library had stirred some controversy over whether it would be open to those who might find something critical of the ex-president. It was later decided that finding anything critical would be impossible. Whether this was because it did not exist or because it could not be found was unclear. Also at the Nixon Birthplace is a $400,000 simulation of the original home built by Nixon's father from a $300 Sears Roebuck kit. Nixon's deep voice is piped in to reminisce about his first nine years in Yorba Linda, amid all kinds of reproduced memorabilia, including the humble family piano that Dick's mother often whipped him into playing, and the mnemonic sound of a passing train to recreate a sense of history. Could it all be real? You bet . . .

Scene 4: UC Irvine—A Campus by Design

Looking out over the empty hills of the Irvine Ranch in the late 1950s, planner William Pereira searched his mind for a powerful metaphor to match the University of California campus he envisioned. As reported by Leon Whiteson in the *Los Angeles Times* (December 12, 1988):

> Pereira's aim . . . was to establish a heart and a sense of place that would offer the first students a feeling for "the destiny of the campus." . . . At the heart of the campus was a series of concentric rings—the innermost containing undergraduate facilities, the outer one housing graduate and research buildings. This ring-within-a-ring metaphor was intended to express a student's progress, from the self-absorbed concentration of the first years of study to the wider circle of the world beyond the campus. While the late architect's master plan was bold, the buildings he fleshed it out with in the 1960s and 1970s were, in the view of many observers, overscaled and boringly detailed . . . a bunch of giant cheese graters. Now all this is changing.

Urban history repeating itself as farce: ring-within-a-ring development representing itself as progress and modernity, disenchantment flourishing when the outer limits are reached, urban memories of old progressive dreams falling apart in the orange sunlight. Now modernity itself is being replaced by deliberately postmodern architectonics . . . a new and different destiny, an enveloping hypersimulation of unlimited expansion, reconcentration, recentering. A new urban space takes shape when the inner rings are left behind as stale plots from a departed past. Whiteson adds, "UCI has inaugurated a $350 million expansion that, by 1992, will feature more than 20 major new complexes designed by the some of the best U.S. and international architects." UCI, which some have translated as "Under Construction Indefinitely," has become a virtual architectural theme park. Among the places to visit:

On the eastern quadrant, writes Whiteson, "Charles Moore's Italianate Alumni House and Extension classroom complex—described by one critic as a stage set for an opera by Puccini—plays off a colonnaded Graduate School of Management by New York–based Venturi, Rauch, Scott-Brown." Actually, the playfulness of Moore's Extension Building, located where UCI's specialized spoke for the social sciences "extends" to the outside world, is less operatic than televisual. Moore himself saw it as the piazza of some imagined Italo-Spanish-California town, bounded by three Baroque church fronts and a rancho-style verandah, into which, on some dark night, a sworded Zorro might ride and slash his *Z* in the dust. Sure enough, during the dedication ceremonies, a masked man dressed in black swooped out of the shadows, presented a plaque to establish authenticity, bowed with a smile beneath his penciled mustache, and cut the air with three swipes of his sword. This instant memory, fantastically faked, made all the necessary reel-world connections.

Elsewhere, more playfulness abounds. To the south, quirky, raw-looking fabrications by Frank Gehry and Eric Owen Moss present images of children toying with giant building blocks. On the west, a "Food Satellite Center" designed by the chic architectural group Morphosis to serve the Humanities Department contains a row of freestanding columns as if it were an instant architectural ruin. Across a mall-like space is a pop-postmodern science library by James Stirling brightly banded in multicolored stucco. To the north of the library is a Fine Arts Village by Robert Stern; and to the south, a horizontally striped green glass and plastic Biological Sciences Unit by Arthur Erickson. Maybe it all comes together in UC Irvine? (See app. 1, source 3B).

Scene 5: Spotting the Spotless in the City of Irvine

Lying just outside, in the exocampus of UCI, is Irvine, the largest New Town (or New City?) in the United States, a jewel in the crown of the master-planning Irvine Company, owner of one-sixth of Orange County (see the shaded area on map 12) and donor of the land on which the university (and Irvine) was built. Always planning ahead, the Irvine Company endlessly produces absolutely real fakes to simulate a thicker appearance of urbanity. Let us enter another scene with Maria La Ganga, *Los Angeles Times,* November 5, 1988.

> Throw out those visions of pool tables and dart boards. Forget about pickled eggs and older waitresses who call you "hon." The city of Irvine [with its more than one hundred thousand inhabitants at the time] just got its very first bar, and none of the above are anywhere to be seen.
>
> For the Trocadero—not surprisingly—is Irvine incarnate, a so-Southern California watering hole located across the street from UC Irvine and characterized by its owners as "an upscale, traditional Jamaican plantation."
>
> As the very first real bar in Irvine history, the Trocadero is as much a symbol as it is a saloon. The Trocadero's owners and site were hand-picked by the Irvine Co., which controls 50% of the city's retail space and has spent decades carefully molding the retail mix in this spotless [the perfect spatial adjective] suburb. . . .
>
> As the new owners Mark and Cindi H. say of their latest endeavor, [it is] a bar where patrons can graze on appetizers including fresh oysters injected with Stolichnaya and topped with orange hollandaise [of course].
>
> About a year and a half ago, the development company approached Mark to design and run this bar-to-be and its very trendy kitchen. Mark, at the time, was co-owner along with brother-in-law Chuck Norris of action-film fame, of a successful Newport Beach bar. . . . Cindy was a modeling school owner who just happened to be Miss California/USA 1981, third runner-up for Miss USA in the same year, and voted by her cohorts as Miss Congeniality and Most Photogenic.
>
> What's a barkeep to do when faced with such an opportunity? Mark sold his bar, married Cindy and went on an extended honeymoon in the Caribbean . . . collecting ideas for the proposed pub. . . . The product of all that honeymoon research was . . . a Honduran mahogany bar and back bar to suggest "manliness," Mark said, marble-topped tables, ceiling fans, palm trees and primary colors for a "feminine" touch.

Cindy exclaimed, "When we went before the Planning Commission to tell them our idea they gave us a standing ovation, they were so pleased to finally have a bar here." The Trocadero survives today as an Italian restaurant sans any Caribbean references. There are still fewer than ten pubs and bars in Irvine despite there being more than 250 in the surrounding communities.

Swinging over to the west bank of the UCI campus, we find another gathering of master-planned spaces of a different sort in a corridor running along the Newport Freeway from Santa Ana to Costa Mesa and Newport Beach. This is the Grand Axis-Mundi of exopolitan Orange County. Here is how the boosterish *Airport Business Journal* described it in 1984.

> It has been said before, but we'll say it again—the MacArthur Corridor is . . . booming at a mind-boggling rate. We all get tired of the millennia of urbanized cities [??] and communities staking their claim that they are the place to be. Developers along the MacArthur Corridor need only sit back and let their projects speak for themselves.
>
> Not since 1849 have Californians witnessed anything quite like it: a massive stampede of fortune seekers eagerly laying claim to any piece of land they can lay their hands on, their eyes fired with a burning hunger, crawling over each other for a chance to cash in on untold riches.
>
> Only this time it isn't gold they're breaking ground for—it's office buildings. MacArthur Boulevard, once a two-lane asphalt path running through orange groves and tomato patches, has widened like a flooded river . . . its banks giving root to towering office complexes.
>
> . . . all signs point to this section of the County . . . becoming *the* major financial center in the county, perhaps California, and perhaps the United States.

These gushing developments along the MacArthur Corridor, as well as wildly ambitious plans for the future, were in the late 1980s remarkably reproduced in miniature in the now nonexistent Irvine Exhibit, a real estate PR extravaganza formerly housed in the Jamboree Center. I will take you along with me on my first and only visit.

To get to the exhibit you must pass through columns of transplanted palm trees and a set of revolving doors to an imposing security desk, where you are asked to leave your cameras behind. Disarmed, you are led to the plush seats of a small theater that vibrates with anticipatory technologies. The whole front wall is a split-screen panorama upon which is soon projected a dazzling array of scenes—of birds and babies, sunsets and shorelines, family outings and businessmen's lunches, clouds and lakes (always lakes) and cuddly animals—all set to stereophonic music and soothing voices announcing the sales-pitch messages that appear, in resolutely capitalized words, on the brochure clutched in your hands.

THERE ARE ONLY TWO LASTING THINGS WE CAN GIVE OUR CHILDREN. ONE IS ROOTS. THE OTHER IS WINGS . . . ROOTS AND WINGS . . . BOTH IN THE COMMUNITY AND THE NATURAL ENVIRONMENT, A BALANCE MUST BE ESTABLISHED IF THE INTEGRITY OF THE SYSTEM IS TO REMAIN SECURE . . . A CONSTELLATION OF TECHNOLOGY AND BUSINESS . . . ADVENTURES FOR THE MIND. A GIFT OF TIME. A GIFT OF FAMILY . . . THE IRVINE EXHIBIT . . . WE CAN HAVE THE DREAM. WE HAVE THE PLACE WHERE WE CAN PUT DOWN ROOTS. WHERE OUR LIVES CAN TAKE WING.

The air is almost drugged with an effort to make you believe, to make you want to consume new promises. But suddenly the flashing pictures stop and the screen-wall becomes transparent, a shimmering gossamer film behind which a secret room appears. Still in your seat, the music still throbbing in your ears, you realize that the whole floor of the secret room is moving, tilting up before your eyes, coming at you slowly to fill up the wall with a portentous overview of Irvine Earth, an exact model (simulacrum?) of the real world of ROOTS AND WINGS. You gather your belongings and move toward the alluring model as it slowly, seductively, tilts back to receive you. It is a fascinating site, detailed down to the lane markers on the freeways and the loose dust where new homes and offices are being built.

But this totalizing "area model" is not enough. After a brief lecture, a guide takes you through marbled halls and up steel-capsule elevators to another floor, where the model itself is reproduced in progressively larger-scale close-up photos. You are moved, room by room, closer and closer to the ultimate one-to-one correspondence between representation and reality, the map and the territory. The final stop is a space almost entirely filled with a giant structure very much like the building you are in, exact in nearly every detail, offices lit and filled with miniature accoutrements, including little people and tiny framed pictures on the walls (made by computers, you are proudly told). You feel like peeking into the second floor to see if you too can be seen there, peeking into the second floor . . .

The experience is finally capped when the beaming guide pushes a button and the apparently solid outer wall disappears, revealing a huge window onto the palm-colonnaded entranceway and the surrounding buildings and grounds of the Irvine Business Complex. You thank the guides, walk back to the security desk, retrieve your camera, and exit, noting how disappointing and dull the real columns of palm trees look in comparison to their artful imitations on the second floor.

Reminiscing, I think again of Jean Baudrillard's reflections on California, when he too stopped off at Irvine. "There is a violent contrast here," he says, "between the growing abstractness of a nuclear universe and a primary, visceral, unbounded vitality, springing not from rootedness, but from the lack of roots." He goes on to describe the United States and, by implication, Orange County as well, as "the only remaining primitive society . . . *the primitive society of the future,* a society of complexity, hybridity . . . whose immanence is breathtaking, yet lacking a past through which to reflect on this."[7]

Scene 7: It's a Mall World after All

On the other side of John Wayne International Airport, mainly in the city of Costa Mesa, the Irvine Empire has its chief competitor for centrality in Orange County. The locals call it South Coast Metro, although there is nothing metropolitan about it. Here one finds the rest of the large business parks (South Coast Metro Center, Center Tower, Home Ranch, Town Center); streets named Town Center Avenue and Park Center Drive; and California's largest shopping mall, with its ten thousand parking spaces. The place reeks of anticipatory pretensions of becoming the true upscale downtown simulacrum, the center of centers in a centerless urbanity. Here too culture is being hopefully centralized with breathtaking immanence, as described by Allen Temko, *Los Angeles Times,* December 20, 1987.

> When America gets around to culture, the pioneers used to say, America will make culture hum. Except for places like Texas, there's nowhere the frontier spirit hums better than in affluent Orange County, which finally has symphony, opera, ballet, Broadway musicals, you name it, in a $73 million Orange County Performing Arts Center, known by its awful acronym OCPAC.
>
> Victory over any barbarian past is signified by a mighty triumphal arch. . . . Never mind that the arch is a structural fake. Its reddish granite cladding is pure veneer, covering a trussed inner frame, all angles and squares, that has nothing to do with a rounded form. The great forward wall is nothing more than a free-standing screen, an enormous advertisement, cut open in the shape of an arch.
>
> Yet the superficial effect is grand . . . the great symbolic portal—which turns out to be not a real entrance at all—swells majestically across the front of Segerstrom Hall, a 3,000-seat auditorium that is OCPAC's pride and joy. At night, when the building is lit, the arch acts as a monumental proscenium

for the social drama attending the performance, revealing open terraces that are crowded on warm evenings, glittering and mirrored spaces within—spectacularly walled in glass—through which a colossal "Firebird" sculpture by Richard Lippold crashes outward into the void, flashing brightly colored metal plumage.

There could be no better emblem for Orange County, crashing through provincialism to the big-time world of music and art.... Despite many architectural flaws, Segerstrom Hall is, functionally, the *finest multipurpose facility of its kind in the country.*

So too, one might say, is all of Orange County: a structural fake, an enormous advertisement, yet for all its flaws functionally the finest multipurpose facility of its kind in the country, the "primitive society" of our future . . .

Scene 8: Olympian Recentering in Mission Viejo

Thus far we have concentrated on the breathtaking industrial-cum-commercial-cum-cultural landscapes of exopolis, only hinting at the existence of residential population. It is time now for another spin outward, to the sleeping margins of exopolis, the superdormitories of the southern half of Orange County, another vast zone of recentering. One place stands out amid them all: Mission Viejo, a congeries of themed housing developments built to attract superjock parents who want their children to bring home gold medals. And in the 1984 Olympic Games, they did.

Taking us along to Mission Viejo are Mark Landesbaum and Heidi Evans, *Los Angeles Times,* August 22, 1984.

Mission Viejo—swim capital of the world, mecca for medalists, home of the perfect 10 high dive, three competition swimming pools but only one public library—is nestled alongside a freeway in the rolling hills of south Orange County. Billed by its developer as "The California Promise," it has emerged as the epitome of the American Dream.

During the [1984] Olympic Games, 200 of the world's best bicycle racers pedaled for the gold here past neat lawns, $1-million lake-front homes, a private gated community and 200,000 cheering fans. Swimmers and divers trained here in Mission Viejo before reaping a harvest of Olympic medals, nine gold, two silver, and one bronze—more medals than were won by France or Britain or, for that matter, 133 of the 140 nations taking part in the Games.

The world-famous Nadadores swim and diving teams train here, and are subsidized by the Mission Viejo Co., the developer. But there are also three wading pools, 19 lighted tennis courts, 12 handball and racquetball courts, five volleyball courts, two outdoor basketball courts, men's and women's saunas, two weight rooms, four outdoor playgrounds, a multipurpose gym, 19 improved parks, four recreation centers, a 125-acre man-made lake, two golf courses, and three competition pools (one a 50-meter Olympic pool), and more—all built or donated, some still owned and operated, by the company.

A local real estate saleswoman and Municipal Advisory Board member summed it up: "It's a community that offers a great life style—a house in the suburbs, and your children kept busy. I think this is an area that people will flock to." Another member of the council adds: "How can anyone from the East have anything but desire to move out here with us? I couldn't speak too highly of the community—I'm in love with it." Some, however, are less devoted. A forty-year old housewife feels "out of step."

> It's just a status thing here.... You must be happy, you must be well rounded and must have children who do a lot of things. If you don't jog or walk or bike, people wonder if you have diabetes or some other disabling disease.... We need a little more Huck Finn around here ... more time to kick tin cans down the street.

She later asked a reporter not to identify her because her comments could "create friction" for her husband with his business and golfing friends, who, she said, "are *very Mission Viejo*."

Imitations and analogs of the corporate New Town of Mission Viejo (itself an imitation of the corporate New Town of Irvine) are filling up the frontier lands of south Orange County, lining Saddleback Valley and other areas with a sprawl of coalescing urblets. Like the originals, they reach out for specialized residential markets and tightly package the local environment and lifestyle, to the point of prescribing through thick contracts the colors you may paint your house, whether you can hang an American (or other) flag outside your front door, and how best to keep up with the residential theme—Spanish Colonial, Greek Island, Capri Villa, Uniquely American, etc. Some say this thickly contracted living is private-sector socialism. The lawyers call it association-administered servitude regimes.

Scene 9: Orbital Landscapes for the Elderly

Forming an integral part of the residential panorama of Orange County are two elderly New Towns, each aging rather gracefully, one near the western border with LA County, the other, called Leisure World, nestled into the Laguna Hills. The Laguna Leisure World is considered to be the largest retirement community in America, a "privatopia" that has many attractions. Around it has developed another specialized orbital landscape, vividly described by James S. Granelli (*Los Angeles Times,* February 2, 1986).

> The one-time bean fields outside Leisure World have sprouted at least nine securities brokerage houses, five banks, 12 savings institutions and numerous other money handlers ... turning a five-block area outside the main gate ... into a supermarket of financial services. And many more brokers, bankers, and lenders are a short distance away.
>
> Retirement communities attracting brokers is not unusual. . . . But Leisure World, which opened in September 1964, is different. The development has an intense concentration of money and is located in a growing area. "It's the largest growth of upper wealth in the county," they say. About 21,000 mostly retired people live in nearly 13,000 units on more than 2,000 acres of land, with an average age of 76 and home values ranging from $40,000 to more than $400,000, not including the land, which is owned by the Leisure World housing corporation.
>
> The residents often were captains of industry—retired corporate executives, bank executives. . . . At least three retired Army generals and two Navy admirals, along with a retired German U-boat captain from World War I, live in Leisure World.

The generals and admirals residing in this targeted El(derly) Dorado bring us to a more secretive series of theme parks being exposed with the in-filling of the outer spaces of the county.

Scene 10: Exopolitan Wars

George Frank, in "Urban Sprawl: A New Foe Surrounds the Military" (*Los Angeles Times,* December 24, 1988), tells the story of the densification of Orange County—how the rapid increase in population and commercial development has been threatening the once constraint-free military establishments of yesteryear.

> A Marine Lt. Col. was still angry about the Japanese attack on Pearl Harbor as he flew over the wide-open farmlands of Orange County. It was 1942 and he was searching for "just the right place" for a mainland airfield where Marine Corps aviators would be trained for the campaign to regain the Pacific.

As he swept over a tiny railroad whistle-stop called El Toro, he spotted a sprawling plot of land covered with bean fields and orange groves. It was perfect: few and far away neighbors; close to the ocean so pilots could practice carrier landings; within range of desert bombing ranges; and near Camp Pendleton, the Corps' then-new 125,000-acre troop-training base. "Orange County was an ideal place for military bases," he recalled almost fifty years later. "It was all open country.... There was hardly anyone living there."

Today, that Orange County airfield—the El Toro Marine Corps Air Station—is under a siege the old Marine could not have imagined in 1942. Tightly packed housing tracts have brought tens of thousands of neighbors creeping closer and closer to the base fences. High-rise buildings, shopping centers and industrial parks are popping up around the airfield.... With the advance of urban development have come the volleys of complaints about the thunderous screams of low flying Marine Corps jets.

The peacetime assault on El Toro is not unique. Base commanders from Boston to San Diego and Seattle to Jacksonville are defending their ground against well-organized community groups, environmental activists, land-hungry developers and demanding local political leaders.

Battle lines are constantly being drawn to reflect the little exopolitan wars over territory and spatial control. Besieged military commanders and weapons testers fiercely defend their once pristine fortresses against many "enemies": well-organized community groups and homeowners' associations fighting for their property rights and values; land-hungry developers and self-proclaimed community builders hunting for new room to accumulate; a few environmental activists desperately seeking sanctuaries for the many endangered species of the exopolis.

Everything in these exopolitan wars seems to revolve around emplacement and positioning, or what Michel Foucault once described as "the little tactics of the habitat" and the "micro-technologies of power." Three more newspaper clippings point out these complicated militarized habitactics. For each, I suggest a background song, to be heard while you are reading.

> *Up a Laser River.* A flash fire at a test facility near San Juan Capistrano [where the sparrows always come back to] will delay indefinitely the final testing of the missile-killing Alpha laser [capable of obliterating whole cities if necessary], a key component of President Reagan's "Star Wars" defense initiative.... [T]he fire broke out at the TRW plant in southern Orange County when a worker opened a valve at the wrong time.... With the vacuum chamber contaminated by smoke and debris, officials said it is impossible to conduct experiments in which the laser beam would be produced and tested in

space-like conditions. (Richard Beene and John Broder, *Los Angeles Times,* January 29, 1988)

SONGS of Silence. Three nuclear reactors are now [1987] being used at the San Onofre Nuclear Generating Station (SONGS) to generate electricity at the largest and, potentially, the most dangerous nuclear power plant west of the Mississippi.... The plant represent one of the most terrifying threats imaginable, short of full-scale war, yet people seldom speak of that. They live in the "Basic Emergency Planning Zone," with its questionable promise that, in the event of something untoward, there will be a sure and hasty evacuation of everyone. The people hereabouts depended on that, even as they depend on assurances that it won't ever be needed. What will it take to arouse them? I tell them that a single meltdown at SONGS could cause 130,000 early deaths, 300,000 latent cancers, and the evacuation of 10 million people.... They listen, but they cannot allow themselves to consciously accept such grim processes. They choose not to live in fear. (Fred Grumm, *Los Angeles Times,* October 11, 1987) [SONGS closed down in 2013.]

Tern, Tern, Tern. Camp Pendleton ... has become the last sanctuary for many endangered species. Pendleton troops engaged in field warfare training must be careful to avoid the nesting areas of the light-footed clapper rail, the Belding's Savannah Sparrow or the California least tern.... "The West Coast is right now in the lead as far as the encroachment problems go," [a Marine colonel] said. (George Frank, "Urban Sprawl: A New Foe Surrounds the Military," *Los Angeles Times,* December 24, 1988.)

Scene 11: Scamscapes—Capitals of Fiction Become Reality

Every day, life in Orange County seems to move one step beyond Umberto Eco's vision of Disneyland as "a degenerate utopia ... presented as at once absolutely realistic and absolutely fantastic," and deeper into Jean Baudrillard's world of hypersimulation, where "it is no longer a question of false representation, but of concealing the fact that the real is no longer real."[8] Perhaps more than any other place, Orange County sustains Baudrillard's vision of the anesthetic enchantment of hyperreality, where serious politics is abandoned to enjoy the many tempting diversions. Rather than being degenerate, however, OC is a generative utopia, a make-believe paradise that makes you believe in make-believing.

Under these transcendental conditions, it is no surprise that image and reality become spectacularly confused, that the difference between true and false, fact and fiction, not only disappears but becomes ... irrelevant. In this next look inside exopolis, another inventive postmodern geography is explored: the fraudulent—or better, metafraudulent—*scamscape,* ecstatic playground for the habitactics of make-believe, as introduced in an untitled article in the Los Angeles *Daily News,* March 24, 1987.

> Orange County owns the dubious title of "the fraud capital of the world," according to U.S. Postal Service inspectors. Five inspectors working out of the Santa Ana post office will handle mail-fraud complaints involving as many as 10,000 victims this year.... It is estimated that the county suffers losses of $250 million a year in [postal] fraud.... Orange County's affluence and the large number of retired people living here combine to make the area a favorite of con men.
>
> Postal inspectors say the hottest current schemes involve precious-metal futures. Underground boiler room operations typically convince investors they can reap huge profits and then spend their money on parties, drugs, and cars.... The operators usually disappear about the time the investors become suspicious.
>
> Another popular scam, envelope-stuffing, is difficult to trace because victims who send in money to learn how to participate are usually too embarrassed to admit they've been had.

More than two hundred boiler rooms—named for the intensity of activity in the barest of spaces—punctuate the scamscape of Orange County, reportedly generating activities that gross over $1 billion a year, more than the local drug barons earn. The typical boiler room is, at its base, a telemarketing center serving to collect money for charities, public television stations, and credit card and loan applications, as well as to promote investment schemes promising quick and easy profits. The basic work is done by "wholesome youth" on telephones with high-tech "confidencers" used to sift out all background noise. Often starting out their employment careers, the youthful telemarketers are trained by experts who instill confidence and entrepreneurship with promises of advancement to higher levels of take-home pay (much of it tax-free, it is hinted). The densest agglomeration of boiler rooms is probably in and around Newport Beach, one fraud inspector said, "simply because it sounds classier on the phone than, say, Pomona."

Bogus "investment opportunities" are promoted by young telemarketers reading from prepared scripts infused with the illusions of make-believe. According to authorities, the average boiler room fraud victim loses between $40,000 and $50,000. One was reported to have invested $400,000 based on a single telephone call, and another, a ninety-year-old widow in Nebraska, sent off $750,000 to a young man who told her he was "a native Nebraska boy brought up with high morals" and was working way through college. During one police raid, a placard was found on a salesman's desk. Effectively capturing the sincerely duplicitous honesties of the boiler room, another of the magical enclosures of the exopolis, the placard proudly proclaimed: WE CHEAT THE OTHER GUY AND PASS THE SAVINGS ON TO YOU!

The boiler room is only one of many indications that Orange County, the place "where you can have anything you want," has become the most active scamscape on earth. The Defense Criminal Investigative Service office in Laguna Niguel, which investigates fraud in the defense industry, is the largest in the country, befitting Southern California's world leadership in the devastating production of offensive weapons. In highly specialized OC, the most serious defense frauds involved product substitution and the falsification of test results, such as was rumored in the case of a local firm that manufactured "fuzes" for the warheads of Phoenix air-to-air missiles—the weapons of choice for "Top Gun" Navy jet pilots.

The frightening function of fuzes is appropriately ambivalent: the fuze both detonates the warhead and prevents it from detonating prematurely. Exceedingly proud of their prowess, workers in an OC fuze factory confidently raised embossed metal signs that read: THE BEST DAMNED FUZES IN THE WORLD ARE MANUFACTURED BEHIND THIS DOOR and hinted that this made thorough testing unnecessary and superfluous. It was never proven that test results were falsified or that flawed fuzes were ignored, but there are stories that fuzes from this OC plant failed in their purpose during the first Gulf War, costing significant loss of life.[9]

Other fraudulent schemes found in the OC scamscape include bankruptcy and foreclosure scams, stock swindling, computer crimes, environmental regulation crimes, real estate cons, and many types of insurance fraud, often committed by "capper lawyers" who stage automobile accidents and occupational injuries to get their percentages. But these everyday scams are small change when compared to the savings and loan industry scandal in the late 1980s. Reportedly costing nearly $500 billion to cover up and repair, this "metafraud" had deep roots in Orange County. Charles Keating's infamous Lincoln Savings and Loan Association, the focus of an influence-peddling investigation that involved Alan Cranston, John Glenn, and John McCain, had branches around the country, but its headquarters was in Irvine.

Scene 12: Orange County Bankruptcy—1994

One could not have written a script that comes close to the denouement that hit Orange County in 1994, not very long after the savings and loan scandal. In December of that year, the scamscape imploded when the county, among the richest in America, declared bankruptcy. Compared to the modern fiscal crisis that hit New York City in 1975, this had to be described as a postmodern fiscal fiasco, emerging not from excess spending on social welfare but from the fraudulent financial hyperrealities of the fulsome scamscape.

When the bankruptcy was announced, it was discovered that OC had been running its finances very much like the savings and loan companies before the meltdown. Just as Keating came to symbolize a new entrepreneurial model of people-oriented investment, the Orange County Investment Fund, run by a folksy tax collector with the almost dementedly appropriate name of Citron, became known throughout the country as a pioneer of the "new fiscal populism." Through the artful financial manipulations of Citron and his crew, OC found a way to make up for the radical downsizing of property tax revenues that followed passage of Proposition 13 in 1978 (product of a statewide tax revolt led by Orange County archconservatives), allowing for continued spending on parks and recreation and other services expected by the county elites.

Tax Collector Citron, the only Democrat in high office, lived modestly and signed public tax bills with a happy face during his twenty-four years in office. He became nationally applauded, however, for expanding county financial resources by plunging head-on into the magical realism of the new bond market, with its lush derivatives, reverse repos, and inverse floaters. Using local government's spectacular comparative advantage in financial markets—the ability to raise tax revenues and issue municipal and general obligation bonds whenever necessary—the Citron-led Orange County Investment Fund essentially gambled the county's well-being on the bond market and fluctuations in interest rates. By early 1994, the fund had reached more than $7 billion; by the end of the year, owing to market changes, the county had lost $1.7 billion and was forced into the largest municipal bankruptcy in U.S. history

The Orange County bureaucracy and voters, given their fiscal obsessions, refused to raise taxes by even a tiny percentage to respond to the crisis. Instead, three thousand public employees were discharged, and there were minor cutbacks to services. Citron eventually pleaded guilty to six felony charges and was sentenced to five years of supervised probation and one thousand hours of community service, although to the end he insisted he had done nothing wrong. While it could have been a warning of what was to come in the crash of 2008, the Orange County bankruptcy was quietly absorbed into the growing speculative bubble that would drench the national economy in unmanageable and unimaginable debt.

It is no mere coincidence, however, that Orange County contained one of the largest clusters of the national mortgage lenders most responsible for the subprime mortgage crisis that sparked the crash of 2008 and led to an almost unprecedented drainage of wealth from the poorest half of the U.S. population. Here were located the headquarters of Argent, New Century, Fremont Investment and Loan, Ameriquest, and Option One, all now either facing bankruptcy or under new management. The Orange County scamscape has been spreading to larger scales in many different ways.

SIMAMERICA: EXPANDING THE SCOPE OF THE ORANGE COUNTY SCAMSCAPE

To place the discussion of these simulated worlds in a wider perspective, it is useful to look back briefly at the specialized and politically successful production of hyperrealities that was practiced in the Reagan-Bush years, from 1980 to 1992, when Los Angeles exploded in one of the most destructive and violent urban uprisings in U.S. history. Without resorting to conspiracy theories or demeaning the patriotic intent of its primary leaders, it can be argued that a reactionary form of postmodern politics consolidated rapidly in the United States after the election of a Hollywood actor and ex-California governor as president in 1980.

A Republican majority had already been constructed around a "southern strategy" that thinly veiled an appeal to white racism in the Sunbelt and suburbia, heavily populated by those fleeing the perceived criminal threats and actual urban riots of increasingly dark inner cities since the 1960s. Crucial to the victory of every Republican presidential candidate starting with Reagan has been the net Republican vote of Orange County.

In power, the Reagan regime acted boldly to sustain the support of the so-called silent majority, one of a dazzling array of hypersimulations used to sell postmodern neoconservatism (often ideologically disguised as neoliberalism) to the American public. Remember, to simulate is quite different from dissimulating, which means pretending not to have what you actually have, lying or covering up, as in the early phases of the Watergate scandal or the "disinformation" programs connected to the Vietnam War. Simulation, in contrast but not contradiction, means pretending to have something that really isn't there and working hard to make others believe that it is, really.

One of the most effective and lasting hypersimulations of the Reagan years was the crusade against "Big Government," a political scam "spin-doctored" to make people believe that smaller government is always better and the country's problems arise from too much active government intervention and regulation. This became the ideological foundation for attacks on the welfare state, various antipoverty programs, and the entire civil rights movement. Arguments about "reverse racism" and "political correctness," while containing grains of truth, were broadcast convincingly to cover up and rationalize a growing tide of reactionary antiminority feeling. Perhaps the majority of (white) American voters were made to believe that the new global economy required belt-tightening austerity and lean-and-mean downsizing; that leniency toward gays and lesbians threatened "family values"; that abortion was a form of murder; that affirmative action actually hurt those it was meant to help. There were even some economists and sociologists willing to create theories and models so that these scams could be made to appear true.

Sunbelt and suburban virtues (including union bashing, the open shop, and the patriotic promotion of xenophobic whiteness) and, above all, the mythic and magical power of the free market and legendary American entrepreneurial skills were combined into a hyperreal substitute for Big Government. What Bush the father inadvertently called voodoo economics encouraged trickle-down theories, made deregulation (or sidestepping existing regulatory legislation) a necessary development strategy, legitimated privatization as a means of rescuing the public sector from real/imagined debt and inefficiency, and led one of the most undertaxed nations in the industrial world to support some of the biggest government programs to subsidize the rich. All this was occurring in a decade of deepening poverty, declining real wages, devastating deindustrialization, and gargantuan ballooning of national debt.

National politics in neoconservative SimAmerica, feeding off the spreading urban scamscapes so vividly exemplified in Orange County, continued to be emptied of substance and any presumption of factuality or objectivity well into the twenty-first century. The "reality-based community" was shunted aside by an army of professional spin doctors artfully promoting the creative

simulations that legitimized the costly wars in Iraq and Afghanistan, rationalized increasing privatization and deregulation, and made liberal
Democrats, labor unions, and even community-based organizations and
welfare agencies appear to be riddled with corruption and obsessed with rais-
ing taxes. Key to the success of these efforts, especially in mobilizing national
attention, was the emergence of a popular television network specialized in
such hypersimulation. What was formerly highly localized became, largely
through media intervention, a national movement with significant electoral
impact.

How then to respond to this ascendancy of SimAmerica? Reinvigorating
the reality-based community is essential but not enough. Renewing the same
old liberalism and/or radicalism will be easily dismissed by consolidated
neoconservative power. Finding some better ways to fight those who most
powerfully shape our lives, our lived spaces and times, is necessary, and this
will require shifts in new directions. I have no easy answers to present here,
but continuing to learn from Los Angeles, every chapter that follows contains hints toward creating more innovative forms of activism aimed at
achieving greater social and spatial justice. Rather than fomenting a revolutionary and total transformation of capitalism, the objective should be making capitalism as socialist as possible.

NOTES

1. The term *non-Hispanic white* developed with clear racist overtones to distinguish largely Caucasian Mexicans from what some thought to be even whiter
Americans. The preferred substitute that developed locally was *Anglo*. *Hispanic* was
also considered unsatisfactory, as was its prevailing substitute, *Spanish-speaking*.
Mexican-American was used to preserve nationality, while *Chicano/Chicana* emphasized Americanization through longer-term residence. Later, in an effort to create
an even larger hemispheric identity, the term *Latino* came into widespread usage.
The old Los Angeles term *Californio* has virtually disappeared, although some
descendants struggle to keep it alive.

2. Edward Soja, "Postmetropolitan Psychasthenia: A Spatioanalysis," in *Urban
Politics Now: Re-Imagining Democracy in the Neoliberal City,* ed. Gideon Boie and
Matthias Pauwels (BAVO) (Rotterdam: NAI Publishers, 2008).

3. The quote comes from an article written by Ron Suskind in the *New York
Times Sunday Magazine,* October 17, 2004. The full quote is: "The aide said that
guys like me were 'in what we call the reality-based community,' which he defined
as people who 'believe that solutions emerge from your judicious study of discernible

reality.'... 'That's not the way the world really works anymore,' he continued. 'We're an empire now, and when we act, we create our own reality. And while you're study-ing that reality—judiciously, as you will—we'll act again, creating other new reali-ties, which you can study too, and that's how things will sort out. We're history's actors . . . and you, all of you, will be left to just study what we do.'"

4. From a pamphlet called *The Californias,* issued by the California Office of Tourism, circa 1992.

5. Allen J. Scott, "New Frontiers of Industrial-Urban Development: The Rise of the Orange County High Technology Complex, 1955–1984," in *Metropolis: From the Division of Labor to Urban Form* (Berkeley and Los Angeles: University of California Press, 1988), 160.

6. Umberto Eco, *Travels in Hyperreality* (San Diego: Harcourt, 1986), 58.

7. Jean Baudrillard, *America* (London and New York: Verso, 1988), 7.

8. Jean Baudrillard, *Simulations* (New York: Semiotext(e), 1983).

9. See Ralph Vartabedian, "Cases of Defense Fraud Boom amid Cutbacks," *Los Angeles Times,* March 26, 1995.

FOUR

Comparing Los Angeles

After my Orange County adventures, with a few exceptions, I stopped writing directly about the Southern California region and began a new, more comparative phase of writing, lecturing, and learning from Los Angeles. Responding to the growing global interest in Los Angeles, I literally and figuratively took LA on tour around the world, responding to invitations to apply what had been learned to other urban contexts. Looking back, during the 1990s I came close to launching a new career as a "city critic," offering my (LA-based) views and impressions of other places very much like a movie reviewer or restaurant critic deals with films or food. Rather than learning more about Los Angeles itself, the emphasis shifted to building on and off the already established literature on LA, although the latter often informed the former in new and unexpected ways. The comparisons begin most notably with Amsterdam.

THE STIMULUS OF A LITTLE CONFUSION: COMPARING LOS ANGELES AND AMSTERDAM

In 1990, I spent three months living in the extraordinarily well-preserved Centrum of Amsterdam, jam-packed with narrow Dutch houses aligned along multiple rings of canals extending outward onion-like to an encirclement of fast-growing outer cities. A cadre of urban geographers and sociologists from the Centrum voor Grootsedelijk Onderzoek (Center for Metropolitan Studies) had invited me to visit as Centrum Professor, strategically settled me in on a volatile and exciting street where the past and present of the squatter movement were visibly demanding attention, and asked me only to give a public lecture and write a formal paper looking at Amsterdam from a Los Angeles perspective. The result was "The Stimulus of a Little Confusion: A Contemporary Comparison of Amsterdam and Los Angeles" (app. 1, source 4A), published first as the Text of a Special Lecture in 1991 and reprinted with revisions in *Thirdspace* (app. 1, source 6B).[1]

The title was taken from an essay by Henry James, collected in his "Transatlantic Sketches" (1875), in which he comments on experiencing the Netherlands for the first time. He wrote: "All these elements of the general spectacle in this entertaining country at least give one's regular habits of thought the stimulus of a little confusion and make one feel that one is dealing with an original genius" (p. 384). So much in Amsterdam was strangely familiar, while deceptively appearing rather ordinary, especially to the outside English speaker. Yet I was bowled over during my stay by the extraordinary urban agglomeration that was the Centrum of Amsterdam and by the abiding Dutch genius for creating a socially and spatially just urbanism, so unlike what I had been experiencing in Los Angeles. In his exploration of Dutch culture and what he called its "embarrassment of riches," the TV-savvy historian Simon Schama described the uncanny ability of the Dutch, especially in Amsterdam, to turn "catastrophe into good fortune, infirmity into strength, water into dry land, mud into gold."[2]

The vibrant Centrum was a slightly confusing yet stimulating assemblage of oxymorons and juxtapositions, a conglomeration of opposite forces that define the moral geography of Amsterdam. Filtering through the urban fabric was the imprint of highly regulated urban anarchism based on a slightly repressive form of tolerance and an odd combination of flexibility and rigidity. Feeling like I had entered some secret world, I discovered preserved in the Centrum, if not all of Amsterdam in 1990, a deep and enduring commitment to libertarian socialist values and participatory democracy (much of which, I understand, is being seriously undermined in the early twenty-first century). As I wrote at the time, "One senses that Amsterdam is not just preserving its own Golden Age but is actively keeping alive the very possibility of a socially just and humanely scaled urbanism . . . the most successful enactment of the anarcho-socialist-environmentalist intentions that inspired the urban social movements of the 1960s."

On Spuistraat

My writing on Amsterdam was divided in two parts. The first, "On Spuistraat," began with a description of the location of this border street in the western and oldest part of the city, near the old city wall and the Singel ("girdle"), the canal moat just beyond. Nearby is the old port and the Central Railway Station, on the teeming Stationsplein, where thousands of visitors from everywhere in the world first enter the Centrum. Angling into Spuistraat is the Raadhuisstraat, the start of the main east-west boulevard that leads to the Royal Palace (once the town hall, or *raadhuis*) and Dam Square. Here is where the city was born more than seven hundred years ago, in a portentous act of regulatory tolerance granting the local settlers toll-free use of the new dam across the Amstel River, Amstelledamme becoming Amsterdam.

In this first part, I tried to show that I could be a microgeographical flâ-neur, exploring the "view from below," in contrast to my usual macrogeo-graphical perch, looking mainly at what might be called Big Picture urban-ism. I started my flânerie by walking around the corner from where I was staying to pass through a large wooden door to the Beguinhof, or Beguine Court. The Beguines were a Dutch lay sisterhood that sought to combine convent-like constraints with freedom to leave and marry, giving to their habitat an odd but oh-so-Dutch mix of discipline and emancipation. Today the major occupants are unmarried ladies keeping up the traditions, along with hordes of tourists, mainly American, eager to see the ancient church where the fleeing English pilgrim fathers securely prayed before setting sail on the Mayflower. On one of my visits, the Loyola College choir from New Orleans was joyfully singing American spirituals to passersby. The Beguine Court at that time was a remarkably peaceful spot despite the flocking tour-ists, seemingly both open and closed to the outside world, like so many spaces in the paradoxical Centrum.

My canal house on Spuistraat was one of more than six thousand monu-ments to the Golden Age (fifteenth to sixteenth centuries) that are packed commemoratively into the Centrum, the largest, most lively and lived-in historic inner city in Europe. With a frontage no wider than my garage door back in Los Angeles, the building, like nearly all others, rose four stories to a gabled peak embedded with a startling metal hook designed for moving fur-niture and bulky items by ropes in through the wide windows. Given the narrow entrance and steep staircase *(trappenhuis)*, I had visions of my great bulk having to be hauled up the same way.

To live in a canal house is to immediately and precipitously encounter Amsterdam. The past is always present in its narrow nooks and odd-angled passageways, its flower-potted spaces and unscreened windows both open and closed to the views outside. You are invited every day into the enriching and communal urban spatiality, an invitation that is at once embracingly tolerant and carefully guarded. Not everyone can become an Amsterdammer, but everyone must at least be given a chance to try.

From my vantage point on Spuistraat, a moving picture of contemporary life in the vital center of Amsterdam visually unfolded. Through my window I could see the vertical class stratification of the canal house across the way, the first floor a comfortable home for a working woman who enjoyed candlelit dinners by her window; the second occupied by a couple expecting their first child and more nervously excitable and reclusive; while on the small, plastic-sheet-covered top floor a solitary male student sat alone eating his meals alfresco. It would not have been surprising to discover that everyone I saw, at one time or another, was part of the squatter movement.

The vertical view from my window was not only a transect of social class but also a reflection of the horizontal story of the squatter movement that was unfolding along Spuistraat. On the corner with Raadhuisstraat, looking north, was one end state of rehabilitated squatting: government-constructed rental housing and small shops for settled squatter renters (a whole bunch of contradictions here). Just next door was some new office construction on a site once occupied by squatters but traded off to the government authorities, probably in return for the comfortable corner compound. Next door to that, closer to my window, was an even earlier phase of the movement, a privately owned building recently occupied by squatters and brightly repainted, graffitoed, and festooned with political banners stretching across the street to another, slightly older, occupation. Painted on the building façade was the obviously absentee owner, caricatured as a fat tourist beached somewhere wearing sunglasses and with tropical drink in hand (figure 6).

Although waning significantly over the next two decades and virtually gone today, the squatter movement in Amsterdam had by 1990 etched itself more deeply into the urban fabric than in almost any other city in the world. Squatting symbolized the tense freedoms and regulated tolerance of a remarkable urban environment that at the time was vibrantly and democratically alive. Now hard to imagine, local authorities then published pamphlets entitled "How to Be a Squatter," radical squatters consistently got elected to the city council, and the spirit of the movement contributed to the fact that Amsterdam had more social housing than any other Western European city.

FIGURE 6 Amsterdam images. From *Thirdspace*, 1996. Photographs by the author.

I did not just sit looking through my windows; I explored the many other resources and attractions of the lively Centrum, from the hash coffeehouses to the numerous museums, the dense shopping streets to the then thriving red light district. Everyday urban life brought about discoveries and encounters almost inconceivable in other cities and, unfortunately, rapidly disappearing in Amsterdam today. The encompassing welfare system of that time, for example, was built on a Dutch variation of the honor system. If you earned a certain income, you were expected to pay for many of the services offered, from medical costs to tickets on a tram or bus. Otherwise, the services were free. While I was there, it was said that the tram system was not collecting as many ticket fares as expected or needed. What was done to increase the number of travelers paying full fare was remarkable indeed. Young people were hired, given fancy red and gold costumes, and told to ask everyone boarding the tram whether they had paid their fare. If not, they were asked to present some form of identification, which the Dutch considered an unacceptable violation of privacy. The attention, however, stimulated enough of that "embarrassment of riches" to raise the collected fares to an acceptable level.

The Centrum came alive in a different way when I got to know A.C.M. Jansen, an obsessively localist geographer who had walked every street in the Centrum many times and had written detailed accounts of the astonishing variety of specialized cafes, beer pubs, and hash coffee shops in the area.[3] Reputed not to even own a bicycle, Jansen, who passed away several years ago, took me on a wonderful walking tour of the Centrum in 1990. He would later write that I, in my look at the Centrum, was one of the few scholars able to capture the exciting flavor of the place without spending at least a year in detailed observance, one of the best compliments I have ever received. By the end of my stay, I could not imagine a greater contrast of city centers than that between Amsterdam and Los Angeles.

Off Spuistraat

Fanning out from my canal house on Spuistraat, I began to explore a larger-scale *regional* comparison of the two cities. Here an appropriate mood was set by a lead quote from the renowned Dutch architect Rem Koolhaas, who has been trying for decades to expand the spatial scope of the architectural imagination.

> From my very first visit to Los Angeles in the early 1970s, I have had the feeling that the major Dutch cities (with Amsterdam in the lead) deny out of sentimental considerations the fact that they are part of a larger whole (an area as large and diffuse as Los Angeles) and as such completely ignore a dimension of an entirely different order from the one which they traditionally know.[4]

At first glance, a comparison of Los Angeles and Amsterdam seems as impossible as comparing oranges and electric shavers. These two extraordinary cities virtually demand to be described as unique and incomparable, and of course to a great extent they are. In their uniqueness, however, they become opposite and apposite extremes of contemporary urbanization, informatively positioned antipodes that are very close to being inversions of one another.

Los Angeles in 1990, although changing rapidly, still epitomized the sprawling, decentered, polymorphous, and centrifugal metropolis, a nebulous galaxy of suburbs in search of a city, a place where history is repeatedly spun off and ephemeralized in aggressively contemporary forms. In contrast, Amsterdam may be the most self-consciously centered and historically centripetal city in Europe, carefully preserving every one of its golden ages in a repeatedly modernized Centrum that makes other remnant mercantile capitalist "Old Towns" pale by comparison.

Moving into the city centers makes the contrast even more dramatic and intense. Downtown Los Angeles and the Amsterdam Centrum cover roughly comparable areas, but only one in a hundred Angelenos live in the city's center, while more than 10 percent of Amsterdammers are Centrum dwellers. Many residents of the City of Los Angeles have never been downtown, and surprisingly few tourists take in its local attractions, at least in comparison to more peripheral sites. Amsterdam's Centrum receives eight million tourists a year and is packed daily with thousands of shoppers. Amsterdammers may not be aware of the rest of the city, but they certainly know the center.

It has been claimed that nearly three-quarters of the surface space in downtown Los Angeles is devoted in some way to the automobile, and to the average Angeleno freedom and freeway are symbolically and often politically intertwined. Here the opposition to Amsterdam reaches its extreme expression. It is the bicycle, not the car, that assumes an almost equally obsessive symbolic and political value for the Amsterdammer, but it is an obsession filled not with unfettered individual expression and automaniacal freedom as much as with a collective urban and environmental consciousness and commitment. This makes the contrasts all the more stark.

Amsterdam's center feels like an open public forum, a daily festival of spontaneous political and cultural ideas played in a low key but all the more effective for their lack of pretense and frenzy. Downtown Los Angeles is almost pure spectacle—of business and commerce, of extreme wealth and abject poverty, of clashing cultures and rigidly contained ethnicities. Boredom is assuaged not by playfulness and sensuality but by overindulgence and bombardment with artificial stimulation; while despair is contained and controlled by the omnipresence of authority and obtrusive surveillance. Young householders—twenty-somethings—made up nearly 20 percent of the Centrum's population in the 1990s, whereas they have been virtually nonexistent in downtown LA. In their place are the homeless, who form close to one-half of the downtown population. The authorities in Amsterdam became disturbed when they discovered a dozen people living on the streets in the Centrum in 1990 (although the number has since almost surely increased).

In compact Amsterdam, the whole urban fabric, from center to periphery, is clearly readable and explicit, a morphological regularity that binds

Amsterdammers to traditional concepts of urban form and encourages its urbanists to be unusually cautious of—but at the same time peculiarly open to—new theories of urban transformation. In comparison, Los Angeles seems to break every rule of urban readability and regularity. It is no surprise, then, that Southern California has become a center for innovative and nontraditional urban theory and analysis.

The core of my oppositional comparison is amply clear, but what about the urban peripheries, or the "larger whole" as Rem Koolhaas called it. Is it possible that the astoundingly antipodal centralities of Amsterdam and Los Angeles blind us to comparisons "of an entirely different order"? Taking a more regional perspective and focusing on the dynamics of urban restructuring, the two cities become more similar and comparable than might initially have seemed possible. Looking first at urban form and extent, the two *city regions,* as they might appropriately be called, have some remarkable similarities.

Defined by the sixty-mile (hundred-kilometer) circle around its downtown center, the Los Angeles city region contains more than seventeen million inhabitants today, roughly the same population as the whole of the Netherlands. In its restructured form, described in chapter 2, Los Angeles has a huge and dense inner city amalgamation of ethnicities, surrounded by increasingly urbanized outer cities. Amsterdam too is part of a larger system of cities. It is the largest city in the Randstad, one of the earliest examples of the new polycentric regional network of cities that have been taking shape in recent decades. Both have become models of the regional urbanization process that will be examined in a later chapter.

Although the open farming area that is described as the "green heart" of the Randstad is radically different from the densely populated pentagonal core of the LA region shown in map 10, both can be seen as surrounded by outer cities. Indeed, the Randstad is defined almost entirely by this ring of outer cities: Amsterdam, Rotterdam, The Hague, Utrecht, and such smaller cities as Leiden, Delft, Haarlem, and just beyond the official borders of the Randstad, the Dutch cities of Eindhoven, Nijmegen, Groningen, and Maastricht, plus the major Belgian metropolis of Antwerp. This extended version of the Randstad has many more similarities to the city region of LA described in chapter 2, including roughly the same population size and nearly the same regional economic output.

Another interesting regional comparison has to do with import and export trade. Rotterdam and the combined twin ports of Los Angeles–Long

Beach are among the largest port complexes in the world. The international airports at LAX and Schiphol are two of the world's largest and have both become the focal point of expansive outer city complexes. I was even told at the time that military bases and surveillance centers could be found within the circumference of a hundred-kilometer (sixty-mile) circle drawn from the center of Amsterdam. There are even further regional comparisons.

The Randstad city region anchors the western side of what is today described as the Euro-lowlands, possibly the most populated "megaregion" in Europe, with more than fifty million inhabitants extending across the Netherlands, Belgium, Luxembourg, and parts of France and Germany. Los Angeles too is the hub of a larger megaregion, which stretches from the San Francisco Bay Area on the north through LA and San Diego to its cross-border outpost in Tijuana, Mexico. The population here is probably more than thirty million.

Amsterdam and Los Angeles are experiencing, albeit in different ways, the same forces of crisis-induced urban restructuring that are unevenly affecting all the world's metropolitan areas: expanding globalization, the formation of a more information-intensive post-Fordist New Economy, the spread of what Mike Davis called security-obsessed urbanism and advanced surveillance technology, and the often paradoxical mixture of deindustrialization-reindustrialization and decentralization-recentralization that is reorganizing intrametropolitan geographies.

Based largely on their FIRE sectors (finance, insurance, real estate), Los Angeles and Amsterdam are in the second tier of the global city hierarchy as defined by Saskia Sassen, below London, New York, and Tokyo. In 1990, LA was growing rapidly as a financial center, and to some it looked as if it would join the top three global cities by the end of the century. Not only did LA fail to reach this level, but its global financial strength probably decreased over the past twenty years. Unlike London and New York but more comparable to Tokyo, banking became more consumer oriented and was scattered over the region rather than concentrated in one financial core, such as Wall Street or the City of London.

Amsterdam's financial position has been more stable, building on its concentration of Japanese and American banks, the large number of foreign listings on its stock exchange (reputedly second only to London in 1990), control over the vast Dutch pension funds, and the strong export orientation of Dutch companies. Significant competition was beginning to emerge, however, in the eastern edge of the Euro-lowlands around the growing financial hub of Luxembourg, the core of what is emerging as a new transnational region including French Lorraine, German Saar, and other parts of eastern Belgium and nearby Germany.[5]

Globalization has filled both city regions with enormous numbers of immigrants, edging both toward becoming minority-majority cities. Amsterdam has had a long history of effective and democratic absorption of immigrant populations, and it looked in 1990 like this would continue with the flood of newcomers from northern Africa, Turkey, and Asia. Tolerance in Amsterdam, however, has reached a tipping point in recent years, especially with regard to the rapidly growing Muslim population, estimated by some to become the majority in Amsterdam around 2020 if present trends continue. Anti-immigrant feelings have intensified in both Los Angeles and Amsterdam in recent decades, leading in both cases to calls for deportation.[6]

As described earlier, Los Angeles contains one of the largest agglomerations of immigrant working poor of any major world city and has already become a majority-minority city. Not only has there been frequent tension between domestic and immigrant populations, but the City of LA's minorities have been unusually active politically, obtaining key positions in the City Council, County Board of Supervisors, and Mayor's office. There can be no doubt, however, that immigrants are better housed in Amsterdam. There has been a significant reduction in the construction of new social housing, and access to affordable rentals has declined, but Amsterdam still has more social housing than any other city in Western Europe (and possibly Eastern Europe as well today), and homelessness is a tiny fraction of what it is in Los Angeles.

Worth mentioning—and exemplified in my look through my window on Spuistraat—is what can be called the functional intermixing of social classes in Amsterdam. Many students and graduates in their twenties are formally unemployed but survive by providing informal personal services, such as housecleaning, babysitting, late-night shopping, entertainment and catering, household maintenance and repair, tutoring, therapies, and body care activities, often to their more successful former student colleagues. This unusually large economic cluster of personal services in the Centrum, probably unmatched in any other downtown area, has softened the impact of gentrification and weakened somewhat the tendency toward income polarization that has typically been part of crisis-generated urban restructuring.

Then and now, the housing situation in Los Angeles has been, by contrast, disastrous. The addition of millions of immigrants has been happening without any substantial change in housing stock, creating the most crowded housing conditions in the United States. In addition to what is probably the largest homeless population in the country, perhaps as many as half a million live in conditions that are not much better than Third World shantytowns. Motels all over the city are filled with "hotbedding" families, who occupy beds in eight-hour shifts; tens of thousands live in backyard garages subdivided into tiny compartments with no kitchen or toilet facilities; some of the old movie houses downtown close to the public at ten-thirty on hot summer nights and allow the homeless to come in for a good night's sleep (for a small fee); two-bedroom apartments are often filled with ten to fifteen people, including children.

Several more general questions arise from this comparison. For example, do we learn more about a city by engaging in small-scale geographies of everyday life and pursuing what some scholars call the "view from below" or by seeing the city as a whole, conceptualizing the urban condition on a more comprehensive regional or "big picture" viewpoint? Another way of looking at this question is to ask whether understanding any city is best achieved through accumulated empirical detail or an applied theoretical purview. My demonstrated response to this question is to refuse to choose one or the other as "best" but rather to recognize the need to combine the two approaches and, at the same time, to search for additional insight through this interactive mixture of perspectives. In short, I reject the either/or option in favor of a both/and also approach.

Neither the view from below nor the view from above should be privileged in understanding the city. I make this point to avoid a tendency in much of the urban and related literature to see the view from below as inherently more revealing and evocative than seeing the city from above. As depicted by Michel de Certeau in his influential book *The Practice of Everyday Life* (1984), the view from above "transfigures" the viewer into a voyeur, who is distanced from the object of understanding, looking down on the city like an all-seeing god, creating little more than an abstracted viewpoint divorced from actual practices and everyday life itself. De Certeau makes these points while contemplating New York City from atop the pre-9/11 World Trade Center. He states that "to be lifted to the summit of the World Trade Center is to be lifted out of the city's grasp. One's body is no longer clasped by the streets . . . nor is it possessed, whether as player or played, by the rumble of so many differences."[7]

An effective counterfoil to the temptations of an exclusive view from below can be found in the writings of Henri Lefebvre, whose work has inspired nearly everything I have written over the past thirty years. Lefebvre, who more than anyone else has expanded our understanding of *la vie quotidienne* (everyday life), insisted that urban life is most effectively revealed by combining a critical spatial analysis of the urban condition writ large (urban reality, he called it) with an equally critical (and spatial) interpretation of the practices of everyday life. The two are indissolubly linked, Lefebvre believes, each shaping the other as products and producers of an encompassing social spatiality. *My Los Angeles* has been and will continue to be framed primarily by a macrospatial or regional perspective, but there are many illustrative probes into the everyday scattered throughout, although never do I dwell very long on the view from below. Is this a weakness? Perhaps.

POLES APART: COMPARING LOS ANGELES AND NEW YORK CITY

The "window" provided by Amsterdam opened up many new insights into Los Angeles—and vice versa, I might add. Comparative urban and regional studies have become an especially rich and insightful way to build on the accumulated literature on urban restructuring and postmodern urbanism, and this remains a challenging frontier of contemporary urban research. Continuing along these lines, soon after my excursion to Amsterdam, I was asked by Manuel Castells and John Mollenkopf to add a Los Angeles point of view to a book project they were involved in: *The Dual City*, a look at New York and its social polarization between managerial and working classes.[8] This comparison was quite different from my look at Amsterdam, not least because I am a native New Yorker, born and bred in the peripheral borough of the Bronx.

The object of the project that led to the 1991 publication by the Russell Sage Foundation of *Dual City: Restructuring New York City* was to put together empirical material and analysis concerning social polarization in New York. Theoretical perspectives were not emphasized, largely because a theoretical framework had already been established. New York was assumed unambiguously to be the "social laboratory for the new society" and the "capital of the American century." Unlike the Los Angeles research cluster, which had similar pretensions to importance, Castells and Mollenkopf did not see New York as paradigmatic and hence applicable in modified ways to all large cities. Rather, it was seen as a "profoundly revealing case," something that every city can learn from but none can reproduce. As I think is true about nearly all the best work on New York City, it is the utter uniqueness of the place, its incomparable exceptionalism, that comes through most clearly, in great contrast to the more comprehensive and comparative viewpoint of the LA scholars.

That NYC was and always had been a dual city of the rich and the poor was also assumed, although the authors readily accepted the idea that dualism greatly oversimplified the class structure. The dual city idea may not be empirically verifiable in its fullest sense, but it was deemed useful nonetheless as the foundation for empirical investigation and scholarly discussion. With relatively little justification, the authors suggested that the dual city was the "social expression of the emerging spatial form of the new society," the global city being its economic expression and the informational city its technological expression.

Although there was some scholarly questioning of the dual city concept and the representativeness of NYC as a social laboratory at the seminars and in the book, there was no such questioning about what for me would be the most controversial and unacceptable premise of the dual city project. From the start, it was assumed that the restructuring process revolved around a *postindustrial* transformation. Some slight attention was given to California voices, representing both south and north, who argued that "manufacturing matters," that much of the postindustrial thesis was a myth, and that economic restructuring was essentially a spatial reorganization of the relationship between industrialization and urbanization, but these arguments were not taken seriously. Whatever else NYC might be, it was definitely and definitively postindustrial.

Although I was welcome to give my viewpoint, it was difficult to say much when the fundamental premise of the project was being questioned. I argued that it was true manufacturing employment had plummeted in the five boroughs and New York City itself was no longer among the very largest industrial cities in the country. But I also pointed out that if the entire metropolitan area is included, its ranking remained relatively high. I also raised a related issue, one that had always bothered me about the literature on NYC and had flavored my childhood in the Bronx. When one spoke or wrote about New York City, too often what was being referred to was only Manhattan. I called this widespread synecdoche, substituting a part for the whole, Manhattanitis.

This did not mean that I thought Manhattan was postindustrial but the metropolitan region was not. Even in Manhattan, it could be said that manufacturing still mattered a great deal, not in the older Fordist sense of mass-production assembly lines, but related to the New Economy. The booming financial services sector, nowhere in the country more vibrant (and concentrated) than in southern Manhattan, was not only a part of the tertiary economy, but also fed vitally into industrial production, especially in high-technology and information-intensive manufacturing. Taken together with remaining industrial activities, manufacturing continued—and continues—to generate a major share of the gross economic product despite the massive loss of mainly Fordist manufacturing jobs. If there had to be a "rush to the *post-*," then *post-Fordist* and perhaps even *postmodern* would be better than *postindustrial*.

Subsequent events have demonstrated much more vividly than I could have at the time the deleterious effects that can arise from a rigid belief in the postindustrial thesis and the related notions that consumption drives the economy and that going shopping and thinking positively are the best ways to counter economic downturns. Economic restructuring in the United States unavoidably involved a breakdown of well-established Fordist industries, but it need not have opened the valves to such a voluminous overseas flight of manufacturing jobs as has occurred over the past thirty years, in part because so many influential people genuinely believed we had entered a postindustrial era. As we in Los Angeles have been arguing, deindustrialization needs to be seen not alone but in conjunction with reindustrialization, the rise of a new industrial economy in new industrial spaces, and a revised (but not disjointed) relationship between industrialization and urbanization processes.

China, now the world's leading producer country, knew this very well and took advantage of the abandonment of manufacturing jobs in advanced capitalist countries, formerly known as the industrialized countries or the industrial world, to achieve a level and rate of development never before attained in so short a time. The lessons of China demonstrate clearly that three key terms do not deserve to be prefixed by *post-* or with anything hinting at "end of": *urban, industrial,* and *capitalism.*

To return to comparing LA and NY in 1990, I saw the Manhattan bias leading to an excessive focus on Wall Street as a generative force in the local, regional, national, and global economies. The dual city project began soon after the minicrash of 1987, when Wall Street and the larger New York economy went into enormous turmoil. A significant recovery had been initiated by 1990, and there was growing confidence that the fulsome financial sector might lead the way to a new era of expansive economic development. Nearly all discussions of the New York economy and real estate development consequently focused not only on Manhattan, but even more so on the tiny island's southern tip, home of arguably the world's largest FIRE cluster.

To an outsider from Los Angeles, this narrowing of focus to Wall Street seemed as misleading as seeing Disneyland as the primary motor of the Los Angeles economy. Using the well-known Tom Wolfe book in which a successful Manhattan broker takes a wrong turn on the highway and ends up lost in the burnt-out offerings of the South Bronx, used by Castells and Mollenkopf in their introduction as a vivid metaphor of the polarized dual city, I revised the book's title to reflect the Wall Street bias I encountered, retitling it *The Vanity of the BonFIREs*.

I was strongly advised to calm down my rhetoric and speculative attacks on theoretical issues in the paper I promised to write. In "Poles Apart: New York and Los Angeles" (app. 1, source 4B), I clarified my point of view, recognizing the enormous contrasts between the two places, but emphasized not so much the polarity of NY-LA as the increasing polarization that was accompanying the urban and economic restructuring processes within these two largest cities of the United States, however one defined this restructuring.

In both NYC and LA, the income gap was widening, conflicts between domestic and immigrant populations were becoming more frequent, the composition of the population was becoming increasingly polarized between the rich (defined as "upper professionals" primarily involved in financial services in New York and a new technocracy of mathematicians, scientists, and engineers in Los Angeles) and the poor (often seen as a welfare-dependent underclass in NY, as an agglomeration of the working poor in LA). In both, most of the population was no longer describable simply as consisting of capitalists and proletarian workers, but was better seen as embedded in a new class structure in which a middle-class squeeze was creating a small but growing bubble of the super-rich at the very top while pouring thousands into a swollen underclass, bottoming out in the largest homeless populations in the United States. There was a strong foundation to claim that Los Angeles and New York were the peak cities of income polarization and economic inequality in the country.

Some basic issues were left unaddressed, especially with regard to the intrametropolitan geographies of New York and Los Angeles, issues that had been dealt with in some detail in the study of Amsterdam. Referring back to the geography depicted in map 10 for LA, how could the new inner city of New York be defined? How far did it spill over from Manhattan into Brooklyn and New Jersey? How did the ethnic makeup of NY's urban core compare with that of LA, and what difference does this make? Where was ethnic segregation more pronounced? To what extent could one compare the entertainment industry and Hollywood cluster to the financial services sector and Wall Street cluster in terms of their size and overall impact on the urban and regional economies? Is overspecialization a problem in either LA or NY? Why is gentrification seemingly more of an issue in NY than LA?

A comparison of the outer cities would have been particularly interesting. In some ways, the NY-LA comparison was an inversion of what was seen when comparing LA and Amsterdam. The vast agglomeration of the immigrant working poor, the rising number of ethnic enclaves, and the growing social polarization between super-rich and super-poor made the two inner cities relatively similar. A dramatic contrast can be seen, however, in the metropolitan periphery. Los Angeles has spawned dense outer cities as its traditional suburbia becomes increasingly urbanized, while there are few if any booming new urban agglomerations in New York's vast suburbia, a major factor in why and how LA passed NY as the densest urbanized area in the country. One wonders whether this relatively unchanging suburbia intensifies Manhattanitis, the tendency to make "downtown" stand in for the entire region. Alternatively, has the extraordinary concentration in Manhattan drained the regional economy of a great portion of its developmental potential?

Comparing Los Angeles and New York should have provoked the realization that American suburbia is changing at very different rates and in different ways. The Washington, D.C., and San Francisco Bay urban regions are today much more like LA than NY. How does Chicago compare? Detroit? Atlanta? One conclusion to be drawn from this is that there is great need for rigorous comparative studies and new descriptive typologies of the differentiation of suburbia. Even where traditional suburban ways of life are fiercely maintained, it would be interesting to explore just how such preservation has occurred in the face of pronounced changes elsewhere. One thing is clear: suburbia is not what it was thirty years ago. These comments open up another round of urban comparisons having to do with the concept and measurement of sprawl.

SPRAWL ISN'T WHAT IT USED TO BE

Sprawl is a nasty term that has become even nastier in recent years, especially in its application to low-density suburbia, specifically to the way many characterize Los Angeles and other western cities. Why is it seen as such a wellspring of ailments? Does it deserve this reputation? More basically, what is sprawl and what should be done about it? Which cities in the United States suffer most from suburban sprawl? What would a comparative study of the extent of suburban sprawl tell us (see app. 1, source 4C)?

Before trying to address these questions, let us look back to how the term entered the English language. The first use of the word *sprawl* can be traced back at least to the early eighteenth century and has most commonly referred to an awkward or clumsy stretching out of the limbs of the body. The word and its meaning seem to have been formed by a combination of three older words: *spread, crawl,* and *straggle,* the latter adding elements of irregularity and clumsy departure from the normal to the simpler notion of stretching out one's arms and legs. Sprawling, then, has always been seen as improper behavior, at least in polite society.

In its use as urban or suburban sprawl (the two adjectives seem to be used interchangeably), these impolite nonurbane uncivilized qualities (to use words that have their root meaning in *city*) have become magnified into an imposing list of decidedly negative associations. Here are just a few of the evils that have been connected to sprawling suburbanization: social isolation ("trapped" suburban housewives, for example), the promotion of poverty and injustice (through inaccessibility of jobs and resources), the destruction of community (as in the "malling" of suburban life), worsening public health (more asthma and obesity), increased flooding and soil erosion (too much cement), higher food prices and the end of the small family farm (loss of agricultural land on the suburban fringe), the extinction of wildlife (as nature disappears), aesthetic degradation (as culture disappears), and global warming (partially caused by car emissions).

Following a long tradition of viewing cities through either utopian or dystopian optics, contemporary debates on sprawl have become increasingly polarized. The bad, "stupid," destructive growth associated with sprawl has spawned its equally exaggerated alternative: good, "smart," sensitive, sustainable development, packed with its own impressive list of green and organic virtues and presented with passion as the repository for all hope against the evil ooze.

It would be easy and entertaining to continue to deconstruct this hyperbolic binary of sprawl versus sustainable development, finding good reasons to toss out both of these overused and substantively misleading terms. There are several reasons, however, to keep these two terms together. First, the great sprawl/sustainability dichotomy has become so deeply ingrained in popular, professional, and academic thinking about cities that it would be impossible to eradicate entirely, no matter how clever the attack. Furthermore, the dichotomy does capture some important aspects of contemporary urbanization and, as such, needs to continue to be critically evaluated rather than simply ignored. Even the flagrant polarization into ping-pong epitomes of good and evil serves some useful purpose, if only to remind us of the deep-seated ideological opposition between utopian and dystopian visions that has always characterized—and, I would add, distorted—Western ideas and writings about cities and urban life.

The main point being made here is that, even with its negative connotations toned down, *sprawl today is no longer what it used to be*—an argument that resonates with the underlying theme of pronounced urban restructuring. Let us look at some recent attempts to measure sprawl statistically in the United States, focusing specifically on the urban region of Los Angeles, long considered the sprawling antithesis to sustainable urban development but today the densest large metropolis in the country. If nothing else, the Los Angeles case strongly suggests the need to rethink such concepts as sprawl, compactness, smart growth, sustainability, and stereotyped comparisons of European and American cities.

Tables 1 and 2 list the ten lowest and ten highest U.S. metropolitan areas of more than a million inhabitants, ranked on two different statistical measures of sprawl. The first set of rankings is based on urban population densities, perhaps the most widely used single indicator of sprawl. It is calculated from 1990 data for the *urbanized area,* defined as a built-up area with census tracts having greater than 1,000 inhabitants per square mile. According to this measure, Los Angeles has, by a substantial margin, the densest urbanized area in the United States, with an estimated 6,062 people per square mile, in comparison to 5,184 for New York City, in second place. Other high-density metropolitan areas include the four of the five largest city regions in California after LA, two in Florida, plus Chicago and New Orleans. Given

TABLE 1 Population Density in the Urbanized Area

(33 largest U.S. metropolitan areas, 1990)

Highest Density		Lowest Density	
1. Los Angeles	6,062	24. Houston	2,547
2. New York	5,184	25. Minneapolis / St. Paul	2,453
3. Miami	4,815	26. Tampa / St. Petersburg	2,416
4. San Jose	4,401	27. Dallas / Fort Worth	2,346
5. San Francisco / Oakland	4,311	28. Cincinnati	2,259
6. Sacramento	3,751	29. St. Louis	2,270
7. Chicago	3,525	30. Pittsburgh	2,139
8. San Diego	3,520	31. Kansas City	2,130
9. New Orleans	3,441	32. Riverside / San Bernardino	1,976
10. Fort Lauderdale	3,351	33. Atlanta	1,590

NOTE: *Population density* = number of people per square mile; *urbanized area* = built-up area with greater than 1,000 population/sq. mi.

SOURCE: *Demographia* 1990 U.S. Urbanized Area Density Profile, www.demographia.com/db-porla .htm.

that Riverside/San Bernardino is listed separately (and among the least dense regions, because of the huge area), the figure for Los Angeles almost surely refers only to the Los Angeles–Long Beach–Santa Ana MSA, that is, Los Angeles County plus Orange County.

At the other density extreme is Atlanta, with just 1,590. As with *Bonfire of the Vanities* for New York, another Tom Wolfe novel, *A Man in Full* (1998), based in Atlanta, captures an essential feature of the urban region. The story revolves around a real estate mogul who has made millions investing in the growth of relatively nearby edge cities around Atlanta. He pushes his luck by going much farther out into the far reaches of the metropolitan area, expecting that jobs and residents will follow. When the investment fails, everything begins to fall apart in the mogul's life. While not spreading out endlessly, Atlanta's sprawl is as extensive as any in the United States.

Nine of the ten lowest-density cities are located inland, with only Tampa/ Saint Petersburg being a major Atlantic, Pacific, Gulf, or Great Lake port. This distinctive regional patterning makes it seem almost as if the urban population of the United States has been spinning outward from the national center of gravity toward the coasts in all directions, packing the coastal fringe with the densest metropolitan areas while densities in the American heartland cities (Atlanta, Dallas, Saint Louis, Cincinnati, Pittsburgh, Kansas City, and

Minneapolis) flatten out. Or is it simpler than that? Perhaps a littoral location cuts off room for expansion, concentrating populations along the shoreline even far from the city center? With a much larger area for low-density sprawl (a full circle rather than a truncated one), might it be that interior cities will always rank lower than coastal cities on density measurements?

But let us return to what many would consider the most counterintuitive finding in this data set, the ranking of Los Angeles ahead of all others as America's densest urban area. Los Angeles passed New York in overall density in 1990, but the two have been moving in opposite directions for at least the past forty years. For the first half of the twentieth century, Los Angeles epitomized the growth of a sprawling, automobile-driven, low-density suburban metropolis. In 1950, it was the least densely populated urbanized area of all U.S. cities of over a million people, with half the density of New York and Philadelphia. Despite a pronounced midcentury U-turn and its dramatic densification, Los Angeles has continued to be mistakenly seen as the most suburbanized, sprawling, and probably unsustainable metropolis of all. What, then, has happened since 1950?

First, Los Angeles added nearly eight million new inhabitants, while New York grew by around 3,750,000, both far ahead of all other large metropolitan areas (low-density Dallas–Fort Worth and Houston were next, with about 2,250,000 newcomers each). The urbanized land area of both Los Angeles and New York expanded significantly in size (although the expansion in LA was much less than one might expect); it was in the density of this new development that the difference between the two was most pronounced. For Los Angeles, which by 1990 included Orange County in its defined urbanized area, the added extensions had a composite density of 6,800 per square mile versus 2,200 for New York. What was happening rapidly in Los Angeles and far less so in New York was a process that has been variably described as peripheral urbanization, the growth of outer cities and edge cities, and with its wonderfully in-built paradox, the *urbanization of suburbia*. In other words, Los Angeles's older suburban rings, once the archetype of American suburbia, are now the densest in the country, and like booming Orange County, many formerly suburban areas now deserve to be called cities in themselves.

There has also been a contrast in the inner cities. The single densest census tract in New York in 1990 remained nearly three times as dense as the equivalent tract in Los Angeles, but even this ratio has dropped significantly since 1950. If one calculates the density for the inner core of the metropolitan region, when this core is defined as comprising 10 percent of the densest census tracts, New York continues in 1990 to have the highest figure in the country, with Los Angeles second. But when the calculation is for the densest 20 percent of the urbanized land area, something very interesting happens. Los Angeles jumps to the first rank, while New York drops below San Francisco/Oakland, Miami, and San Jose. In Los Angeles today, many inner city areas have reached the same density as in Manhattan, due primarily to the fact that more foreign immigrants have moved into the inner city of Los Angeles, perhaps as many as five million since 1965, than into any other inner city in the United States. New York has experienced heavy in-migration too, but its rate of domestic out-migration—and I might add sprawling low-density suburbanization—has been greater than in Los Angeles.

Table 2 contains more recent data and introduces a more complex measure of sprawl but shows much the same pattern. Derived from a study that appeared in *USA Today* in early 2001, it calculates a sprawl index based on two measures: a "compactness index" that measures the proportion of the total metropolitan area population (based on adjacent counties) living in the urbanized area (presumably defined as in Table 1), and the change in density in the metropolitan area between 1990 and 1999, which emphasizes recent growth. Both were estimated for forty-eight urban areas with over a million in population, rather than the thirty-three used in the 1990 study. On the compactness index alone, Los Angeles ranked third, following Salt Lake City and Miami/Fort Lauderdale. In the overall calculation, Salt Lake City (located on the largest interior water body in the United States) topped the list. Los Angeles was fifth and New York sixth.

It should be noted that the metropolitan areas used in Table 2 combine cities that were considered separately in Table 1, so that San Francisco/Oakland now includes San Jose (and Silicon Valley), Miami and Fort Lauderdale are combined, and Los Angeles is significantly expanded, not only by the explicit inclusion of Orange County but also by the addition of Riverside and, almost surely despite its not being mentioned, San Bernardino County, two of the largest counties in land area in the country. San Bernardino/Riverside was treated separately in Table 1 and was ranked as having the second-lowest density, after Atlanta. It is reasonable to assume that their addition to the LA metro definition accounts in large part for Los Angeles not scoring higher (that is, less sprawl) on Table 2.

The ten least sprawling cities contain all but two of those listed as the most dense in Table 1, and continue to include mostly coastal cities. Atlanta's

TABLE 2 *USA Today* Sprawl Index

(48 metropolitan areas >1 million, 1999 data)

Low Sprawl		High Sprawl	
1. Salt Lake City	60 (2)	39. Indianapolis	299
2. SF / Oakland / San Jose	62 (5)	40. Louisville	306
3. San Diego	66 (4)	41. Memphis	329
4. Miami / Fort Lauderdale	69 (1)	42. Rochester	338
5. LA / Riverside / Orange	78 (3)	43. Grand Rapids	357
6. New York Metro	82 (6)	44. Atlanta	392
7. Oklahoma City	94	45. Austin	413
8. Chicago / Gary / Kenosha	112 (9)	46. Greensboro, NC	437
9. Norfolk	116 (7)	47. Charlotte, NC	454
10. Providence	138	48. Nashville	478

NOTE: The index here combines rank on (a) % total metro population living in urbanized area (shown in parentheses); and (b) change in density 1990–99 for 271 metro areas. Higher indexes indicate greater sprawl.

SOURCE: *USA Today,* February 22, 2001, http://usatoday30.usatoday.com/news/sprawl /masterlist.htm.

sprawl is now exceeded by four other southern cities, while every one on the list of the most sprawling cities is located inland from the coasts. More can be gleaned from these tables, but one highly counterintuitive point emerges. According to the best statistical measures of sprawl, Los Angeles is near the top of the list of the densest and most compact, and thus in this statistical sense probably the *least sprawling—and most sustainable?*—major urban region in the country.

Adding further to the confusion over what sprawl is and what effect it has on urban life is a comprehensive study by Anthony Downs, senior fellow at the Brookings Institute and a well-known urban analyst. Looking at 162 metropolitan areas, Downs devised a sprawl index based on nine indicators and compared this index to several measures of urban decline, including crime and poverty rates. No significant correlation was discovered. That is, there was no evidence that sprawling suburbs had anything to do with what was happening in the central cities. Downs stated, "My goal was to find out whether there was a link between aspects of sprawl such as low density development, the leapfrog out to suburbs and the use of automobiles and urban decline. It turned out there wasn't. At least I couldn't find one."[9]

Such reputable studies seem to challenge a broad range of presumed truths and both theoretical and policy assumptions about sprawl. They suggest that compactness is not automatically a virtue, nor will densification alone resolve problems of poverty and urban decline. Similarly, large-scale but low-density suburban development in itself may have no discernible effect whatsoever on the conditions in inner cities. Such interpretations of the causes of poverty and urban decay, more common in the eastern half of the country, may actually divert attention from the real sources of the problems. And furthermore, the causes of urban poverty and decline may be quite different today than they were thirty years ago. One conclusion is clear: new ways to understand sprawl and its relation to the restructuring of the modern metropolis must be sought and developed, controlling for both negative and positive biases.

BACK TO SCHOOL: NY-LA-CHI COMPARISONS

The three largest cities in the United States—New York, Los Angeles, and Chicago—have probably generated a more voluminous literature than other America cities and played a larger role than other cities in the evolving field of urban studies. There are many differences, however, in how each of these cities has been studied and represented in the literature. Studies of Chicago peaked early with the development of the very influential Chicago School of Urban Ecology in the interwar years. During its heyday, the Chicago School significantly shaped the development of the social sciences, social theory, and in particular the discipline of urban sociology. It began to decline after 1950 but was revived somewhat, mainly by urban geographers, in the 1970s. Although the heritage of the Chicago School still persists, Chicago itself is not as central as it once was in the development of urban theory or as the focus for original and representative empirical research.

In some ways, studying Los Angeles is the obverse of how Chicago has been studied. For the first three-quarters of the twentieth century, there were very few high-quality academic studies of LA and, far from seeing it as representative of urban development elsewhere, scholars often dismissed it as a bizarre exception, of little interest in the development of general urban theory. In the late 1970s, however, there was an explosion of writing about Los Angeles that would project it into a central role in urban studies and lead to discussions and debates as to whether there had emerged a distinctive LA School comparable to the earlier Chicago School. As far as I can tell, no city other than Chicago and Los Angeles has developed a significant critical mass of interacting scholars and collectively shared scholarship deserving to be described as a school of urban studies.

New York City has never developed a distinctive school of urban studies, although during the interwar years there arose a regional planning school of sorts centered in New York and the Regional Planning Association of America. The leading figure of this group, which included other regional thinkers such as Clarence Stein and Benton Mackaye, was Lewis Mumford, often considered one of the greatest urban scholars, social critics, and "public intellectuals" of the twentieth century. None of the regionalists, however, developed a strong university base or affiliation that might have generated a larger community of like-minded scholars. The creative center for regional thinking shifted after 1975 to Los Angeles, building on the work of John Friedmann, Allen Scott, Michael Storper, and other geographers and planners at UCLA and USC, forming the core of what some would call the Los Angeles School.

With some important exceptions, urban studies of New York have tended in the past to be rather parochial, overwhelmingly focused on Manhattan and highly celebratory of the city's unique features rather than seeking a more general understanding of the contemporary urban condition. Permeating much of the work is the belief that there is no other place like New York, although every place can learn something from the exceptional experiences of Gotham. Even when addressing a wider audience, many of the best writings on New York seem introverted, looking inward more than reaching out for comparative insight.

Starting with Lewis Mumford and Jane Jacobs, the individual achievements of New York–based scholars, both in studying New York City and in their wider influence in urban studies more generally, are more than impressive when added together. To name just a few, there is Richard Sennett, William H. White, Christine Boyer, Sharon Zukin, Peter Marcuse, Cindi Katz, John Mollenkopf, and more recently, Saskia Sassen, Harvey Molotch, Robert Beauregard, Neil Brenner (now creating a major urban studies presence at Harvard), and adding to the growing cluster of urban scholars at CUNY Graduate Center, Neil Smith, Ruth Gilmore, and perhaps the best-known and most frequently cited urban scholar in the world, David Harvey. As of this writing, however, there are still very few signs of significant collective interaction among this impressive group of urban scholars, and few noteworthy joint publications about New York City.

Another differentiating feature of the scholarship on New York compared to Chicago and Los Angeles is its much weaker spatial perspective, at least until very recently. Part of the reason has been the almost complete absence of an established and prominent geography department at any public or private universities in New York City. Columbia shut down its geography department many years ago, CUNY (even as CCNY) never had one, neither has NYU. David Harvey and Neil Smith (recently deceased) are distinguished professors of anthropology, although there has been some talk of creating a department of geography at CUNY.

An assertive and consequential spatial perspective has, from the start, been at the definitive core of the Chicago School and what I prefer to call the Los Angeles Research Cluster (LARC). Not everyone agrees with this claim, so let me elaborate further. In my view, the Chicago School was perhaps the most influential effort in at least the first half of the twentieth century to explain individual and collective behavior in the modern world from an explicitly geographical perspective. Its emphasis on what was called urban ecology—how the urban environment and geography shape social life—united a diverse group of scholars at the University of Chicago around a bold and ambitious conceptualization of the city. Reflecting this broader philosophical view in his introduction to a later edition of the school's classic work, *The City: Suggestions for Investigation of Human Behavior in the Urban Environment,* originally published in 1925, Morris Janowitz argues that the city is not some residual arrangement but "embodies the real nature of human nature." It is an "expression of mankind in general and specifically of the social relations generated by territoriality."[10]

The Chicago School scholars rarely used the terms *spatial* and *geographical,* preferring instead *ecology,* a term first used by German natural scientists in the 1880s. Although they used concepts borrowed from botany and other natural sciences, the Chicago School urbanists rarely looked at the actual physical or natural environment. Their ecology revolved primarily around the well-known concentric zone model first developed by Ernest Burgess and some subsequent elaborations of it. Most of the voluminous literature produced by the Chicago School saw all forms of human behavior in the city as shaped by location within one or another of these concentric zones. Vice, gangs, slums, street-corner society, and other urban phenomena differed as one moved from one zone to another. Although culture and other factors intervened, explanation was primarily rooted in natural processes, such as invasion and succession, in the concentrically zoned "urban environment."

Its distinctive form of ecological explanation would, however, lead to the school's relative decline after 1950. Seeing it as a naive form of extrasocial (i.e., environmental) determinism, the discipline of sociology reacted against any suggestion of urban or spatial causality, contributing to a retreat from spatial thinking in the social sciences and a deadening of the explanatory power of the urban. Present-day sociology looks back to the Chicago School with some nostalgia, seeing it as pioneering the study of race and ethnicity and other social aspects of the city. Almost invisible, however, is its core emphasis on geographical causality.

The Chicago School survived by moving along two paths, both diverging from roots in sociology. One was based on the continued use of the concentric zone model in a highly mathematized field of urban economics. The other built on the long-standing ties at the University of Chicago between sociology and geography. The earliest indication of this connection was the effort in 1923 by Harlan Barrows, the chair of geography and a nationally influential geographer, to change the name of the Geography Department to Human Ecology. As the influence of the school in sociology began to die out in the 1950s, geographers at the University of Chicago (Chauncey Harris, Edward Ullman, and Brian Berry) took the lead in maintaining and, some would say, enhancing the urban ecological tradition.[11]

A powerful critical spatial perspective has shaped the study of urban restructuring and features prominently throughout *My Los Angeles*. Especially in such concepts as the search for a spatial fix and the depoliticizing effects of postmodern urbanism, space was the major explanatory factor, but this was not the almost naturalized and extrasocial environmental explanation of the Chicago School but rather a different form of explanation arising from the socially produced and "socialized" space that featured in the innovative work of Henri Lefebvre. This difference was politically significant, for if "we" produced a city-space that was unjust and oppressive, rather than it being given to us by God or Mother Nature, we can change it for the better.

In the field of urban studies more generally, Chicago and the Chicago School models continue to receive attention today, but mainly as a remembrance of things past rather than as an active influence. Over the past thirty years, there seems little doubt that Los Angeles has become a more prominent focus for the building and analysis of urban theory. This does not necessarily mean that a Los Angeles School has replaced the Chicago School, for there is not much left to replace. Moreover, other trendsetting and representative cities have emerged to compete with Los Angeles for exemplary prominence.

However it is described, the accumulated literature on Los Angeles has contributed significantly to our understanding of the contemporary urban condition, as well as broader aspects of societal development and change, especially as seen from an explicitly *causal* spatial perspective. This emphasis on urban and regional explanation and causality is the research cluster's most distinctive characteristic. A critical spatial perspective, more than anything else, unifies the diverse scholars involved in studying LA. It also helps to explain why some excellent research and researchers on Los Angeles have not been included within the putative school's boundaries.

The debates associated with the LA School reached a peak as well as a turning point with the publication in the August 18, 2000, issue of the prestigious *Chronicle of Higher Education* of an article by D. W. Miller called "The New Urban Studies: Los Angeles Scholars Use Their Region and Their Ideas to End the Dominance of the 'Chicago School.'" Although Allen Scott and I were interviewed, the article was primarily built upon Michael Dear's vision and version of Los Angeles and the so-called LA School of Urbanism. The online publication of this article stimulated heated arguments and commentary across the country and internationally. In many ways, this broadcasting of the LA School debates marked the end of the first phase in its development and the beginning of another, marked by wider attention and recognition but also greater critical dismissal.[12]

In retrospect, the most important achievements of the Los Angeles Research Cluster-cum-school have been in gaining practical and theoretical understanding of two areas of analysis. The first involves the restructuring processes that have been dramatically reshaping cities and the contemporary world over the past three or four decades. The second revolves around exemplifying the generative power of cities and city regions and demonstrating how this stimulus of urban agglomeration affects economic development, technological innovation, cultural creativity, and the formation of social movements With regard to both these areas of achievement, Los Angeles and Southern California have proven to be an extraordinarily rich and revealing laboratory.

NOTES

1. "The Stimulus of a Little Confusion" was reprinted as often as any of my writings. See M. P. Smith, ed., *After Modernism: Global Restructuring and the Changing Boundaries of City Life* (New Brunswick, NJ: Transaction, 1992); Leon Deben,

Willem Heinemeijer, and Dick van der Vaart, eds., *Understanding Amsterdam: Essays on Economic Vitality, City Life, and Urban Form* (Amsterdam: Het Spinhuis, 1993); H. Hitz et al., eds., *Capitales Fatales: Urbanisierung und Politik in den Finanzmetropolen* (Zurich: Rotpunk, 1995); Iain Borden et al., eds., *Strangely Familiar: Narrative of Architecture in the City* (New York: Routledge, 1996); I. Borden et al., eds., *The Unknown City: Contesting Architecture and Social Space* (Cambridge, MA: MIT Press, 2001); N. Brenner and R. Keil, eds., *Global Cities Reader* (New York: Routledge, 2006). See the list following source 4A in app. 1.

2. Simon Schama, *The Embarrassment of Riches* (Berkeley and Los Angeles: University of California Press, 1988), 25.

3. See, for example, Jansen's "Hotelling's Location Game and a Geography of Hashish and Marijuana," *Geoforum* 20 (1990).

4. Rem Koolhaas, "Epilogue," in *Amsterdam: An Architectural Lesson* (Amsterdam: Thoth Publishing House, 1988), 108–19.

5. SaarLorLux, or *La Grande Région*, as it is sometimes called, combines the Duchy of Luxembourg with French Lorraine, German Saarland and parts of Rhineland-Palatinate, and most recently Belgian Wallonia, forming a transnational EUREGIO with a population of nearly five million.

6. Over the past two decades, there has been a marked reversal between LA and Amsterdam in minority and cultural politics. Once the hive of progressive social movements and effective minority integration, Amsterdam and the Netherlands as a whole have become much more reactionary. Political organization among minority groups has become highly fragmented and relatively ineffective, and anti-immigrant feelings are reversing many of the trends discussed earlier. While anti-immigrant feelings are also strong in Los Angeles (and across the country), immigrant minorities have played a vital role in the emergence of successful and socially innovative labor-community coalitions, as will be discussed in chapter 8.

7. Michel de Certeau, *The Practice of Everyday Life* (Berkeley and Los Angeles: University of California Press, 1984), 91.

8. Manuel Castells in 1990 was still a professor of city and regional planning and sociology at the University of California–Berkeley and already the most highly cited scholar in his field, a position he maintains today as professor of communications at the University of Southern California. John Mollenkopf has since 1981 been a professor of political science and sociology at the City University of New York. He too has a bicoastal background, having taught at Stanford University and lived elsewhere in California. Both are well known to have rich spatial or regional imaginations and at the time of my visit had a positive and welcoming attitude toward the Los Angeles research cluster-cum-school.

9. Anthony Downs, "Some Realities about Sprawl and Urban Decline," *Housing Policy Debate* 10, no. 4 (1999): 955–74; Haya El Nasser, "Researcher: Sprawl Doesn't Hurt Cities." *USA Today,* February 16, 2000.

10. Morris Janowitz, "Introduction," in *The City: Suggestions for Investigation of Human Behavior in the Urban Environment,* ed. Robert E. Park and Ernest W. Burgess (Chicago: University of Chicago Press, 1967), ix. The first use of this title

was in an essay by Robert Park published in 1916 in *American Journal of Sociology* 20 (1916): 577–612.

11. Especially important was Brian J.L. Berry and John D. Kasarda, *Contemporary Urban Ecology* (New York and London: Macmillan, 1977). Using various forms of multivariate statistical analysis, the new quantitative geographers developed factorial ecology to integrate the various spatial models of the Chicago School.

12. After the publication of the *Chronicle* article in 2000, the LA School became closely identified with Michael Dear's particular envisioning, especially given the lack of interest among other local researchers in advertising themselves as a school. His views are made clear in Michael Dear and J. Dallas Dishman, eds., *From Chicago to L.A.: Making Sense of Urban Theory* (Thousand Oaks, CA: Sage Publications, 2001); and Dear, "Los Angeles and the Chicago School: Invitation to a Debate," in *The Urban Sociology Reader,* ed. J. Lin and C. Mele (New York: Routledge, 2005), originally published with critical responses in the inaugural issue of *City and Community,* 2002; "Urban Politics and the Los Angeles School of Urbanism," *Urban Affairs* 44 (2008): 266–79; and "The Los Angeles School of Urbanism: An Intellectual History." See also Dear, *The Postmodern Urban Condition* (Oxford: Blackwell: 2001).

FIVE

On the Postmetropolitan Transition

As practically everything described as "postmodern" in the 1990s became almost unavoidably embroiled in seemingly impossible-to-resolve conflicts of interpretation and emphasis, I stopped trying to defend and clarify my particular take on critical postmodernism (an oxymoron to many) and shifted to interpreting more directly the dramatic transformation of the modern metropolis that I saw so vividly unfolding in Los Angeles.[1] Unable to be more specific in "Six Discourses on the Postmetropolis" (app. 1, source 5D), I called the emergent new form the "postmetropolis" and accordingly redefined what was happening after 1965 and especially after 1980 as the "postmetropolitan transition," an ongoing process that emphasized a movement away from the established form of the modern metropolis but without a confident identification of what the end state of this transition might turn out to be.

Focusing on the postmetropolitan transition led me to recompose the extensive literature that had accumulated around economic restructuring and contemporary urbanization processes more generally into six "discourses," defined as distinctive clusters of interrelated writings on specific thematic aspects of urban change. My definition of discourse was simple and straightforward, without the theoretical complexity of "discourse analysis" as it appeared in the writings of philosophers and critical social scientists.

The six discourses represented different ways of conceptualizing and interpreting urban restructuring and the postmetropolitan transition. The literature surveyed went well beyond the Los Angeles case to illustrate more general processes that were affecting urban areas everywhere. In most cases, the references selected for emphasis were decidedly spatial in their perspective and purview. One could say, only somewhat facetiously, that if there indeed was an LA School, the six discourses identified would represent something like its specialized component departments, each studying different facets of the same processes.

The 1992 Justice Riots, as they came to be called, building on earlier events at Tiananmen Square and the Cold War–ending fall of the Berlin Wall in 1989, added a new twist to my treatment of the postmetropolitan transition. Perhaps, I thought, we were seeing the slowing down of crisis-generated restructuring and the beginning of a new postmetropolitan era of crises arising not out of the conditions underlying the urban unrest of the 1960s but from the new social and spatial orders of postmetropolitan urbanism created by neoliberal globalization and urban economic restructuring. In other words, the postmetropolitan transition was leading to a shift from crisis-generated restructuring to *restructuring-generated crises*.[2] With this possibility in mind, we look next at the major research clusters that have evolved around understanding the postmetropolitan transition.

POSTMETROPOLITAN DISCOURSES AND THE NEW REGIONALISM

The six discourses or research clusters can be broken down into three pairs. The first two discourses focus on the most convincing arguments that have developed about the *causes* of restructuring and the postmetropolitan transition; the second pair depict the major spatial and social *consequences* of the causal forces; while the third pair represent hard and soft reactions to these consequential effects and help to explain why the volatile postmetropolis has not exploded more often, given the negative consequences of restructuring. As a shorthand indicator, I give particular names to the urban expressions of these discourses, but I feel no particular attachment to their use. The following are chapter titles from *Postmetropolis* (app. 1, sources 5D and 6C).

1. The Postfordist Industrial Metropolis: Restructuring the Geopolitical Economy of Urbanism
2. Cosmopolis: The Globalization of Cityspace
3. Exopolis: The Restructuring of Urban Form
4. Fractal City: Metropolarities and the Restructured Social Mosaic
5. The Carceral Archipelago: Governing Space in the Postmetropolis
6. Simcities: Restructuring the Urban Imaginary

The most voraciously absorptive of the two causal or explanatory discourses on urban change focuses on the *globalization of capital, labor, and culture.* By the 1990s, almost everything new and different was being explained as a product of globalization, and an ever-increasing literature grew around its seemingly unstoppable force. So attractive and encompassing was the globalization discourse, however, that I refused to put it first, purposefully choosing to have it follow what I considered to be the most powerful and explicitly spatial approach to explaining the postmetropolitan transition, the *restructuring of the geopolitical economy of urbanism,* or, from another viewpoint, the formation of a new post-Fordist mode of urban industrial capitalism—what many now simply call the New Economy.

Setting aside any formal ranking, it has become increasingly clear that these two causal discourses are tightly intertwined and in many ways inseparable. Their differences have to do more with emphasis than substance. The New Economy or industrial urbanism discourse explains urban change largely through endogenous processes and models, coming from within and working from the bottom up, while the forces of globalization tend to be exogenous, generated from outside the city and working, for the most part, from the top down. The endogenous approach tends to deal with local and localized processes, while the exogenous view is more macroanalytic and broadly based, giving rise to the familiar catchphrase "Think Global—Act Local." The intertwining of the two discourses and processes, however, reconstructs this catchphrase by focusing attention on all that falls between the global and the local, the macro and the micro, endogenous and exogenous forces. I refer here to the meso- or regional scale.

Hybridizing the two causal discourses has been a *new regionalism,* an emergent integrative discourse that has become increasingly central to understanding the postmetropolitan transition. I call it an integrative rather than causal, consequential, or reactive discourse because of its hybridizing power, which connects not only micro and macro analytics and endogenous and exogenous forces but also the established literatures on urban and international political economy, pioneered in the first case by David Harvey and in the second by the world systems theories of Immanuel Wallerstein.[3] The new regionalism and the spatial turn that is sustaining it will be discussed in more detail in the next chapter.

There is another discourse that needs to be mentioned, for it too generates explanations of urban change. I refer here to the body of literature on the revolutionary changes in information and communications technology.

Studied most influentially by such notable urban scholars as Manuel Castells, this field has generated such ideas as the Informational City, the information mode of production, cybercities, the Network Society, and the increasing power of the "space of flows" over the "space of places."[4] It might appear that this should form another causal discourse, but I have chosen not to do so for several reasons. First, I am suspicious of all forms of technological determinism and see information technology as a facilitative rather than a causal force helping to accelerate and consolidate globalization and the formation and growth of the New Economy.

Also explaining my decision not to identify information technology as the focus of a causal discourse in itself is its frequent inclusion of arguments that diminish, if not dismiss, the significance of space and place in the informational cities, network societies, and space of flows. Like the related literature on the clearly premature demise of the nation-state, some have written about how the Internet and other new technologies signal the "death of distance" and the "end of geography," how abstracted flows of information and communications detach people from place, making the advantages of agglomeration obsolete and diverting attention from the generative power of cities. Though they by no means define the entire IT discourse or directly reflect the views of Castells, such aggressively antispatial stances nonetheless unhelpfully complicate the assertive spatiality of the other causal discourses. I recognize the importance of the information and communications revolution as a facilitative force but do not discuss it as a causal or explanatory discourse in itself.[5]

LOOKING FIRST AT THE NEW GEOPOLITICAL ECONOMY OF INDUSTRIAL URBANISM

The first discourse revolves around the changing relations between urbanization and industrialization, highlighting the importance of industrial restructuring as opposed to postindustrialism and related "end of" theories. It deals mainly with endogenous processes, with the "inner workings" of the evolving new geopolitical economy. Basically, the argument that has emerged from analyses of Los Angeles and other city regions interprets the postmetropolitan transition as arising, first of all, from the crisis-driven development of a new form of *industrial urbanism,* variably described as post-Fordist, flexible, global, information intensive, neoliberal, postmodern, or postmetropolitan, but decidedly not postindustrial. The New Economy that is part of the foundations of the postmetropolis remains a form of urban industrial capitalism and not its replacement.

From the point of view of the first discourse, the key processes driving the reorganization of the modern metropolis are *deindustrialization and reindustrialization.* Every urban region in the world has been experiencing these processes, though at different rates and intensities, some deindustrializing much more rapidly than they reindustrialize, such as Detroit and most other cities in the American Manufacturing Belt; others emerging as centers of the New Economy without experiencing much deindustrialization, such as Singapore and major cities in the newly industrialized countries (NICs) as well as formerly suburban areas like Silicon Valley and Orange County. Los Angeles (with OC) and the Bay Area (San Jose–Oakland–San Francisco) have been among the few major urban regions that have experienced unusually intensive examples of both deindustrialization and reindustrialization, a key factor in their becoming particularly rich research laboratories for this first discourse.[6]

Described differently, what was happening was, on the one hand, a breakdown or *deconstruction* of Fordist assembly-line mass production, mass consumption, and related forms of demand driving mass suburbanization, largely through the vertical disintegration of corporate structures and the production process;[7] and on the other, a rebuilding or *reconstitution* of a New Economy of flexible specialization, global outsourcing and subcontracting, increasing privatization, and a horizontal or spatial reintegration in new industrial agglomerations or clusters—the "new industrial spaces" mentioned above.[8] The New Economy is thus associated with a new geography, a pronounced reorganization of the urban form or morphology of the modern metropolis, which has taken shape through related processes of decentralization and recentralization.

Map 13 provides both a composite sketch of the industrial geography of Los Angeles around the turn of the twentieth century and a model of how to cartographically portray other urban regions from an industrial urbanist perspective. The geography is clearly still centered on the downtown core of the City of Los Angeles, demonstrating the persistence of older centralities. The Inner Area circle (dotted line) contains the four major industrial clusters of the inner city: Most central is the clothing or garment industry, by 2000 probably the largest cluster of garment manufacturing in the United States. Nearby is a smaller circle representing a specialized jewelry cluster; to the

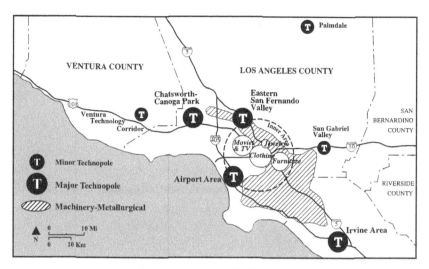

MAP 13 Industrial geography of Los Angeles. From *The City*, 1996.

southeast is one of the largest furniture manufacturing districts in the country, while to the northwest is the benchmark movie and television cluster of LA in Hollywood.

These four "anchoring" industries of Los Angeles are all craft-based industries, one of the three most propulsive sectors of the New Economy, along with high-technology manufacturing and financial services (FIRE). Research on these industries has shown that they initially were concentrated in large specialized clusters in or close to the city center, but over the past few decades they have become more centrifugal, diffusing outward from the old centers. The movie and television industry, for example, has been shifting from Hollywood to other areas, such as Burbank, Culver City, and Santa Monica. As with garment manufacturing, the old specialized district remains but no longer dominates the industry to the same degree it once did.

These and other craft-based industries tend to be highly conscious of design or fashion and fad and are connected to what has come to be defined as the cultural or creative industries. As the other two propulsive sectors of the post-Fordist New Economy, high tech and FIRE, have seemingly reached their peak expansion, the (typically craft-based) culture industries have become the new favorites of urban planners and developers all over the world, leading Allen Scott to shift his attention to Hollywood and to define the New Economy as *cognitive-cultural capitalism.*[9] A booming new literature has emerged around the culture industries, examining how they cluster and how these clusters work to generate economic development and cultural creativity, thus contributing significantly to the recent work on the generative power of cities and attracting the attention of urban planners all over the world.

The large patch described as machinery-metallurgical is not a new cluster but rather the most prominent residual from the Fordist industrialization of Los Angeles. Once a continuous urban zone ranking in size with the Ruhr in Germany, it was a major target of deindustrialization and now consists of scattered sites dispersed over a wide area, from the San Fernando Valley through South Central Los Angeles to the early industrialized area of northern Orange County. This industrial zone once contained the largest cluster of automobile assembly, tire and glass manufacturing, and iron and steel industries west of the Mississippi River. Today, almost every one of these sites has closed down, as discussed in chapter 1.

Outside the inner zone are the major new technopoles or high technology industrial clusters of Los Angeles, the most prominent, best-known, and paradigmatic of which is centered on Irvine in Orange County. Thanks to the work of Allen Scott, Orange County has joined Silicon Valley in Northern California as a primary reference point and exemplary model for studying the development of industrial districts or new industrial spaces all over the world. Also notable are three technopoles stretching from the oldest, in the eastern San Fernando Valley, through the cluster in Chatsworth-Canoga Park, to an expanding new technology corridor in neighboring Ventura County; the now much smaller and disintegrating aerospace cluster in the LAX Airport Area; and two smaller, somewhat stagnant outliers in the San Gabriel Valley and the Palmdale area in northern Los Angeles County.[10]

THE GLOBALIZATION OF PRACTICALLY EVERYTHING

Globalization has been a vital component in the restructuring of every major urban region and a definitive exogenous force in the postmetropolitan transition. Looking at Los Angeles, globalization has been a primary influence in creating arguably the most economically and culturally heterogeneous urban region the world has ever seen. Los Angeles, as well as New York, London, and Paris, are giant crucibles for the development and expression of multicultural diversity and reconstituted urban identity.

As mentioned earlier, Los Angeles has experienced a net growth of nearly eight million people since the 1965 Watts Riots, more if one includes what some estimate to be more than a million undocumented workers. Migrants from Mexico have been by far the largest component of this migration, swelling the population of the East Los Angeles barrio, replacing poor whites and blacks in the southeast quadrant of LA County to the point of reaching 95 percent of the population in some areas, and spreading into almost every census tract in the region. Add to this a million or so immigrants from Central America—El Salvador and Guatemala in particular—and one can understand why Spanish has again become a dominant everyday language in LA, as it was before the post-1848 "Americanization" process.

Percentagewise, the expansion of the Asian and Pacific Islander population has been even greater than Latinos, as they have replaced African Americans as the second-largest minority. There are today at least one hundred thousand of each of the following ethnic groups: Chinese, Pilipino, Koreans, Vietnamese, Thais, Iranians, Armenians, and Indians, along with substantial numbers of Samoans, Cambodians, Hmong, various Pacific Island groups, Pakistanis, and Bangladeshis. African American numbers have decreased in LA County, as has their degree of residential segregation. Watts, for example, has become predominantly Latino, while the center of Black Los Angeles has shifted significantly to the west, toward the predominantly African American city of Inglewood.

Nearly all immigrant groups have defined ethnic enclaves, although there are also large areas of ethnic mixture and diversity and high rates of ethnic intermarriage. Most segregation indexes have been declining in Los Angeles, once one of the most racially segregated cities in the country. Even with the formation of ethnic enclaves and the extraordinary transformation of southeast LA County from 80 percent Anglo to more than 90 percent Latino, the number of census tracts where more than 70 percent of the population consists of one ethnic group has declined significantly. The older segregation of white, wealthy, suburban populations has been diluted practically everywhere by the admixture of wealthy Asian residents; many Asian enclaves, such as Koreatown, actually have Latino majorities; and ethno-racial diversity has been spreading throughout the region.[11]

Studying this globalized ethnic geography has led to some interesting research questions and discoveries. Enclave formation, for example, has been shown to have both positive and negative consequences, occasionally isolating some groups from the mainstream economy but perhaps more often providing a welcoming base for newcomers and in some cases acting as a generative source, like other agglomerations, for new economic and cultural ideas and innovations. Increasing multicultural diversity also has a double edge, providing creative hybridities while multiplying the sources of interethnic and intercultural conflict, as various political quarrels around the world, (e.g., Armenia–Turkey, China–Taiwan, Serbia–Kosovo, North Korea–South Korea) get played out on the streets of LA.

Two remarkable but quite different zones of multiracial population that have emerged in LA illustrate these cultural complexities. The first was initially based in Monterey Park (population 60,000 in 2010), northeast of downtown. Beginning in the 1970s, large numbers of well-educated and affluent Chinese Americans and Taiwanese settled in Monterey Park, dubbed the "Chinese Beverly Hills" by real estate agents in Taipei. As the Chinese population grew in influence and began to introduce Chinese language signage on shops and street names, an unusual alliance of Anglo and Latino residents emerged to urge the passage of ordinances making English the official language of the city and forcing all Chinese signs to include English translations.[12]

Monterey Park, the first majority Chinese-ancestry municipality in the continental United States according to the 1990 census, would later in the decade become the staging point for the creation of the country's largest suburban Chinatown. Strong efforts to control growth and the effects of continued Anglo-Latino antagonism led to a rapid eastward spread of Chinese residents and new Chinese immigrants along the northern edge of the Latino barrio, into Arcadia, Temple City, Rosemead, San Marino, and through the San Gabriel Valley to Rowland Heights, Walnut, and Diamond Bar, perhaps the most extensive example of the Chinese urbanization of American suburbia. Today, in much of this area, the Asian population accounts for more than two-thirds of the total, and Mandarin is rapidly replacing Cantonese as the dominant Chinese dialect, reflecting the changing composition of Chinese in-migration.

Another zone of even greater ethno-racial diversity is centered in the municipalities of Carson and Gardena, extending eastward along Route 91 to Artesia and Cerritos. According to standard measures of diversity, the 150,000 or so residents of Carson and Gardena stand out as the most diverse urban population in the United States, with roughly 25 percent of the total classified as Latino, Anglo, African American, and Asian–Pacific Islander. As an emblem of this peak diversity, the first Museum of Cultural Diversity opened in Carson in 1997. Nearby California State University–Dominguez Hills is reported to be the most culturally diverse campus in the country. Little is known as to whether this peak diversity will have any significant lasting effects, but as a new kind of globalized urban environment, it is likely to appear in many other urban regions. Like enclave dynamics, these zones of extreme diversity deserve vigorous new research efforts.

Although always differing in intensity and specific expression, every city in the world is being globalized and becoming subject to the complex interplay of "glocalized" capital and labor, culture and politics. Once fairly autonomous internal activities, such as local decision-making processes and planning in both the public and private sectors, are increasingly influenced by these global forces, while at the same time globalization is absorbed in many different ways and shaped into many different urban outcomes. Globalization has also been a powerful driving force behind all forms of crisis-generated restructuring and has deeply affected the emergent New Economy, so much so that many urban social movements (beginning, I will argue, with the 1992 Justice Riots in LA) have shifted their focus to explicit struggles against the unjust and uneven effects of the globalization process and the New Economy that accompanies it.

OFF-THE-EDGE CITIES: STRETCHING OUT THE JOURNEY TO WORK

The next two discourses look at the spatial and social impact of globalization, economic restructuring, and the postmetropolitan transition. Like the causal discourses, these consequential or resultant discourses are tightly interwoven and difficult to separate. The restructuring of urban spatial form, for which I use the term *exopolis,* has close connections to the restructuring of the social order in what I call the Fractal City. Here I will focus on just one of the effects of socio-spatial restructuring: the *growing disjuncture in the distribution of jobs, housing, and supportive public transit,* which I will call the jobs-housing imbalance.

Like the conditions of peak cultural and economic diversity, extreme examples of the jobs-housing imbalance have produced new kinds of urban environments and aggravated urban problems, which were present in the traditional metropolis but at a much smaller and less problematic scale. The reorganized geography of the postmetropolis, for example, has led to many

kinds of "spatial mismatches," some of the most serious involving the growing disconnection between the distribution of jobs and the residential location of job seekers. This mismatch between supply and demand reaches its
cruelest peak in the explosive growth of homelessness over the past thirty
years.

Homelessness—the absence of both housing and jobs—has always been
part of the industrial capitalist city. Marx called the unemployed and poorly
housed the lumpenproletariat and saw their existence as a way of disciplining
workers and providing a contingent labor force during times of expansion.
Their numbers were reduced significantly during the boom decades following the Second World War, especially with the rise of an expanded middle
class. After 1970, however, homelessness grew rapidly, especially in states with
a weaker welfare system, such as the United States. Agglomerative forces
continue to concentrate homelessness and limited facilities for the homeless
in and around city centers, along what in LA and other cities is called Skid
Row, but centrifugal forces have spread the homeless throughout the entire
urban fabric, making it more difficult to provide necessary services, especially
as the number of homeless increased dramatically.

Estimates of the size of the homeless population in Los Angeles vary
greatly, but most studies show that more than one hundred thousand, including increasing numbers of women and children, spend at least one night a
year "sleeping rough," as it is sometimes called. Here again there is a disjointed and unjust geography, with the spatial distribution of Mission houses
and single-room occupancy hotels rarely matching the geography of need for
the homeless. There are stories of "elite" homeless sleeping on golf courses and
"invasions" of foreclosed properties throughout the region, as a new and
more complex geography of homelessness embeds itself in the postmetropolitan landscape.

Downtown Los Angeles remains, however, the site of the largest concentration of homeless in the United States. Some estimate that the homeless
form the majority of the residential population of the Central City area. They
exist on the cusp of many contradictory forces characterizing the new inner
city. During the week, they tend to stay away from the skyscrapered business
district, but they become more visible on the empty streets on the weekend.
Some planners and policy makers work hard to provide adequate housing
services, while others seek ways to expel them entirely. Asian warehouse own-
ers in the area known as Toy Town, just north of Skid Row, vacillate between
fighting off a potential homeless invasion (through such strategies as turning

on sprinkling systems overnight in warehouse doorways) and welcoming the cheap labor they provide during peak delivery and unloading times.

Homelessness, however, is just the cruelest tip of an even larger iceberg of housing poverty. The amassed working poor in LA and other urban regions, while having (often several) menial jobs, cannot easily afford formal housing, especially given the highly inflated rental market. This has led to the creation of an "informal" city of slums in nearly all the major city regions of the world, leading Mike Davis to speak of a "planet of slums" containing more than one billion inhabitants.[13] Like so many features of the postmetropolis, informality has a double edge as a sign of relative poverty as well as a strategy for survival and a source of innovative action among the world's growing mass of urban poor.

In Los Angeles and other U.S. cities, the slums are frequently disguised and much less visible than they are in, say, Rio de Janeiro or Nairobi. Backyard garages, mentioned earlier in the comparison with Amsterdam, probably still house more than two hundred thousand people in LA, and the region's motels continue to be filled with "hot-bedding" families sleeping in eight-hour shifts. In addition, nearly every housing survey shows Los Angeles to have the most overcrowded formal housing in the United States. It is difficult to find extensive shantytowns or favelas as such, but perhaps as many as half a million people live in roughly similar conditions. Recognizing the social volatility of such conditions, the United Nations proclaimed after the 1992 riots in Los Angeles that urban poverty and inequality will become "the most significant and politically explosive problem" of the twenty-first century, as conditions similar to those in Los Angeles spread to other urban regions.

Still another new kind of urban environment is being created by regional urbanization and the jobs-housing imbalance. This one is found in the outer cities, and it affects households with jobs and affordable housing but overly long journeys to work. With increasing overall density, the average times of journeys to work have probably remained stable or dropped somewhat in the LA region, but there are areas where commutes of two hours or more are common. While only 6 percent of Americans travel that far to work, 15–17 percent of worker commutes in Orange, Ventura, and most of LA County average two hours or more. The figure jumps to 25 percent in Riverside and San Bernardino counties, while in such "off-the-edge cities" as Palmdale and Lancaster, in northern LA County, figures reach between 30 and 40 percent.[14] This highly uneven geography of work commutes is a characteristic feature of the stretched-out postmetropolis, where aggregate average statistics can be very misleading.

Flushed by the success of the Orange County and West San Fernando Valley outer cities and intensified by the fear of the immigrant-packed inner core of the new Los Angeles, a remarkable anticipatory building boom has taken place in the outer fringes of the city region over the past thirty years, attracting millions of newcomers to densifying suburbia. In the 1990 census, more than half the fastest growing small cities in the United States were found in LA's outer fringe. Where jobs were relatively abundant and accessible, such as in Irvine and Mission Viejo in OC and Thousand Oaks and Simi Valley near the border of LA and Ventura Counties, thriving middle-class communities formed. In other areas, where industrialization and local job growth stalled, whole cities were left stranded, creating a socio-spatial crisis of unprecedented proportions.

In Moreno Valley, located about sixty miles from downtown Los Angeles and almost as distant from Irvine, the jobs-housing imbalance became seriously out of whack in the last two decades of the twentieth century. In 1990, Moreno Valley was the fastest-growing city over 100,000 in the country, expanding from 18,900 in 1970 to 49,000 in 1984, the year of its incorporation, to 120,000 in 1990, then leveling off in the 1990s but booming again to 193,000 in 2010. Attracted by affordable housing and developer promises of imminent job growth, and distanced from the perceived problems of the inner city, mainly young lower-middle working-class families, including a high proportion of minorities, flocked to the area. Almost 20 percent of the inhabitants today are African American, 54 percent are Latino (mainly Mexican), 8 percent are Asian and Pacific Islander, and there are residents from Central America, Southeast Asia, Cuba, Puerto Rico, Somalia, the Balkans, and many other areas, making Moreno Valley one of the largest and most exemplary "ethnoburbs," another new term coined to describe the changing urban geography of the postmetropolis.

When the jobs did not come fast enough (the hoped-for expansion of employment in what was once nearby March Air Force Base, for example, never occurred), many were forced to travel to their old employment sites, more than fifty miles away. Thousands of working residents had to rise well before dawn to drive or be taken by a fleet of vans and buses to their distant work sites, returning home in the late evening with precious little time to spend with spouse and children. Day care centers had to remain open from 4 A.M. to 9 P.M., and without a large industrial or commercial tax base, public services declined, schools were overcrowded, freeways became gridlocked, and family life came under increasing stress. For a long period, divorce, suicide, and spouse and child abuse rates skyrocketed as the still attractive ethnoburb became, in part at least, a pathological postsuburban slum.[15]

Something similar happened in the high desert of northern Los Angeles County, but on an even larger scale. Propelled by the possibility of a new international airport and the existence of a small technopole associated with Edwards Air Force Base, the cities of Palmdale and Lancaster boomed together, creating in the Antelope Valley an urbanized region of nearly half a million people. Antelope Valley (the native pronghorn antelopes disappeared in the late nineteenth century) became covered with a sea of peach and beige stucco houses with red tile roofs that sold at bargain prices, at least by comparison with the city far to the south. Palmdale grew from 12,000 in 1980 to 152,000 in 2010. The figures for Lancaster over the same four decades are slightly larger, increasing from 37,000 at the time of incorporation in 1977 to 157,000 in 2010. The racial makeup of Palmdale is almost exactly the same as Moreno Valley, while Lancaster is slightly more Anglo and African American and less Latino. Both are today excellent examples of ethnoburbs. although both had earlier "redneck" and racist reputations.

In many ways, the development of Antelope Valley imitates the much earlier growth of Orange County and vividly illustrates the story of outer city expansion and densification. Similar to OC, where the Irvine Company owned one sixth of the land area and served as a master planner, most of the Antelope Valley is being developed by the Tejon Company, a private corporation controlling the vast Tejon Ranch and serving some of the same functions as master planner. Not only has this lightly settled high desert area been filled in by nearly half a million newcomers, but it is predicted to double in population by 2020, with much of the growth concentrated in highly planned new towns, such as Centennial, a somewhat smaller version of Irvine expected to reach seventy thousand inhabitants in the next twenty or thirty years. In a lengthy article in the *New York Times* real estate section (March 18, 2007), Jon Gertner reports on the planned development of Centennial under the evocative title "Playing SimCity for Real." According to the CEO of Tejon Ranch, the Centennial project isn't the last of its kind in crowded postsuburbia; rather it is "the first great American community of the 21st century," provoking many comparisons with the Orange County experience described in chapter 3.

With the end of the Cold War and the steep decline of the region's aerospace industry, as well as the ensuing real estate crisis and economic recession in the early 1990s, the booming Antelope Valley became the site of what one reporter called a "middle-class implosion" filled with road-blocked dreams and a new "class struggle," as excessively long journeys to work began to have a pathological effect on family life and personal health.[16] In the 1990s at least, the rates of child and spouse abuse soared, leading to creation of the largest psychological center specializing in domestic violence in the United States. Homicide rates were the highest in LA County, and even before the crash of 2008, mortgage foreclosure rates reached unusually high levels. There were also rising numbers of suicides, divorces, and violent juvenile crimes (especially in shopping malls). As foreclosures multiplied, many brand-new but empty homes were filled for a short time with underclass squatters from the inner city, while others became crack houses and garment sweatshops, further indications of a city turned inside out.

These off-the-edge cities look new and attractive to the outsider driving by, and I would not be surprised if most residents said they enjoyed living there, that they would find it difficult to find a pleasant and affordable home anywhere else. There are also arguments that the pathological conditions are temporary growing pains, part of a cycle that will eventually lead to stable prosperity. Even if it is only a stage in the urbanization of suburbia, however, it carries excessively high costs and demands more public attention, especially as the problems are not likely to disappear entirely.

Enclaves of "invisible" middle-class immiseration are as characteristic of the restructured urban form as are the more familiar concentrations of immigrant working poor in the inner city and engineers and computer specialists in the burgeoning outer city technopoles. Accompanying the restructuring of urban form and made worse by movements against tax increases and for smaller government are new rounds of fiscal crises, as local governments edge toward bankruptcy, imitating in other ways the Orange County example.[17]

Countering some of the arguments presented here has been an extraordinary explosion of specialized logistics warehouses in the Inland Empire over the past ten years, turning this area of off-the-edge cities into the country's most attractive and fastest growing industrial real estate market. Vast warehouses, some larger than thirty football fields, serve as gigantic distribution centers for both American and East Asian markets. The old Norton Air Force Base near San Bernardino is now home to a 480,000-square-foot facility for Quaker Oats, while Amazon has set up its warehouse on what was once the base's golf course and clubhouse. Pep Boys occupies the old parade ground. This enormous cluster of distribution centers at the old Norton base is being developed by Hillwood Investment Properties, owned by the Ross Perot family of Texas.[18]

Notably, there is almost no manufacturing activity in this once industrialized Inland Empire outer city and, although there has been significant job growth, the wages are not high, though possibly more than for restaurant work. Logistics clusters have been growing in many city regions of the world, but little is known about the nature and intensity of their spillover effects. They are nevertheless likely to be a major focus for urban and regional planning in the future.

SUBURBAN REDOUBTS: RESISTING THE URBANIZATION OF SUBURBIA

Almost opposite to the off-the-edge cities is the privatopian paradise of Palos Verdes, perhaps the country's, if not the world's, largest concentration of gated and guarded communities aggressively acting as private residential governments to prevent incursions of the poorer classes.[19] The Palos Verdes Peninsula juts out like a large Pacific island floating next to the vast lowland basin of Los Angeles. Its eastern edge laps over into the burgeoning port of Los Angeles–Long Beach, but its verdant and decidedly insular highlands stand out as the world's first *privatopolis,* a collection of gated and guarded private utopias that provides one of the ultimate expressions of the security-obsessed urbanism discussed by Mike Davis in *City of Quartz* and effective suburban resistance to regional urbanization. There is nothing quite like it anywhere else, although gated communities are now found in almost every large city region in the world.

Four geographically interwoven cities make up this privatopian complex (table 3). The smallest is the purest. Rolling Hills began in 1935 as reputedly the first master planned and gated new town in the country. Its first installation was the gatehouse, which is today the main entrance to the tightly guarded private residential community. For thirty years, the gatehouse also served as city hall and community center, jumbling together public and private governance. Built to provide and maintain a "ranch style equestrian environment," Rolling Hills was incorporated in 1957 as a single gated and guarded enclave. Some say that the elected city council has relatively little to do other than collect horse manure. For shopping, schools, police, and other

TABLE 3 The Privatopias of Palos Verdes

City	Year Incorporated	2010 Population	% Anglo + % Asian = % "Elite" Population	% Latino of Any Race
Rancho Palos Verdes	1973	41,600	62 + 29 = 91	8.5
Rolling Hills Estates	1957	8,000	68 + 25 = 93	6.2
Rolling Hills	1957	2,000	77 + 16 = 91	5.5
Palos Verdes Estates	1939	13,000	77 + 17 = 94	4.7

vital services, the residents depend on—some say exploit—outside sources. The development contains no public infrastructure, no traffic lights, no city-owned roads, sewers, or services. The Rolling Hills Community Association, a private and dominant second layer of government, controls access to the city, monitors architectural design, and maintains the advertised "unique lifestyle found only behind the gates."

Rolling Hills Estates is a larger and more diverse version of Rolling Hills. It consists of thirty distinct gated or walled-in "neighborhoods," each with its own HOA (homeowners association) and distinctive architecture, maintained, like most gated communities, through thick contracts defining the accepted colors houses may be painted, where cars must be parked, and other detailed proscriptions. Lawyers have dubbed these agreements "association-administered servitude regimes." Whatever they are called, these contractual obligations and the HOAs that serve as their judge and jury are the leading edge of the growing privatization of residential life, not just in Palos Verdes but in themed housing developments and specialized common interest developments all over the country.

Palos Verdes Estates, incorporated before the Second World War, was master-planned (along with Rolling Hills and nearby Torrance) by the Olmsted Brothers, descendants of the designers of Central Park in Manhattan, and it reflects continuing ties to New York banking interests. It is a little more of a city and is the only one of the four to have its own police department.

The largest (with almost twice the population of the other three combined) and most recently incorporated of this cluster is Rancho Palos Verdes, located mainly uphill from Portuguese Bend in an area that is considered to be the most unstable fault zone in North America. At least five magnitude 6+ earthquakes have hit the peninsula in the twentieth century, and tremors are familiar to all residents. While there are gated communities in the Rancho, the city has also become very environmentally conscious and has set aside many ecological reserves within its boundaries. These ecological preservation areas are another means, in addition to powerful private residential government, to avoid the high-density development occurring all over the map of LA.

This privatopian cluster is one of the richest urban/suburban areas in the country, mainly Republican but with an admixture of more liberal New York City migrants. As can be seen from the table, the whole peninsula is more than two-thirds Anglo or non-Hispanic white. As is true of other wealthy, predominantly Anglo areas of Los Angeles, there is a sizable Asian population, which, when added to the Anglo residents, pushes the "elite" population to over 90 percent. In addition to being a redoubt of the wealthy, the defensible-space-minded population is also one of the most vigorously "localist" in the region. A recent civil rights court case involved peninsula surfers violently attacking "invaders" from the north in Lunada Bay, reputed to be one of the best surfing beaches in the world. The defenders of their surf turf put up signs saying "locals only," they installed surveillance cameras, and a few accepted, with appropriate insignia, their depiction as surf nazis.

Intensified localism, whether advanced by private residential governments or strategically planned by local environmentalists, has made Palos Verdes stand out in the midst of regional urbanization as a bastion of traditional white and wealthy low-density suburbia. Mike Davis rejects any possibility that something positive can develop from this "homegrown revolution." The chapter in *City of Quartz* by this name includes subheadings that represent his most vicious metaphorical messages: "Sunbelt Bolshevism," "The White Wall," "Suburban Separatism," "Defending the Fat Life," "Revolt Against Density," "The Watts Riots of the Middle Classes," "Homeowners Soviets," "Nimbys and Know-Nothings."

Other ways of describing the gated-community phenomenon are as a bridgehead for the corporate privatization of residential governance and family life, as a preserve for extreme conservative politics, and as a product of the "secession of the rich," a way for the wealthy to abandon any commitment to the city and urban development, much worse in its urban effects than gentrification, which at least involves some willingness to participate in urban life. Reflecting the harder surfaces of an emerging mode of social regulation, gated communities also serve in part to deflect political activism and avoid unrest, not just through attempted isolation and insularity but also by channeling political participation away from the city beyond and toward those little tactics of the habitat that occupy so much of the time of these association-administered servitude regimes.

So is there nothing positive that can be said about the spread of gated communities and such specialized privatopias as Leisure World and Sun City? Are they not examples of participatory local democracy created through freedom of choice, albeit by the relatively wealthy? What if anything should be done about them? Should their spread be forcefully stopped? Should they be disbanded? Perhaps these questions will answer themselves as increasing regional urbanization makes escape from the perceived dangers of urban life more difficult. I would not be surprised, however, if Palos Verdes lasts longer than anywhere else.

METROPOLARITIES: MANUFACTURING INEQUALITY

Interwoven with the jumbled spatiality of the globalized post-Fordist city region is a reconstituted social structure that has become similarly fluid, fragmented, decentered, and rearranged in complex patterns that are only beginning to be recognized and effectively studied. One overriding conclusion emerges from this complexity: urban restructuring and the post-metropolitan transition have *accentuated socioeconomic inequalities and ideological and political polarization.* Again, inequality has always characterized the industrial capitalist city, but over the past thirty years inequality and polarization have become worse than ever before, while also taking on new forms.

Although there are significant continuities with the past, the contemporary urban social order can no longer be defined only by such traditional models of social stratification as the class-divided dual city of the bourgeoisie and the proletariat; or the neatly layered hierarchical city of the rich, the middle class, and the poor; or the racially divided city of Black versus white that split America in the 1960s. These older polarities have not disappeared, but a much more polymorphous and fractured social order has taken shape from the restructuring of social boundaries and the multiplication of crosscutting divisions, based not just on class, race, and gender but on new polarities related to sexual preferences, relative location, cultural identity, and especially the differences between immigrant and domestic populations.

The urban social mosaic remained relatively stable in the metropolitan era from the last decades of the nineteenth century to around 1980. There was a prominent dividing line between the urban and the suburban, some degree of concentricity based mainly on life-cycle stage (empty nesters and single-person households in the center, young families with children in the suburbs), distinct wedges of rich and poor extending from center to periphery, and clearly segregated racial zones. Over the past thirty years, however, the mosaic has been spinning almost like a kaleidoscope. This spatial restructuring was intertwined with a restructuring of urban systems of social stratification, and marking both was an intensification of inequalities, injustices, and what I called "metropolarities."

As with spatial restructuring, many new terms have emerged to reflect the polarized restructuring of the social order. Rarely used before the 1960s but so commonplace today that its origins in the postmetropolitan transition are often forgotten is the term *yuppies,* for young urban professionals who have become synonymous with rapid upward mobility. Yuppie ambitions are driven by hopes of joining the super-rich, an expanded category of millionaires and billionaires that make up the top one percent of the income ladder. Among the more successful yuppies are the not-so-young upper professionals (better called uppies?), leaders of the executive-managerial class of overseers that has been described as the "new dominant class" of the contemporary city.

In many North American and Western European city regions, yuppies and upper professionals in particular have become aggressive infighters in the public domain of planning and urban policy. They may not constitute a cohesive class and probably do not control the highest peaks of economic and political power, but they increasingly influence daily life in the city and shape the development of the urban landscape. They are the primary agents of gentrification, struggling to establish and maintain their distinctive lifestyles and living spaces literally and figuratively in the heart of the city. Through gentrification as well as the normal planning processes, many poor neighborhoods are transformed—and many former residents and local shops displaced—as old spaces are filled with trendy food stores, clothing boutiques, entertainment zones, and other accoutrements of yuppie life.

The new professional-executive-managerial class tends to be younger and more focused in the Central City than their Fordist predecessors, who typically moved quietly to the suburbs, living in privatized households far from the downtown core. Except for those escaping the city to peripheral gated communities, the present generation demands a central place in the urban fabric and has the public and private power to make the city-building process suit its own image and needs. Upper professionals and their families are reputed to make up one-third of the population of Los Angeles, New York City, and other large urban regions. Along with the 30–40 percent of the population classified as working poor or welfare dependent, they form the new majority of the postmetropolis.

The bottom of the income ladder has its own new terminology, starting with the aforementioned immigrant working poor and welfare-dependent underclass, which the well-known African American sociologist William Julius Wilson called, in an effort to define the extreme opposite of the super-rich, "the truly disadvantaged" or, in an earlier version, "the permanent urban underclass."[20] Expanding the size and diversity of the poor are larger than ever numbers of homeless and a growing population of "new orphans," elderly poor abandoned by their children or (only in the United States) patients without health insurance dropped off on the streets by hospital staff. Bands of runaway homeless youth, also attracted to the big cities, compete for space in desolated "landscapes of despair," while older forms of domestic slavery and peonage have reemerged in new guises. In LA and other Pacific Rim ports, hundreds if not thousands of immigrants from Indonesia, Thailand, China, and Central America are "imported" each year. Their documents are taken away, and they are either "sold" to wealthy households as live-in domestic servants or forced to live in total isolation and work for little or no wages and under the worst sweatshop conditions.

Squeezed between these two extremes of social stratification is the once expansive middle class, now significantly reduced in size as a few trickle up to the rich and many more drop down the income ladder, deflating the great middle-class "bulge" that characterized the postwar boom years. After leading the world in social mobility and job growth, the United States has fallen behind many other countries during the postmetropolitan transition. As is true of so much of the postmetropolis, the middle class is no longer what it used to be.

By now there can be little doubt that one of the outstanding features of the postmetropolitan transition and the formation of a New Economy has been an extraordinary concentration of wealth in the upper one percent of the population and an accompanying reduction in the income share of the bottom 50 percent. In the United States in 2000, the approximately thirteen thousand richest families, 0.1 percent of the population, earned more than the twenty million poorest families. The average income of these richest families was three hundred times the income of the average family, as against seventy times the average in 1970.[21] What some now call the "fortunate fifth," the upper quintile of the income ladder, has consistently been earning more (and is typically taxed at a lower rate) than the remaining four-fifths. There is nothing to suggest that this income polarization has decreased, especially after the crash of 2008. More controversial, however, has been how to explain and interpret this polarization and what to do about it.

Ironically perhaps, the extreme Left and extreme Right have somewhat similar responses to income inequality. Both see it as an integral part of capitalist development, a kind of generative and possibly even necessary condition. There is nothing new here, they say. Deepening inequality represents continuity, capitalism as usual, not radical change. Even if aimed in very different directions, the outcome of this agreement is normalization of the problem, calming the need for active intervention.

Also tending to normalize the condition are those who believe income inequality arises primarily because of the powerful attractions of such large city regions such as Los Angeles and New York, as large numbers of both the rich and the poor flow hopefully into the urban economy, creating the startling statistics on polarization and widening income gaps. Again, everything is normal—no need to stir up new anxieties.

A variation on this interpretation, rarely uttered in academic debates but enjoying much wider popular acceptance, is the idea that uncontrolled immigration (of the poor) is the primary cause of the income gap and the source of many other economic problems. From this perspective, what needs to be done is clear. If one really wants to reduce the statistical gap, governments need to reduce the number of immigrants in any way they can. Controlling the numbers of the super-rich rarely enters the picture, for it is typically assumed that the desire to become rich drives the economy and should never be constrained. These widespread attitudes contribute significantly to the deep cultural and political divide between domestic and immigrant populations, not just in Los Angeles but in many other city regions in North America and Europe.

Further complicating the debate, there are also some who claim that income polarization is not as bad as it seems. That it appears to be worse than at any other time in U.S. history is mainly a statistical artifact, they say, arising from the choice of statistical measures. After all, median household income has not been declining over the past thirty years, and at least before 2008, one could use different data to show that there was much less inequality and poverty than claimed. Crisis-generated restructuring has been (perhaps necessarily) painful for some but, on the whole, has been successful in avoiding major economic decline, even if some cracks have appeared in the past ten years.

Just as liberals praise the survival strategies of the poor, others argue that the middle class has developed strategies to maintain their economic position and lifestyle, ameliorating the effects of the widening income gap. Fitting well into the postmetropolitan discourse, for example, has been the enormous surge of women with children into the labor market, reflecting the "liberation" of often highly educated women from the unpaid housework of classical dormitory suburbia.[22] Another strategy is illustrated by double-income-no-kids households (DINKS), as well as other collective arrangements beyond the traditional nuclear family, which has probably changed as much as any other social institution in the past thirty years and now represents a minority of all households. Again, the message is that the income gap is not as serious a problem as some are claiming.

Given these dismissive interpretations and the prevailing influence of neoliberal discourse and ideological spin, it is not surprising to find that relatively little attention was given, until very recently, to protesting what must surely be the most extreme income polarization in U.S. history. Only in the aftermath of the crash of 2008, when the whole system seemed to have broken down—and especially with the ongoing Occupy movement, which started in 2011—did economic inequality become a major public issue. Not surprisingly, the Occupy movement was most demonstrative initially in New York and in Southern and Northern California soon after.

It is worth repeating the observations made in a United Nations report that appeared just after the 1992 Justice Riots in LA. "An urban revolution is taking place on all six inhabited continents," it states, "brought about by conditions very similar to those in Los Angeles: crime, racial and ethnic tension, economic woes, vast disparities of wealth, shortages of social services and deteriorating infrastructure." Recognizing that the largest gap between wealth and poverty in the developed world exists in the United States and that this gap is greatest in New York and Los Angeles, where it now compares with Karachi, Bombay, and Mexico City, the UN report concluded by predicting that urban poverty will be the most politically explosive problem of the twenty-first century.[23]

A NEW MODE OF REGULATION?

The final two discourses arise from the socio-spatial effects of globalization, the New Economy, and the IT revolution but have an added dimension relating to social control, or what some scholars call the mode of regulation. Crisis-generated restructuring, the fundamental driving force behind the development of Los Angeles since the 1960s, has always involved two objectives. The first and most obvious is to find ways to restore expansive economic growth and profitability after realizing that older, established ways—business as usual—will no longer be productive. The second, usually not given the same degree of attention, is to sustain this new form of capitalist development by devising improved means to ensure social peace and avoid active rebellion and resistance.

Building a New Economy and finding improved forms of social control and discipline have involved specifically spatial strategies. In other words, crisis-generated urban restructuring involves what David Harvey called an attempted "spatial fix," a reshaping of geography and the built environment in the hope of meeting the emerging needs of the post-Fordist, flexible, information-intensive, and globalized New Economy. All six discourses on the postmetropolitan transition reflect, in different ways, this attempted spatial fix and its intended as well as unintended consequences.

Fordism and its associated Keynesian policies of welfare provision and demand stimulation were themselves products of crisis-generated restructuring and a relatively successful spatial fix, the crisis being the Great Depression and the challenges of World War II. The new economy and geography defined by the Fordist-Keynesian spatial fix was based on assembly-line mass production, mass consumption, automobile-driven mass suburbanization, and the attendant expansion of the metropolitan model of urbanism. These dramatic changes did not take place on their own; they were stabilized in the United States by what some called a "social contract," a widespread agreement among big labor unions, large corporations, and a supportive federal government wherein blue-collar workers and the expanding middle class refrained for the most part from major bouts of social unrest and rebellion in return for rising wages, guaranteed jobs, and expanding social welfare.

Social movements arose around issues of class, race, and gender. Occasionally, as with the civil rights movement, they vigorously challenged the status quo. Disruptive social unrest was rare, however, at least until the urban riots and antiwar protests of the 1960s. A New Economy (and new geography), eventually described as post-Fordist, began to emerge in reaction to these urban and related crises and soon reached a turning point in the worldwide recession of 1973–74. This downturn fostered the rise of reactionary neoliberal and neoconservative ideologies that would peak in the Reagan and Thatcher regimes. These expanding political forces then blamed economic decline on that earlier social contract (symbolized by the New Deal and Great Society policies) and sought ways to redress what they saw as too much government intervention and excessive entitlement benefits to workers, making restructuring at times a euphemism for cutting labor costs and union busting.

It became clear, at least for the new neoliberal regimes, that for the New Economy to grow and its social and spatial forms to work effectively, new modes of social and spatial regulation and control needed to be developed. This leads us to the last two discourses, which focus on how urban geographies and urban life in general were increasingly affected by processes, developments, and events that worked in large part to prevent the restructured postmetropolis, with all its inequalities, cultural tensions, and social pathologies, from exploding.

The first discourse deals with the *fortressing* of the postmetropolis and the rise of what Mike Davis called "security-obsessed urbanism," symbolized by the notion of the postmetropolis becoming a "carceral archipelago," its population incarcerated and insulated in actual as well as virtual prisons, walled-in spaces, armed-guarded housing estates, and barbed-wire-protected shopping malls, all with ever-present surveillance cameras and technologically advanced alarm systems. While this new form of socio-spatial control spread quickly all over the world, the most assertive discourses about it arose in and about Los Angeles.

The carceral city discourse was most closely associated with one author and one book: Mike Davis's *City of Quartz* (1990). It was also more heavily dominated by Los Angeles examples than any other discourse—although Davis's book inspired studies of similar phenomena in many other city regions. Davis's singular achievement heavily shaped how Los Angeles was viewed around the world in the 1990s. In his well-crafted prose, driven by his Neomarxist commitments, Davis depicted Los Angeles as an archetypical carceral city, where militarized police and abundantly armed citizen militias stood guard over the largest urban prison population in the country. Spreading well beyond the actual jam-packed prisons and their supportive "prison-industrial complex" was a carceral landscape with residents increasingly and most often voluntarily enclosed in prison-like fortresses walled off from the threatening and perplex-ing new urban conditions. LA was seen as enmeshed in a dense web of defended and gated spaces, wherein, it was implied if not directly announced, trespassers would be shot.

For almost a decade, Davis was the voice of Los Angeles, writing such provocatively titled essays as "L.A. Was Just the Beginning: Urban Revolt in the United States" (1992), "Beyond Blade Runner: Urban Control and the Ecology of Fear" (1992), "Who Killed Los Angeles?" (1993), "Cannibal City: Los Angeles and the Destruction of Nature" (1994), and the full-length book *Ecology of Fear: Los Angeles and the Imagination of Disaster* (1998). Though it was surprising just how many avid readers accepted Davis's apocalyptic noir vision of LA, it was not a surprise that (perhaps jealous) local historians, academics, and journalists began an aggressive campaign to attack Davis as a fact-manipulating, footnote-mangling, politically dangerous, antiurban poseur. The always sizable army of LA boosters, seeing him only as a droning voice of negativism, drove Davis out of Los Angeles for several years. He would return to Southern California, where he lives today, although never again to be as influential as he was in the 1990s.

Here are some excerpts from *City of Quartz,* focusing specifically on the carceral cityscape.

> Welcome to post-liberal Los Angeles, where the defense of luxury lifestyles is translated into a proliferation of new repressions in space and movement, undergirded by the ubiquitous "armed response." The obsession with physical security systems, and, collaterally, with the architectural policing of social boundaries, has become a zeitgeist of urban restructuring, a master narrative in the emerging built environment of the 1990s.

> We live in fortress cities brutally divided between fortified cells of affluent society and places of terror where the police battle the criminalized poor. The Second Civil War that began in the long hot summers of the 1960s has been institutionalized into the very structure of urban space. . . . In cities like Los Angeles, on the bad edge of postmodernity, one observes an unprecedented tendency to merge urban design, architecture and the police into a single comprehensive security effort.

> The LAPD's pathbreaking substitution of technological capital for patrol manpower . . . was a necessary adaptation to the city's dispersed form. . . . [T]echnological surveillances and response supplanted the traditional patrol-man's intimate "folk" knowledge of specific communities. . . . The LAPD introduced the first police helicopters for systematic aerial surveillance. After the Watts Rebellion of 1965 this airborne effort became the cornerstone of a

policing strategy for the whole city. . . . To facilitate ground-air synchroniza-
tion, thousands of residential rooftops have been painted with identifying
street numbers, transforming the aerial view into a huge police grid.

There still is no better description of the dark side of Los Angeles in the 1990s
than *City of Quartz,* even though crisis-generated restructuring is barely
mentioned, postmodernity is discussed only at its "bad edge," globalization
is avoided almost entirely as an explanatory factor, the IT revolution seems
confined to the Los Angeles Police Department, and local community struggles are made to appear hopeless. No other discourse is so disconnected from
all others, so demanding that it be seen exclusively on its own terms, detached
from any alternative interpretation of the contemporary city.

Whereas the fortressing of LA and security-obsessed urbanism were
indicative of a hard-edged approach to controlling urban unrest, another
discourse has emerged to provide a softer way of smothering political activism and social upheaval. It relates more to how the city is mentally or psycho-
logically perceived and imagined than to physical forces shaping the urban
built environment. Stated most bluntly, what is described in the literature as
the Disney-like theme-parking of the city, the precession of simulacra, the
rising power of political and cultural spin doctors, widespread absorption in
virtual reality, and the population's increasing inability to tell the difference
between what is real and what is imagined all contribute to anesthetizing
political consciousness and preventing rebellion and unrest. A key word here
is *diversion,* which means "to deflect or divert away" as well as "to amuse and
entertain." In this Simcity discourse, as I have described it, social control is
mixed with diversionary enchantment and entertainment.

It is worth recalling the encounter between the second President Bush's
advisors and the gathered critics of his regime (discussed in chapter 3). The
critics were defined as the "reality-based community," whereas the Bush team
created its own (simulated) reality, and that is the reality that matters most.
Such simulated realities now not only affect political opinion and judgment
but also heavily shape what we eat, what we wear, how we entertain ourselves,
with whom we mate, and many other activities of everyday life. With the
precession or prioritizing of simulacra—exact copies of probably nonexistent
phenomena—the average person finds it increasingly difficult to tell fact
from fiction. Actual cities become Simcities filled with Simcitizens acting in
real life almost as if they were playing the computer game of SimCity . . . in
SimAmerica.

Evolving alongside these developments has been the eponymous computer game of SimCity, in all its versions the most popular and perhaps influential computer game ever created. The classic version of SimCity appeared in 1989 and described itself as "the Original City Simulator." Its accompanying user manual contained a serious essay on the history of cities and city planning, encouraging players—or Sims—to become city-building authorities, deciding on tax rates, zoning plans, and disaster relief for their SimCitizens. A more pragmatic and moralistic tone accompanied its successor, SimCity 2000, which appeared in 1993 and billed itself as "the Ultimate City Simulator," discouraging any attempt to build an "ideal" city. SimCity would continue with SC 3000 (1999), SC4 (2003), SCDS and SC-Societies (2007). The Sims appeared in 2000, while the *Sim-* prefix would be used many times over with such names as *Earth, Farm, Town, Copter, Life, Isle, Tower, Park, Ant,* and *Mars.* Growing even further in scope and scale was another game, Second Life, which went beyond city building to simulate everyday life in all its details.

Perhaps the most amazing development of the SimCity series, at least for the discussion here, was the announcement of SimCity 2013, which operates in a specifically *regional* context, with a polycentric network of cities that seems uncannily to reflect the latest thinking about regional urbanization.

NOTES

1. My last attempt to defend critical postmodernism and the notion of postmodern urbanism was at an unusually open-minded and supportive international conference, *Postmodern Cities,* held in Sydney, Australia, in 1993, and organized by Kathy Gibson and Sophie Watson. Gibson and Watson also edited the book *Postmodern Cities and Spaces* (1995), which included not only my "Postmodern Urbanization" (app. 1, source 5A) but also a reprint of my earlier article "Heterotopologies: A Remembrance of Other Spaces in the Citadel-LA" (source 2D). I would rarely use the term *postmodern* again in my writings, although I would continue to be referred to as a postmodern geographer (see also app. 1, source 5C).

2. This idea that Los Angeles and a few other major urban regions were beginning to move from crisis-generated restructuring to restructuring-generated crises was discussed in the final chapter of a book I jointly edited with Allen Scott, ambitiously titled *The City: Los Angeles and Urban Theory at the End of the Twentieth Century* (app. 1, source 5B). Another version, filled with illustrative detail from Los Angeles, runs through the core chapters of *Postmetropolis: Critical Studies of Cities and Regions* (source 5D).

3. Harvey's key works are *Social Justice and the City* (Baltimore, MD: Johns Hopkins University Press, 1973), and *The Limits to Capital* (Oxford: Blackwell, 1982). Wallerstein begins his look at the world system in *The Capitalist World-Economy* (Cambridge: Cambridge University Press, 1979).

4. Manuel Castells, *The Information Age: Economy, Society, and Culture,* vol. 1, *The Rise of the Network Society* (1996); vol. 2, *The Power of Identity* (1997); and vol. 3, *End of Millennium* (1998) (Malden, MA: Blackwell). See also Castells, *The Informational City: Information, Technology, Economic Restructuring, and the Urban-Regional Process* (Berkeley and Los Angeles: University of California Press, 1989).

5. For an excellent argument supporting this view of IT, see Edward E. Leamer and Michael Storper, "The Economic Geography of the Internet Age," *Journal of International Business Studies* 32 (2001): 641–65.

6. If one includes the financial services industry (FIRE) as an important component of the New Economy and recognizes the recent growth of high technology and media industries, then perhaps New York City needs to be included here, as experiencing intensive forms of both deindustrialization and reindustrialization.

7. Allen Scott was one of the first to show how industrial restructuring was initiated by vertical disintegration, the shift away from corporate ownership of the entire production-to-consumption process (from raw material procurement to sales of the final product) and the related inflexibility of assembly-line mass production, via such tactics as outsourcing and subcontracting. When the transaction costs of such tactics became too high, there was a horizontal reintegration into new specialized clusters.

8. Industries have always found some advantage in clustering together. What is different today is the renewed and intensified advantage arising from the breakdown of Fordism and the associated emergence of highly generative new industrial spaces or districts.

9. Allen J. Scott, *On Hollywood: The Place, the Industry* (Princeton, NJ: Princeton University Press, 2005); and *Social Economy of the Metropolis: Cognitive-Cultural Capitalism and the Global Resurgence of Cities* (Oxford: Oxford University Press, 2008). See also his *Cultural Economy of the City: Essays on the Geography of Image-Producing Industries* (London: Sage, 2000).

10. In a series of publications, Scott theorizes regional industrial development and the formation of a post-Fordist industrial geography by downplaying the importance of natural resource endowments and easily calculated locational factors, and shifting primary attention to local social and political mobilizations and geographical concentrations of technological sensitivities and skills. Combined with his work on vertical disintegration and detailed industrial case studies, this creative expansion of traditional location theory has helped make Scott one of the world's leading geopolitical economists, attracting substantial additional academic attention to the Los Angeles–Orange County experience.

11. The best mapping of the ethnic geography of Los Angeles can be found in James P. Allen and Eugene Turner, *The Ethnic Quilt: Population Diversity in*

Southern California (Northridge: Center for Geographical Studies, California State University Northridge, 1997).

12. Leland Saito, *Race and Politics: Asian Americans, Latinos, and Whites in a Los Angeles Suburb* (Champaign: University of Illinois Press, 1980); Timothy Fong, *The First Suburban Chinatown* (Philadelphia: Temple University Press, 1994); John Horton, *The Politics of Diversity: Immigration, Resistance, and Change in Monterey Park, California* (Philadelphia: Temple University Press, 1995).

13. Mike Davis, *Planet of Slums* (London: Verso, 2007).

14. Sonia Nazario, "Suburban Dreams Hit Roadblock," *Los Angeles Times,* June 23, 1996.

15. Tom Gorman, "Moreno Valley: Boom Town Going Bust Turns to Voters," *Los Angeles Times,* October 28, 1996; and "Bad Times for Boom Town," *Los Angeles Times,* January 12, 1994.

16. Sonia Nazario, "Class Struggle Unfolds in Antelope Valley Tracts," *Los Angeles Times,* June 24, 1996.

17. Orange County led the way in California's most successful tax revolt, leading to the passage of Proposition 13 in 1978, which many argue financially strangled local government throughout the state; encouraged the tactics that led to the Orange County bankruptcy; fostered the declining quality of education, infrastructure, and health services; and contributed significantly to the election of Ronald Reagan in 1980.

18. Roger Vincent, "Warehouse Empire: Companies Are Setting Up Massive Distribution Centers in Riverside and San Bernardino Counties," *Los Angeles Times,* April 14, 2013.

19. A balanced and insightful picture of the spread of gated communities can be found in Evan Mackenzie's *Privatopia: Homeowner Associations and the Rise of Residential Private Government* (New Haven, CT: Yale University Press, 1994). A sequel has recently appeared: *Beyond Privatopia: Rethinking Residential Private Government* (Washington, DC: Urban Institute Press, 2011).

20. William Julius Wilson, *The Truly Disadvantaged: The Inner City, the Underclass, and Public Policy* (Chicago: University of Chicago Press, 1987); and *When Work Disappears: The World of the New Urban Poor* (New York: Vintage, 1996).

21. My main source here is the Nobel-prize-winning economist Paul Krugman, starting with "For Richer: How the Permissive Capitalism of the Boom Destroyed American Equality," *New York Times Magazine,* October 20, 2002; see also *The Great Unraveling: Losing Our Way in the New Century* (New York: W. W. Norton, 2003); and *The Return of Depression Economics and the Crisis of 2008* (New York: W. W. Norton, 2008). For Los Angeles, see Paul Ong and Evelyn Blumenberg, "Income and Racial Inequality in Los Angeles," in *The City,* ed. Scott and Soja, 311–35.

22. Without equal pay for equal work and in the absence of benefits for part-time work—and often full-time work as well—educated suburban women become a superexploitable resource comparable in many ways to undocumented immi-

grants. The millions in both groups have prevented a steep decline in household incomes over the past thirty years.

23. Reported soon after the event in Robin Wright, "Riots Called Symptom of Worldwide Urban Trend," *Los Angeles Times*, May 25, 1992. There was no mention of the specific UN report referred to.

————

SIX

A Look Beyond Los Angeles

There are currently around five hundred megacity regions with populations of over one million. Each one, including Los Angeles, can be seen as a product of two interacting forces, one involving general trends that affect them all to varying degrees, the other reflecting a multiplicity of particular local conditions and influential forces that make each different from the others. The objective of each of the six discourses discussed in the preceding chapter was to generalize about the particularities of the postmetropolitan transition as it has been expressed in Los Angeles. In this chapter, we move beyond the illustrative details of the Los Angeles case to focus on a more general understanding of the contemporary urbanization process.

Using Los Angeles as the primary source for both theory building and empirical illustration has its advantages, for there are few megacity regions that have accumulated such an extensive literature on the geohistory of urban change over the past forty years.[1] I think it is also safe to say that there are very few megacity regions that have been as "trendsetting" as Los Angeles during this period. This does not mean, however, that we can directly translate the Los Angeles experience to another city region without careful qualification. I say this not just because every city is unique or because, as some critics of the LA research cluster claim, there are so many unusual conditions associated with Los Angeles that to compare it to London or Singapore or, for that matter, Peoria or Scunthorpe, is absurdly presumptuous. Trends and tendencies are not determinations, however, and their applicability does not depend on contextual similarity.

One of the core arguments of *My Los Angeles* is that one can learn a great deal about other cities by studying Los Angeles from a more generalist and spatially informed perspective. This is not to say that other cities will follow the LA model in some numbingly mimetic manner. There is much that is unique to LA, much that will never be repeated anywhere else. Yet many other aspects of Los Angeles are eminently generalizable, applicable in some degree to every city region in the world, north and south, east and west. To sustain this argument, this chapter is divided into two sections. The first is a brief exposition of the theoretical foundations of *My Los Angeles,* the second a discussion of the empirical trends that I predict, based on what I have learned from Los Angeles, will shape all the world's major city regions in the next several decades.

PUTTING SPACE FIRST

A distinctive feature of *My Los Angeles* is the foregrounding of a critical spatial perspective, putting space first in matters of analysis, interpretation, and explanation. Such foregrounding of a spatial perspective is relatively new and not widely practiced in the social sciences or in the development of either liberal and radical (e.g., Marxist) social theory, at least over the past 150 years. Why this is so is a question that I have addressed in many different ways in my research and writing (app. 1, sources 6A, 6B, 6C). I briefly summarize my ideas here to make explicit what I mean by a critical spatial perspective, why it is so central to my approach to studying and learning from Los Angeles, and why, until very recently, relatively little attention was given to it in Western social theory and philosophy.

In an attempt to explain the relative neglect of spatial perspectives in the Western intellectual tradition, I developed a critique of what I called social historicism, an ontological and epistemological bias that privileges, or gives unquestioned priority to, social and historical modes of explanation, theory building, and empirical analysis.[2] In this privileging, I have argued, sociality and historicality, or social and historical perspectives, far outweigh and at times almost obliterate spatiality and spatial explanation. Although originating in the late nineteenth century—it has not always been there in Western thought and philosophy—this sociohistorical bias has persisted to the present, despite the unprecedented and transdisciplinary diffusion of a spatial perspective throughout the human sciences over the past two decades.

I first identified and discussed this sociohistorical bias in an article entitled "The Socio-Spatial Dialectic" (app. 1, source 6D), published in 1980, at a time when Marxist approaches dominated urban studies and powerfully influenced postpositivist developments in geography. As a Marxist-oriented geographer at the time, I was deeply disappointed by the way even the best Marxist geographers ignored socialized spatiality and spatial explanation. Brilliant analyses dissected the way social processes, especially those arising from the needs of capitalist accumulation, shape space and human geography more generally, but very little attention was paid to how spatial processes and existing geographies shape social life and social relations, especially those related to class. With a few exceptions, such as David Harvey's concept of capitalism's search for a spatial fix (discussed in chapter 1), there almost seemed to be a taboo against explicitly spatial or geographical forms of explanation.

I could to some degree understand why other social scientists and Marxists failed to apply a strong spatial explanation, but why should geographers explicitly avoid seeing socially created space as an explanatory factor? Rather than accepting this inherent privileging of the social over the spatial, shouldn't social and spatial forces be seen as mutually formative and equally important in explaining the empirical world? It is easy to see how the social shapes the spatial, but the created geographies, I argued, in turn shape the social; hence my call for a balanced socio-spatial dialectic.[3]

The immediate response to these arguments in the early 1980s was similar to the way many Marxists had reacted to the work of fellow Marxist Henri Lefebvre a decade earlier regarding what can be called urban spatial causality—how urban geographies influence the development of capitalism and class struggle (including the nascent idea of a spatial fix). He and I were called spatial fetishists. That "space matters" was widely recognized, but to claim that space shapes social class and that spatial relations are as important as social relations was a step too far. Although geographers and many urbanists, and not just on the left, eventually accepted some version of the socio-spatial dialectic, to this day it is much more common to study how social processes shape spatial form than the other way around—to study how spatial processes, such as urbanization, affect social forms and relations.[4]

I also argued in 1980 that geography and history were similarly related. They were mutually formative and inseparable, with neither inherently more important than the other. Privileging history over geography, historical explanation and historical materialism over geographical explanation and geographical materialism, I argued, was philosophically, logically, and politically unacceptable. This was even more controversial and unacceptable than the socio-spatial dialectic. Not even the most open-minded Marxists at the time would easily agree with this critique of Marxism's inherent and almost entirely unquestioned social historicism.

In *Postmodern Geographies* (app. 1, source 6A), I blamed both the persistence of social historicism and the timidity of modern geography for the weak development and application of critical spatial perspectives in Western social thought and the relatively low prestige of the discipline of geography, especially in the United States.[5] Modern geography's failure to project a strong spatial perspective not only involved geographers obsessed with positivist science but, as I argued, modernist Marxist geographers as well. As a result of this powerful social historicism, in most of the Western world, historians were considered much more favorably than geographers as intellectuals, social critics, and political observers.

Drawing mainly on Lefebvre, Michel Foucault, and John Berger, as I did in "The Socio-Spatial Dialectic" (included as a chapter in source 6A), I raised the same question they examined in different ways: why is it we think of time (and its concrete and configured extension as history) as dynamic and developmental, involving process and change, while space (and its concrete configuration as human geography) tends to be seen as naively given, fixed, inert—merely background, container, stage, environment. Surely time and space, as nearly all physical scientists would agree, were coequal parameters of reality, one not inherently more important than the other. Everything in the natural and social worlds is spatiotemporal, or geohistorical. Yet there can be little doubt that Western social thought, especially Marxism or historical materialism, has, since the late nineteenth century, favored critical historical analysis and interpretation over critical spatial thinking.[6]

What, then, is *critical* spatial thinking? Is there anything distinctive about critical thinking and critical theory more generally? There is both a very specific and a very general answer to these questions. Critical theory in its specific sense refers to the Frankfurt School of Critical Theory, which developed mainly in the mid-twentieth century and was led by such key figures as Max Horkheimer, Theodor Adorno, and Walter Benjamin. The Frankfurt School was definitively neo-Marxist, focused on updating Marxism to deal with the increasingly complex problems of twentieth-century capitalism. Like critical theory more broadly conceived, the Frankfurt version, currently sustained in the work of Jürgen Habermas, defines theory around its practicality, its usefulness in changing the world for the better.

Critical thinking and critical theory, spatial or otherwise, do not primarily focus on truth seeking or formulating universal laws of human development, like positivist science, but instead "verify" knowledge in practice, or *praxis* (defined broadly as the transformation of knowledge into action). This emphasis on practice and knowledge's usefulness in changing the world for the better resonates well with progressive forms of urban- and regional-planning theory. It is not surprising, then, to discover that critical spatial thinking over the past thirty years has been strongly influenced by new forms of Marxist thought and has been led to this day by geographer-planners, scholars who deal with the practical and political applications of geographical knowledge. Examples range from Manuel Castells and David Harvey to Allen Scott, Michael Dear, and Michael Storper to Neil Brenner, Mustafa Dikeç, and Mark Purcell. It is also notable that most of these geographer-planners play important roles in *My Los Angeles*.

In an effort to better understand the origins of social historicism and the relative submersion of critical spatial thinking, I recently dug more deeply into the philosophical debates in the last half of the nineteenth century, when both the social sciences and scientific socialism (or Marxism) emerged and came to dominate liberal and radical socialist thought. Especially influential in these debates were the German historicists (or historists, from *historismus*), including Leopold van Ranke, Wilhelm Dilthey, Heinrich Rickert, Wilhelm von Humboldt, Johann Herder, Wilhelm Windelband, and their intellectual offspring, Georg Simmel, Max Weber, and Martin Heidegger, author of the most powerful and influential codification of historicism, *Sein und Zeit,* or *Being and Time.*[7] As the social sciences were taking shape, these philosophers of history began to debate whether there was a better way of studying society and human life than the scientific method that prevailed in the natural sciences.

Their answer was history and the historical narrative, but not the speculative and "nomothetic" history of Marx and scientific socialism, which continued to seek "laws" of human development, but rather a new, more empirically rigorous "idiographic" discipline of history, built on an objective understanding of human experience, local culture, and the "contextual" particularities of time and place. It was thought that free will and social consciousness, rather than external or natural constraints, must drive explanation in the social sciences. In this sense, the social sciences, along with Marxism, were antithetical to any form of physical geographical determinism or environmental explanations of human action and behavior.

This antinaturalism pitted the idiographic discipline of history against the then quite influential discipline of geography, which at the time was deeply involved in some version of environmental determinism, or possibilism, as its weaker version was called. Although very little has been written on this subject, the social sciences and scientific socialism held an antigeographical (and prohistorical) bias from the start. Geography had its own scientific version internalized as physical geography, so had little attraction to the German historicist debates and ended up quite isolated from the central debates in Western social theory and philosophy.[8]

Until the past decade or two, social historicism prevailed, almost entirely unquestioned and nearly unrecognized. With a few perturbations and exceptions, such as the rise of the "naturalistic" Chicago School of Urban Ecology in the interwar years (also influenced by late nineteenth-century German science and philosophy) and the critical and theoretical spatial thinkers that emerged after the urban crises of the 1960s (Lefebvre, Foucault, Berger, Harvey, and Castells), historicism was hegemonic in Western social thought and philosophy, at least until the full development of the spatial turn in the 1990s.[9]

The spatial turn springs to a significant degree from a focus on urban spatial causality, the explanatory power associated with socially produced urban space. This increasing interest in spatial thinking can be seen as a kind of ontological and epistemological rebalancing from the distortions caused by the "historical turn" in the late nineteenth century. Over the past fifteen years or so, forms of spatial thinking have spread well beyond the traditionally spatial disciplines (geography, architecture, urban and regional studies) to nearly every humanities and social science discipline, as well as into such fields as critical legal studies, comparative religion, even accounting.

I tried to build on—and promote—this spatial turn in a lengthy manuscript I submitted to Blackwell Publishers in 1985. Following the advice of a sympathetic editor, I split the manuscript into two parts, the first emphasizing my theoretical arguments and the second focused on the six discourses and empirical examples discussed here in chapter 5. It was thought that the two volumes would be published around six months apart, as they were almost complete at the time of submission.

The first volume to appear was *Thirdspace* (app. 1, source 6B, published in 1996), to which I added the subtitle intended for the combined manuscript, *Journeys to Los Angeles and Other Real-and-Imagined Places*. The second volume, *Postmetropolis* (source 6C), did not appear until 2000, as I decided to make it more of a textbook by adding several introductory chapters on the new debates—stirred on by the work of the urbanist Jane Jacobs—on the origins of cities, as well as some discussion of the historical development of urban studies from Manchester through Chicago to Los Angeles. I also added a section on developments after the Los Angeles riots of 1992, a prelude to my next book, *Seeking Spatial Justice* (source 8A).

Thirdspace redefined my critique of social historicism around a modified version of the triad that features so prominently in the work of Henri Lefebvre. The triad represented three different ways of looking at space: first as empirically defined perceived space, which emphasized "things in space," or what Lefebvre called spatial practices; conceived space or representations of space, which emphasized thoughts about space, ideologies and imageries; and finally the most unconventional and creative notion of *lived space,* which combined the previous two spaces but contained much more that is never completely knowable.[10] Building also on Foucault's conceptualization of "heterotopology" as a different way of looking at space, I used the terms *firstspace, secondspace,* and *thirdspace,* the latter representing the core of my approach to critical human geography—as well as to understanding Los Angeles.

I saw this thirdspace perspective as the product of what I called a "critical thirding as othering," which is a rejection of the either/or logic of binary thinking, wherein one is forced to choose between two opposing alternatives as if they were the only possible choices. These binaries flooded the modernist literature: subject-object, body-mind, male-female, black-white, core-periphery, socialism-capitalism, city-countryside, perceived and conceived space. A critical thirding was aimed at breaking down and opening up these "big dichotomies" to different alternatives, starting with a third possibility, an "other" rather than simply another. Thirdspace, like Foucault's notion of heterotopology, was not a specific kind of space but a way of looking, with maximum breadth and scope, at any space one chooses. All spaces can be seen and interpreted heterotopologically as thirdspace.

From a *Thirdspace* perspective, no space is completely knowable; there is always something that is hidden, beyond any analytical point of view, shrouded in impenetrable mystery, like Borges's Aleph or, for that matter, Los Angeles or any other "real-and-imagined" city anywhere. This encourages a sort of intellectual nomadism in urban studies, as one respects but is never satisfied by the knowledge one has accumulated, always ready to move on to new ground, to adapt to new and different circumstances. From this itinerant perspective, there are no permanent laws of human life (or urban development), only tendencies and contingencies, understood best by at least trying to combine social, spatial, and historical modes of interpretation. This constant search for new increments of knowledge, rather than the stubborn defense of earlier accomplishments, forms the foundation and focus of all the chapters in *My Los Angeles*.

Postmetropolis: Critical Studies of Cities and Regions (source 6C), although not always seen that way by readers and reviewers, is an intentional homage to *Thirdspace* and perhaps even more deserving of its subtitle: *Journeys to Los Angeles and Other Real–and–Imagined Places*. In not always obvious ways, *Postmetropolis* is organized around the triad of firstspace, secondspace, and thirdspace perspectives. Part 1, "Remapping the Geohistory of Cityspace," was my attempt to push the core approach of traditional geographical analysis to a new level, focusing on Jane Jacobs's radically revisionist work on the origins of cities and how the stimulus of urban agglomeration (I called it synekism) serves as a primary factor first in the full-scale emergence of the agricultural revolution, and later in every major development in the history of human society, bringing new light to Lefebvre's idea that all human societies are realized, from the start, as *urban* societies. What an amazing thought! There may never have been a human society not significantly influenced by urban spatial causality.

This leap back twelve thousand years, like all the historical references in *Postmetropolis* (and *My Los Angeles*), is meant to give greater insight into the past forty years of urban development. As such, it reflects what I consider to be the most important breakthrough in contemporary social science, an expression of urban spatial causality that I, even in my most hyperbolic moments, would not dare to claim. It is now being argued quite seriously that cities, or urban agglomerations, generate a force that is the *primary* cause of all economic development, technological innovation, and cultural creativity. And according to Jacobs, this has been true for the past ten thousand to twelve thousand years.

That the powerful generative force of cities has hardly been touched upon in the Western social science literature, as well as in Western Marxist traditions, is the strongest condemnation of the effects of social historicism. That it is now being explored seriously for the first time is the greatest tribute to the impact of the spatial turn and innovatively putting space first, at least in the form of urban spatial causality. In a wonderful turn of phrase, which refers to the revolutionary moment when hunters and gatherers settled down in the first urban settlements, Jacobs observes, "Without cities, we would all be poor." We would have remained hunter-gatherers, as we had been for over 99 percent of the history of *Homo sapiens*.

The publication of *Postmetropolis* was delayed at least two years by my fascinated exploration of geohistorical archeology, as I followed Jane Jacobs back to Çatalhöyük in contemporary Anatolia and beyond. In the spirit of tracing back the origins of cities and appreciating the importance of urban agglomeration and clustering, I concluded part 1 with a lengthy discussion of the historical evolution of municipal incorporations in Southern California (nearly 190 of them). The first formal city here was the City of Los Angeles, incorporated in 1850, followed by Anaheim in 1878, Riverside in 1880, and Santa Monica and Santa Ana in 1886. As far as I can tell, this was the first and only geographical mapping and historical chronicle of municipal agglomeration and incorporation in the Los Angeles region. It would be interesting to do similar geohistorical analyses of municipality formation in other large city regions.

While firstspace perspectives generate many new mappings and remappings, secondspace focuses attention on conceptual ideas, thoughts about (city) space and the urban restructuring process. These concepts or ideas translate into the six discourses, each an attempt, from its own viewpoint, to theorize and explain urban change since the Watts Riots in 1965. As described earlier, these discourses are not confirmed theories of postmetropolitan development as much as tentative but assertive conceptualizations of various aspects of the restructuring process and what I called the postmetropolitan transition. Here again the discussion expands well beyond Los Angeles.

In a way, I felt trapped in part 3 of *Postmetropolis*. How could I possibly meet the ambitious objectives of an unbounded and almost infinitely complex thirdspace approach? I decided to try to squeeze out something new from an unconventional look at the so-called Justice Riots of 1992. Wondering whether this would turn off many more academic readers, I composed chapter 13, "LA 1992: The Spaces of Representation," a clear reference to Lefebvre's lived space, entirely around extracts from the works of others, ending with an abridged version of the lengthy free-verse poem that I wrote as a conclusion to the original manuscript submitted to Blackwell. I thus presented the riots through a concatenation of its many interpretations and representations, shaping the flow of reactions, to be sure, but also allowing multiple voices to be heard distinctly.

In a final chapter, "Postscript: Critical Reflections on the Postmetropolis," I searched for something positive to say about contemporary Los Angeles, after noting in great detail its extremely inequitable and unjust geography and social order. This led to another remarkable discovery arising from the application of a critical spatial perspective. I discovered in Los Angeles an extraordinary resurgence of labor-community coalitions, many using explicitly spatial strategies to struggle for social and spatial justice amid the efflorescence of restructuring-generated crises, a topic I will discuss in greater detail in chapter 8. Whether part 3 was successful as thirdspace I cannot say. What is most satisfying, however, is that each of the three parts of *Postmetropolis* contains glimpses of significant new discoveries arising from the application of a critical spatial perspective to our general understanding of the urban restructuring process.

BEYOND LOS ANGELES: GENERAL URBAN TRENDS IN THE TWENTY-FIRST CENTURY

As I have said before, every city needs to be seen as a combination of the general and the particular. We may never be able to calculate the exact proportions of each, but, while always respecting uniqueness, every city will express to some degree identifiable trends and tendencies that are shared by all cities, either simultaneously or synchronically (over the same time period). Focusing on these general trends is an essential step in developing good urban theory; this approach presents the urban analyst with a rich conceptual framework for comparative studies, as illustrated in the comparison between Amsterdam and Los Angeles in chapter 4.

Learning from Los Angeles and referring mainly to the five hundred or so megacity regions of greater than one million inhabitants that exist today, what follows is a discussion of what I consider to be the most important general trends affecting urban development around the world in the near future. It is worth emphasizing that none of these trends will be experienced in exactly the same way in any of the megacity regions of today. Indeed, gathering good comparative data on the differences in their expression is a necessary foundation for future advances in critical urban and regional studies.

The Urbanization of the World

Continuing globalization will increasingly carry with it the urbanization of the entire world, or what some call planetary urbanism.[11] This will lead the study of globalization in two directions, first into a more cogent and policy-oriented understanding of the dynamics of climate change and environmental degradation; and second, into a thorough examination of the increasing urbanization of the Amazonian rainforest, the Siberian tundra, the Saharan desert, the Antarctic and Greenland icecaps, and all formerly nonurbanized areas, as urban industrial capitalism influences to some degree every square inch of the earth's surface. The urbanization and related industrialization of the world does not mean that the rainforest will be covered with skyscrapers and factories, but rather that the entire world will be enmeshed in a new urban hierarchy, a multiscalar network—literally a worldwide web—of urban centers extending from the giant megacities to the smallest urban settlements.

What is being created is the first truly global urban system, weaving together the separate national urban systems of the past. As the world urbanizes, communication, trade, and other flows will increasingly connect megacity regions regardless of national boundaries. The urbanization of the world relates to arguments that globalization ties together sovereign and autonomous nation-states and instigates the beginning of what some have called, rather prematurely, a borderless world. Similarly, there are claims that globalization heralds—also prematurely, it seems—the end of the Westphalian nation-state system. We can say with much greater confidence, however, that globalization is superseding internationalization by creating a global scale and system that is increasingly free from national control. Globalization and planetary urbanism, however, will never erase all national boundaries or spell the end of the nation-state.

One consequence of global urbanization is the gradual disappearance—or, perhaps better, the urbanization—of the rural. Everywhere on earth will be enmeshed in a globalized system of urban regions, which will contain not only familiar city forms but also wilderness, open space, and agricultural and animal husbandry areas. This global system of cities will contain nodes that range in size from gigantic city regions, much larger than the old metropolitan areas, to tiny villages and hamlets. The globalization and global city discourse will accordingly expand to include debates on the new regionalism, sustainable development, green industries, climate change, poverty, inequality, immigration, racism, cultural identity, and identity politics.

The world's five hundred megacity regions, or "megaregions'" as I suspect they will increasingly be called, will continue to concentrate a lion's share of the world's wealth, innovative potential, and total population. According to the latest UN Habitat statistics, the world's forty largest megaregions alone, covering a tiny portion of the planet's land area, contain less than 18 percent of the world's population but account today for nearly two-thirds of all economic activity and 85 percent of technological and scientific innovation. As these figures become more widely known, greater attention will be given to theories of urban agglomeration, the generative effect of cities, and the impact of what some economics textbooks now call Jane Jacobs externalities.

There seems little doubt that these five hundred megaregions will contain most of the world's population within the next few decades. Moreover, they will continue to coalesce into immense conurbations for which, almost surely, new descriptive terms will emerge. It is difficult to predict whether *megaregion* will continue to be the best way of describing the Pearl River Delta and its 120 million people (with Hong Kong, Shenzhen, Dongguan, and Guangzhou each growing to more than five million) or nearly the same number living in the interconnected megaregions of southern Honshu (Tokyo-Yokohama and Nagoya-Kyoto-Kobe-Osaka). *Megaregion* already does not fit the huge urban corridors that are growing rapidly between Delhi and Mumbai (possibly extending to Bangalore, Hyderabad, and Chennai) in India, in South America linking Rio de Janeiro, São Paulo, Buenos Aires, and Santiago, and in coastal West Africa from Lagos to Dakar.

Several other generalizations are relatively easy to make about the urbanization of the world. Most new urban dwellers will be in what we used to call the Third World and now persist in calling, geographically inaccurately, the Global South. Africa south of the Sahara (to avoid the equally offensive "sub-Saharan" underground prefix) will almost surely experience the fastest rate of urban growth and probably also the fastest rate of industrialization, both starting from a relatively low level. All these predictions, however, pale in significance compared to what will happen in China. The great new global wave of urbanization, or the new urban age scholars talk about, is due primarily to the most rapid and remarkable societal urbanization and industrialization in history, which has been taking place over the past twenty years or so in China.

China is not quite majority urban today, but it will surely become predominantly urban very soon and may be 75 percent urban in the relatively near future. We are talking here about at least eight hundred million Chinese living in cities, a majority with the financial resources to live at least a lower middle-class lifestyle. The unprecedented rate of urban-industrial growth seen in the past is not likely to continue, not only because of the international economic crisis and reductions in international trade, but also because of Chinese government policy. Almost incomprehensible to most Western observers, China now seems to believe that annual rates of economic growth under 10 percent are desirable, as national policy shifts from maximizing speed of growth to reducing social and spatial/regional inequalities.[12]

China's rapid urban industrialization and its global leadership in industrial production have many implications. Chinese development makes the concept of postindustrialism look increasingly irrelevant and misleading, almost as if it were a trick played on U.S. policy makers to relinquish the country's productive capacity. It also confirms the idea that the current wave of globalization differs from those in the past primarily in its spread of urban industrialism beyond what for more than the past century was defined as the industrialized (and developed) world. The wave began with the so-called Asian Tigers, the first of the NICs (newly industrialized countries), later exploded in scale and scope in China, and is at least beginning to do the same in India and, although somewhat less so, also Brazil, Mexico, and several other large countries.

This has radically changed the old international division of labor. The First and Third Worlds have been thoroughly redefined, the Second (Communist) World has virtually disappeared, and new power blocs are emerging and will continue to grow in the future. China and India are sometimes combined today as Chindia, home to more than a third of the world's population, while we increasingly hear talk of the BRIC countries—Brazil, Russia, India, and China. More than ever before, globalization, urbanization, and industrialization are simultaneous and interactive processes. In a peculiar way, the entire world has become what Immanuel Wallerstein once called "semi-periphery," areas that are to varying degrees both exploiter and exploited.

Also reflecting the urbanization of the world and the changing international division of labor has been the expansion of supranational regionalisms. Although European unification may continue to be challenged by reassertive nationalisms, supranational organizations will almost surely increase around the world. More difficult to predict is how far beyond regional trading alliances these organizations will go. Will trading blocs such as MERCOSUR, ASEAN, and NAFTA become more involved in environmental, transportation, and labor issues? Will labor unions globalize as swiftly as corporate capital? These remain open questions.

Accompanying the urbanization of the world has been and will continue to be the globalization of the urban, fed by the continuation of massive world-wide immigration flows and the spread of the New Economy of information-rich, flexible capitalism. It is probably safe to say that the population of almost every megaregion in the world will become more culturally and economically heterogeneous in the future.[13] In the inner city of many megaregions—and some outer cities—immigrant minorities will outnumber domestic populations, accentuating debates on the nature of citizenship, cultural identity, and urban democracy.

The most culturally diverse megacity regions today are probably Los Angeles, New York, and London. At least two, if not all three, are among the cities with the greatest income gaps and are likely to continue in these positions. More languages are spoken in these three megacity regions than in any other, although Paris, Amsterdam, and a few others may catch up in the next few decades.

A new cultural politics will develop, dealing more with questions of difference, identity, representation, and participation than with traditional goals such as economic equality. At the same time, however, movements to limit immigration are likely to increase as the tension, conflict, and struggle between domestic and immigrant populations increases. Immigrants are likely to play an increasingly political role in forming new labor-community coalitions and social movements organized around specifically urban issues, such as poverty, homelessness, the right to the city, and the search for social and spatial justice (see chapters 8 and 9).

As the urbanization of the world continues, the differences between what we have called First and Third World urbanization and cities, as well as other regionalized comparisons, such as between European and North American cities, or northern versus southern (Mediterranean) European cities, or between cities of the Sunbelt and Frostbelt, will decrease significantly. These differences will not disappear entirely, but variations within regional categories will begin to increase in comparison to differences between regions. New ideas and realizations will arise from this convergence. It will become increasingly empty and misleading, for example, to demand that urban studies shift its attention to the cities in poor countries simply because the greatest number of urban dwellers are located there; instead it will be apparent that, due to their increasing similarities, cities of the developed world can learn just as much from cities in poorer countries as the other way around.[14]

Many seemingly paradoxical features will characterize urban globalization. The economic base of megaregions will cease being called postindustrial and instead be seen as the outcome (a thirding?) of simultaneous and interactive processes of deindustrialization and reindustrialization on the one hand and decentralization-recentralization on the other. The New Economy will spread everywhere and generate much debate on how best to name the new mode of capitalism that has emerged over the past forty years. *Postindustrial* will be rejected, as will *post-Fordist,* given that so much of the world was never Fordist. *Global, information-intensive,* and *flexible* will be widely used, and with the decline of the financial services sector after 2008 and the spread of high technology to nearly all sectors of the economy, the cultural or creative industries will continue to be seen as the most propulsive and profitable sector, especially with regard to tourism, which will continue to be the world's largest industry.

Another surprising paradox has been and will continue to be the simultaneous homogenization and differentiation of the global cultural economy and its urban expressions. Many aspects of cities will become more and more alike, sustaining such ideas as Coca-colonization, Americanization, and so on, while at the same time it will be apparent that in other significant ways cities are becoming more heterogeneous, as the particularities of space and time shape the forces carried by globalization. All this will prioritize the need for effective comparative urban studies to combat tendencies to overgeneralize and to fall into simplistic either/or conclusions, prematurely trumpeting the "end of" this or that.

Although it will not mean the end of poverty, global inequalities and political polarization are not likely to grow significantly in the immediate future. Existing levels of inequality will be damaging enough, as these persistent inequalities lead to growing contrasts in health levels, lifespan, infant mortality, and other social and physiological pathologies. Leading the way toward actual reduction of social and spatial inequalities will probably be China, which has already curtailed its rate of economic growth to focus more attention and resources on degraded rural areas and the huge "floating populations" in its cities. One of the great questions of the twenty-first century will be whether China can succeed in its search for social and spatial justice to the same degree as it succeeded in rapid urban industrialization, bringing half a billion people from the edge of poverty to middle-class lifestyles.

The urbanization of the world is expressed at the intrametropolitan scale by the continued urbanization (and industrialization) of suburbia. Not only will suburbanization in a traditional sense slow down almost everywhere, but suburban areas will become increasingly differentiated and heterogeneous through variations on the urbanization process. Although some suburbs will be able to resist significant change, most will experience increasing density and cultural diversity, as the boundary between urban and what was once suburban erodes and the two mix together in various ways. This will also occur in colonial and some European cities, where the wealthy were concentrated near the city center. Central cities, as well as former suburbs, will become increasingly diverse in terms of culture and social class.

This trend can be described as the "unbounding" of the modern metropolis. The boundary between urban and suburban will increasingly erode, as will the hinterland boundary of the central city, as the reach of every megaregion becomes global in scope and scale. The hinterland, or what has been called the functional region of the city, will have to be described at multiple scales. Unbounding will also mean a weakening of segregation in many cases, including African American ghettoes as well as tight and defensive enclaves of gay men and women, such as the Castro in San Francisco or West Hollywood in LA. As gay rights become increasingly recognized and accepted, defensive "ghetto formation" becomes less attractive or necessary.

Even the almost sacrosanct system of administrative and government boundaries will be shaken up somewhat, as new ideas of governance and regulation arise to adapt to the new economic geography. This contrast between the radically restructured economic geography and the obstinately rigidified political geography exists at many scales, from the local to the global, and the governance crises associated with this disjunction will become a growing focus of attention.

Although the continued urbanization of the megaregional peripheries and their organization into networks of urban agglomerations (that is, the formation of polynucleated city regions) is easy to predict, it is more difficult to gauge what will happen to the inner cities. Most of the world's megaregions will have already lost significant numbers of inner-city residents and jobs, striking the fear of uncontrollable decline in all those who see the "health" of urban regions as revolving around the condition of their "hearts." Especially where welfare has been curtailed by central governments, city and regional planners have been forced to become more entrepreneurial and vigorously engaged in city marketing and Internet branding in an effort to attract increased investment and tourist dollars. Nearly every old downtown is looking for its own renewing "Bilbao effect," although very few will be successful.

Until neoliberal and other conservative policies are challenged and changed, there will be a widening national income gap between the super-rich and the working poor, as well as a tightening squeeze on the incomes and lifestyles of the middle class, except perhaps for the less developed countries that are growing the most rapidly. In part as a reaction to this enormous concentration of wealth, the informal economy will grow in size and function, playing a key role in mobilizing politically active slum populations. At the same time, security-obsessed urbanism in some form will spread to all city regions. Surveillance cameras will become part of everyday life everywhere, not just in big cities.

Although resistance will grow to the privatization of residential life and the growth of gated communities, various forms of residential associations and what in the United States are called common interest developments (CIDs) are likely to increase in number, with the fastest growth in specialized communities for the elderly. The "digital divide" will grow in importance as access to the Internet becomes increasingly politicized. The spread of scamscapes and spin-doctored politics, however, will probably slow down as the so-called reality-based community grows stronger. As the precession of simulacra slows, as many theme parks will close as are newly created, and the same is likely to be true for "reality-based" television shows.

Megaregions will move in many different directions. Some will have thriving outer cities but severely declining downtowns, with Detroit as the extreme example. Some, like Osaka, will comfortably survive massive outflows of population from the old downtown into dense and expansive outer cities, which will continue to be called suburbs. Some old downtowns will be redefined by large-scale immigration flows. New ethnic enclaves are likely to expand in number, but there will also be growing areas of ethnic and cultural admixture and hybridity. It is difficult to say whether enclave formation or mixture and hybridity will bring the greatest advantage to the city, but both will be intensive areas of study and analysis.

The iconic success story of the urban-industrialization of suburbia is Silicon Valley, the postmetropolitan equivalent of the rise of the Asian Tigers as NICs in the global economy. This new industrial space is focused around

San Jose, now the third-largest city in California (after LA and San Diego) and the main hub of the country's eighth-largest Combined Statistical Area (CSA) in the Bay Area (San Jose–San Francisco–Oakland). Its success is rooted in its regional identity and informal governance, described by Annalee Saxenian in her most recent book on Silicon Valley as a "regional advantage in a global economy."[15] Such regional advantage will help sustain a growing call for more effective regional governance, as governance crises and social movements for regional equity spread across all scales from the global to the local.[16]

These changes will make urban life more complex and threatening. This will not only intensify feelings of urban paranoia and obsessions with security; it will create the conditions for urban unrest and rioting in nearly all megaregions of the world. One hope for the future is that these threatening conditions may encourage creative coalition building and more innovative urban-based social movements.

Continuing the Spatial Turn

As an academic and intellectual trend, the spatial turn is likely to continue to expand and affect an increasing number of subject areas. In many, the spatial discourse will move from the periphery to the mainstream of debate and discussion. As occurred with history in the late nineteenth century, when nearly every discipline had a historian within its academic ranks, nearly all the human sciences, and perhaps the natural sciences as well, will have a spatial specialist exploring the relevance of a critical spatial perspective. Being an economic or social or cultural geographer will become just as significant as being an economic, social, or cultural historian. This diffusion of spatial thinking will create many challenges within the discipline of geography, which will be forced to redefine itself, probably around methodological emphases or, like history, around regional specializations and area studies.

Carried along with the spatial turn are several other developments in the field of urban and regional studies. The urbanization of the world, for example, will also involve an urbanization of Western social theory and philosophy. To some degree, everyone in the social sciences and humanities will have to be an urbanist of sorts, especially as the generative force of urban agglomerations becomes better known and studied. Foregrounding a critical spatial perspective after a century and a half of relative neglect will lead to radically new ideas in many subject areas, as it is increasingly revealed that many of our most trusted theories and concepts are rooted in a spatially weak social historicism and would be turned topsy-turvy by putting space first as an interpretive framework. An extreme case of this has been the idea, arising from the work of Jane Jacobs, that urbanization, the formation of cityspace, was a necessary component in the full-scale development of agriculture and animal husbandry, the so-called Neolithic or agricultural revolution.

Related to Jane Jacobs's ideas will be a reassertion of the urban in urban industrial capitalism. As urban spatial causality was increasingly rejected or ignored in the past, the urban began to disappear from discussions of industrial capitalism and sociology. It was difficult to ignore the fact that most social actions and societal development took place in cities but even more difficult to think they arose because of cities. But just as Jane Jacobs turned upside down the causal relation between urbanization and the agricultural revolution, so too will we come to understand that the Industrial Revolution, for example, was essentially urban generated.

Historians and others may protest, saying that the first factories were located at power-generating sites along rivers in decidedly rural areas. But so too did the domestication of plants and animals develop in nonurban areas at first, probably six thousand or more years before the creation of the first city-states in Sumeria. The full-scale agricultural revolution, however, developed in conjunction with urbanization and the growing need for food and shelter that arose as hunters and gatherers settled in the first cities scattered around southwest Asia. People did not settle down to become farmers; they became farmers because they settled down. In the same way, it can be argued that the Industrial Revolution fully developed only with the concurrent development of the industrial capitalist city and its distinctly urban populations, the proletariat and industrial bourgeoisie. From the beginning, industrialization as factory-based manufacturing was an urban phenomenon arising primarily from the stimulus of urban agglomeration.

Also carried along with the spatial turn and what some call a new urban age has been a growing appreciation for the *new regionalism*. There is little doubt in my mind that the new regionalism will have a growing influence on urban studies in the twenty-first century, fostering a blending of the urban and the regional similar to the way the urban and suburban are becoming interwoven. The notions of *city region* and *regional city* are urban inflections on this new regionalism, as are *megaregion* and related terms.

There are several important differences between old and new regionalisms. First, the discovery of the generative power of cities, or the stimulus of urban agglomeration, has reinvigorated regional analysis, as these generative effects are rooted in cohesive regional economies—in the network of agglomerations that defines the polycentric city region. This has led to a major retheorization of regions and regionalism, led by the geographer-planner Michael Storper in his pathbreaking *The Regional World: Territorial Development in a Global Economy* (1997).[17]

Although Storper does not use the term *new regionalism,* he argues that regions are vitally important social units, on a par with social formations based on kinship and culture, economic exchange and markets, and political states and national identities, the traditional foci of the social sciences. Moreover, he asserts that cohesive city regional economies are the foundation for the propagation of economic development, technological innovation, and cultural creativity, emitting a force that is comparable to, if not stronger than, market competition, comparative advantage, and capitalist social relations.

Even in its most exaggerated claims, traditional regional development theory never went this far in its assertive regionalism. Regions were viewed in the past primarily as places in which things happen, background repositories of economic and social processes. Today, regions are seen as powerful driving forces in themselves, energizing regional worlds of production, consumption, and creativity, while at the same time shaping the globalization of capital, labor, and culture.

The new regionalism also differs from the old in its larger coverage of scale. The old regionalism tended to focus mainly on subnational regions, such as Appalachia, Quebec, and Catalonia, with occasional forays into metropolitan regionalism. The new version continues to look at subnational regionalism, which has been flourishing in recent years, but extends also to supranational regionalism (e.g., the European Union and the multiplication of regional trading blocs) and to local issues, such as the new field of community-based regionalism, whereby community-based organizations mobilize regional coalitions to foster their goals.

Some critics on the left see the new regionalism as little more than the adaptive tactics of neoliberal policy and ideology, a clever extension of entrepreneurial approaches to urban and regional planning. Some liberal geographers feel threatened by the new regionalism, seeing it as just a renewal of an invasive and economistic regional science. A number of social scientists welcome the new regionalism but confine it to supranational organizations and ignore new ideas about the stimulus of urban agglomeration. As the new regionalism becomes more clearly defined and recognized, these critiques and misrepresentations will disappear and what today is called a new urban age will increasingly be seen as an age of the city region or the regional city.

What I see happening in the future is an increasing integration of urban and regional studies. This increasing fusion of urban and regional theory, empirical analysis, social activism, planning, and public policy is nowhere more evident than in a closely related major urbanization trend that will become even more prominent in the upcoming decades. I refer here to the fundamental shift from a metropolitan model of urban development to what I call, with deep connections to the new regionalism, *regional urbanization,* the subject of the next chapter.

NOTES

1. I want to emphasize again this concentration on the past forty years. A number of historians, some without a relevant geographical imagination, have criticized the LA research cluster-cum-school for not covering more of the history of Los Angeles or for not being sufficiently appreciative of the historian's craft. To me this is a little like criticizing a makeshift homeless shelter for not being conceived and built by an architect.

2. Ontology involves basic statements about human existence or "being." Epistemology refers to how we can be confident that our knowledge of the world is sound and accurate. The scientific method, for example, is an epistemology.

3. The idea of a socio-spatial dialectic can be found in the work of Henri Lefebvre, especially in *La production de l'espace* (Paris: Anthropos, 1974), translated as *The Production of Space* (Oxford: Blackwell, 1991).

4. Memories of geography's past history of environmental determinism accentuated its fear of any form of spatial causality. These fears, however, do not recognize the social origins of human geographies, as elucidated so well in Lefebvre's *La production de l'espace.* If we produce our geographies, we can also change them for the better, make them more socially just and equitable, through concerted social action.

5. Over the middle decades of the twentieth century, geography was squeezed out of the American educational system. Geography was rarely taught as a separate subject in K–12 curricula as it became increasingly absorbed into social studies and taught by nongeographers. At the university level, established geography departments disappeared from the Ivy League (leaving only a small department at Dartmouth today), Stanford, and most recently, the University of Chicago. As opportunities to learn about modern geography in grade school, high school, and university dwindled, geographical ignorance became rampant in America and, without a strong base to draw on, doctoral students and faculty at the best remaining

geography departments were disproportionately foreign born and trained, with especially large numbers coming from Britain, Canada, Australia, and New Zealand.

6. I want to emphasize that this does not translate as being antihistory or denying the importance of historical interpretation. Nor does it mean that we should now shift to privileging space over time, except perhaps as a strategic foregrounding to expose the narrowing effects of social historicism.

7. For more on the German historicists and their offspring, see Georg G. Iggers, *The German Conception of History: The National Tradition of Historical Thought from Herder to the Present* (Middletown CT: Wesleyan University Press, 1983).

8. Unlike geography, history had virtually eliminated its "physical" or "natural" side by this time. When one spoke of history, it was assumed to be human or societal history, whereas one always has to distinguish between human and physical geography. Indeed, it was well into the twentieth century before a distinct field of human geography that was not shaped by environmental influences emerged.

9. See the introduction, note 9, for more on the spatial turn.

10. Lived space also has echoes of "lived time," or what might be called the historicist definition of biography. What I think Lefebvre is saying is that the biography of an individual or of a society or culture is spatiotemporal, not just temporal alone. His critique of historicism is almost always implicit.

11. Neil Brenner and Christian Schmid, "Planetary Urbanization," in *Urban Constellations,* ed. Matthew Gandy (Berlin: Jovis, 2012), 10–13.

12. For a fascinating view of the future of China, see Zhang Weiwei, *The China Wave: Rise of a Civilizational State* (Hackensack, NJ: World Century, 2012).

13. Some Chinese cities may prove to be exceptions if we count only foreign nationals. Even here, however, more diverse immigrant flows are likely, ranging from returning overseas Chinese, including from Taiwan, to what are currently reported to be large African migrant populations in places like Guangzhou, where some claim as many as two hundred thousand mainly West Africans have settled. See Bill Shiller, "Big Troubles in China's Chocolate City," *Toronto Star,* August 1, 2009.

14. I think about this as I remember how some have called Los Angeles the "capital of the Third World," given its absorption of immigrants from nearly every country on earth.

15. Anna Lee Saxenian, *Regional Advantage: Culture and Competition in the Silicon Valley and Route 128* (Cambridge, MA: Harvard University Press, 1994); and *The New Argonauts: Regional Advantage in a Global Economy* (Cambridge, MA: Harvard University Press, 2006).

16. Manuel Pastor Jr., Chris Benner, and Martha Matsuoka, *This Could Be the Start of Something Big: How Social Movements for Regional Equity Are Reshaping Metropolitan America* (Ithaca, NY, and London: Cornell University Press, 2009). Pastor, an economist and professor of geography, is also director of the Program for Environmental and Regional Equity at the University of Southern California (USC). Matsuoka teaches at Occidental College and completed her dissertation in Urban Planning at UCLA on the topic of community-based regionalism.

17. Storper, a professor of urban planning at UCLA, has been an integral part of the LA research cluster from the start. *The Regional World* was published by Guildford Press. It subtitle reflects the widespread use of *territory* and *territorial* as substitutes for *region* and *regional,* a practice I hope will not continue in the future, especially if it is used at the expense of asserting the importance of regional concepts and thinking.

SEVEN

Regional Urbanization and the End of the Metropolis Era

Regional urbanization has been referred to many times in earlier chapters. What I plan to do here, in addition to providing further clarification and elaboration of the concept, is to argue as strongly as I can just how profound a change regional urbanization represents in both the nature of the urbanization process and how we think about cities and urban change. Defined as a transformative shift from a metropolitan model, regional urbanization requires much more than a simple name change to define and describe this latest morphing of the industrial capitalist city. It signals instead a fundamental structural, behavioral, and analytical transformation that deserves to be described in epochal terms, as the beginning of a pronounced paradigm shift, a profound metamorphosis, a far-reaching deconstruction and reconstitution of the modern metropolis that is creating a new breed of cities. As such, it demands an accompanying transformation in nearly every aspect of urban theory and practice.

I became aware of this epochal shift from a metropolitan to a regional model of urbanization as the direct result of more than three decades of observing and studying the urban restructuring of Los Angeles. This intensive experience has convinced me that the restructuring of LA is much more than an uninterrupted accumulation of incremental changes and piecemeal reforms. Although the modern metropolis is still around, there has been a profound break with the past in the development of Los Angeles, followed by a redirection of the urbanization process toward an urban future that no longer fits our conventional categories, models, or theories. Represented vividly in this new Los Angeles is the globalized city cum region, a polycentric network of urban agglomerations that contains within its regional grip one of the most heterogeneous collections of cultures and economies the world has ever seen, a new *megaregional version of the industrial capitalist city.*

The metropolitan to regional shift does not negate the concepts of urban restructuring, postmodern urbanization, and the postmetropolitan transition; rather it amplifies them to another level of significance. Urban restructuring remains the core concept, but it is a neutral notion with no end state in mind. Each subsequent "revisioning" gets a little more specific, but only with recognition of regional urbanization as the process of change and the city region or regional city as its definitive product does urban restructuring attain its appropriate denouement.

I also want to emphasize that this shift does not spell the end of the industrial capitalist city or industrial capitalism itself. As I said earlier, the prefix *post-* is often apt but should not be used in front of three related terms: *urban, industrial,* and *capitalism.* The present is not posturban, postindustrial, or postcapitalist. This does not mean that it is the same old urban industrial capitalism that has existed since the Industrial Revolution. Economic restructuring has brought about radical changes in our modes of production and consumption, creating a New Economy and New Geography that together define the end of the metropolis era and the rise of a new urban-regional age.

URBAN RESTRUCTURING WRIT LARGE

The rising force and recognition of regional urbanization completes the story told in *My Los Angeles* and at the same time initiates a new story, one that enlarges the concept of regional urbanization in scale and effect, well beyond the confines of Los Angeles. Before turning to this new narrative, however, the now completed story deserves a brief recapitulation, if only to set the scene.

As you remember, I began with the aftermath of the Watts Riots in 1965, by seeing in this explosive event and other urban uprisings around the world in the late 1960s a crucial turning point. Together these worldwide urban crises marked the end of the long postwar economic boom in the advanced industrial countries and the start of a diverse series of attempts to create a new form of industrial capitalism capable of restoring sustainable economic growth while maintaining sufficient social control to prevent renewed social unrest.

We called what was happening "crisis-generated urban restructuring," an open-ended concept that was intended to describe a middle ground between total transformation and piecemeal reform, for it was certainly less than revolutionary and more than a minor readjustment. By the time of the deep global recession in 1973–74, the term *restructuring* was being used to describe significant structural change short of total transformation in many different areas. The world order of First, Second, and Third Worlds was being restructured; Fordist and Keynesian national economies were restructuring; so too were many corporations, the housing and labor markets, even universities and television programming. It was no great jump to apply this concept to what was happening in cities, but doing so opened a new channel of urban research that has continued to this day.[1]

Studying the political economy of urban restructuring from an explicitly spatial perspective stimulated a local cluster of planners and geographers determined to make sense of the changes taking place in the region after 1965 to dramatically expand their research. At first, they found an admixture of different processes, some reflecting the devastating deindustrialization that was occurring in the American Manufacturing Belt or Frostbelt, others suggesting a rebirth of industry, a reindustrialization typical of Sunbelt and specifically Pacific Rim cities. What followed built upon this coming together of diverse restructuring processes.

Not the least of the early discoveries was that LA was the largest industrial metropolis in the United States at the time, larger in terms of manufacturing employment than Detroit, New York, or Chicago, and that it had been North America's leading industrial growth pole since the Great Depression. Industrial Los Angeles stood out not just because of its size, however, but more so for its combination in one urban area of intensive processes of deindustrialization and reindustrialization at a magnitude that was almost surely greater than in any other modern metropolis.

These unusual conditions were shaping (and being shaped by) a new intra-metropolitan geography, marked in its core by the gathering of perhaps the largest multicultural agglomeration of immigrant working poor in the world, and in its once sprawling suburban periphery by the growth of a series of dense outer cities, the largest and most propulsive being centered around the Orange County industrial complex, Southern California's version of Silicon Valley. Capitalism in crisis was trying to do what it had successfully done several times in the past: creating a new geography to fit an emerging new economy. This renewed attempt to create a spatial fix, as David Harvey so vividly called it, was a major force behind the shift from metropolitan to regional urbanization.

Several approaches emerged in early studies of regional urbanization in Los Angeles. While some maintained a strong geopolitical economy perspective on urban restructuring, emphasizing *post-Fordist* industrialization and the rise of a more flexible capitalism, other LA researchers shifted to an emphasis on the *postmodernization* of Los Angeles and the complex relations among race, ethnicity, gender, and class that were defining a new cultural politics of difference and identity. Postmodern and post-Fordist urbanism, however, were not the only products of urban restructuring, even for those who explored their fulsome exemplifications in the LA region. There emerged a growing need to find ways to combine the various approaches to studying what was clearly becoming a more profound transformation of the modern metropolis than anyone had expected.

Summarizing the greatly expanded literature on urban restructuring, I used the relatively neutral terms *postmetropolis* and the *postmetropolitan transition* to capture the many changes taking place in the modern metropolis and to keep the scope of urban research open to a multiplicity of viewpoints. This openness was indicated by the identification of six distinctive but intertwined discourses, subschools of thought on the deep and broad transformations so vividly represented in Los Angeles and many other major world cities. Woven together in these discourses was a rich picture of the many directions the modern metropolis was taking at the end of the twentieth century, but the potential end state was still not well defined.

Only in the past few years, however, did it become clear to me how best to define the emerging new urban form. The urban restructuring process was not just continuing to unfold in complex new patterns; rather it was leading to a profound sea change in the metropolitan model itself, a true metamorphosis from one city type to another. The modern metropolis, with its clear division between urban and suburban worlds, was experiencing a deconstruction or breaking down and a reconstitution or re-creation as a polycentric regional network of agglomerations that some began to call a city region or regional city.[2] To continue to see only the metropolitan city would be to miss the new dynamics almost entirely.

EMPIRICAL EXPRESSIONS

Although few would explicitly posit a transformative paradigm shift, abundant evidence of a radical change in urban form and function was rapidly accumulating. The growth of outer cities and the urbanization of suburbia were already being discussed in the mid-1970s, while more recently there has been talk of the end of the metropolis era, the metropolis unbound, the endless city, the great inversion, and a megaregional America.[3] A terminological explosion flooded the urban literature with new words and concepts aimed at describing the peculiar fusion taking place among the urban, the suburban, and the nonurban realms that is an integral part of the regional urbanization process.[4]

Just in the past few years, for example, researchers have begun to identify and explore "territories in-between," "in-between cities," "middle landscapes," "hybrid geographies," "metroburbia," "periurbanization," "rurban development," and other unseen "shadowlands," where urban, suburban, and nonurban ways of life are mixed together in unconventional ways.[5] Although not a clear departure from the metropolitan model, the urban-suburban fusion has featured prominently in the study of East Asian cities, generating such concepts as *desakota* (Indonesian) and *chengzhongcun* (Chinese) for the mixture of village and city. New names are also emerging for the regional cities that have formed around Jakarta (Jabotabek) and Singapore (SIJORI, for Singapore, Johor, Riau).

A special place in this debate is held by *Boomburbs: The Rise and Fall of America's Accidental Cities*, written by Robert Lang and Jennifer Lefurgy and published by the Brookings Institution Press in 2007. Not only does this book propose a vivid new term for the cities of substantial size growing in suburban America, such as Mesa (outside Phoenix and reputedly the largest), Anaheim, Plano (Dallas–Fort Worth), Naperville (Chicago), North Las Vegas, and Coral Springs (Miami), but it suggests that a major break with the past has occurred and will continue to shape the future development of cities. In the end, however, these cities are described as "accidental"—almost artificial and certainly unexpected. Lang, one of the most regional-minded urban scholars in the United States today (see note 3), comes very close to defining regional urbanization but cannot quite break from a metropolitan mentality.

In a further reflection of the concept, if not the literal meaning, of regional urbanization, the United Nations started listing the largest cities of the world by city region rather than metropolitan area or Greater X or Y, although it never solved the problem of multiple definitions by country. Along similar lines, the U.S. Census Bureau has developed the term *urbanized area* in part to capture the new trends. This relatively new census category, measuring the entirety of what used to be called the built-up area, first revealed the startling "discovery" that Los Angeles had passed New York City in 1990 as the densest urbanized area in the United States. Nothing signified the direction that regional urbanization was taking more dramatically than this remarkable densification of postmetropolitan and postsuburban Los Angeles.[6]

Evidence for a significant shift in the urbanization process has been accumulating from all over the world—from Los Angeles, Washington, D.C., and the Bay Area to Delhi, São Paulo, and Shanghai. One of the earliest descriptions of the new trends was Peter Muller's Association of American Geographers Resource Paper, *The Outer City: Geographical Consequences of the Urbanization of the Suburbs,* published in 1976. Muller quotes earlier observations, such as L. H. Masotti arguing in 1975 that "suburbia is becoming the city of the 70s" and G. Breckenfeld stating, in 1972, that "regional centers have turned into minicities," resulting in a "little-remarked but momentous change in urban geography. . . . [I]nstead of a single nucleus there are several: the old downtown and a band of satellite centers on the periphery."[7]

In nearly all cases, however, observers have tended to interpret what they see as a continuation of rather than a break with the familiar metropolitan model, often assumed to be eternal. Somewhat of an exception were two of the later and best-known descriptions of the new trends: Joel Garreau's *Edge City: Life on the New Frontier* (1991) and Deyan Sudjic's *100-Mile City* (1993). Both described what seemed like a major break with the past. They speculated that what was emerging was the most radical new development in the recent history of cities, hinting that the death knell might be sounding for what we knew as the industrial capitalist city. Their views were certainly not regional and, if anything, leaned toward a postindustrial thesis.

Given its specific reference to Los Angeles, it is worthwhile quoting Joel Garreau's effusive introductory remarks in *Edge City:* "Americans are creating the biggest change in a hundred years in how we build cities. Every single American city that is growing is growing in the fashion of Los Angeles, with multiple urban cores. These new hearths of our civilization—in which the majority of metropolitan Americans now work and around which we live—look not at all like our old downtowns. Buildings rarely rise shoulder to shoulder. . . . Instead, their broad, low outlines dot the landscape like mushrooms, separated by greensward and parking lots."[8]

Using Garreau's definitions, let us look more closely at the edge cities of Los Angeles, for they are key signifiers of the polycentric regional urbanization process. Updated to 2012, Garreau's list of edge cities surrounding Los

Angeles's old downtown has reached thirty, still the largest number in any metropolitan area in the world, as it was when the book was first published in 1991. Washington, D.C., comes next with twenty-five, New York City and Chicago with twenty-three, and the Bay Area with twenty-one. No other U.S. metropolitan area except Houston (thirteen) has more than ten.

Fifteen of LA's edge cities are in Los Angeles County, and ten are in Orange County. There is no separate list of old downtowns, but many of the original edge cities of Los Angeles, including the Miracle Mile along Wilshire Boulevard and lawyer-filled Century City, are no longer included on the edge city list for 2012. Obviously excluded are the old downtowns of the City of Los Angeles, Long Beach, Santa Monica, and Pasadena, all of which—atypically perhaps—have experienced significant renewal since 1991 and may have grown faster and farther than some of the listed edge cities.

An even better view of the polynucleated network of agglomerations surrounding the City of Los Angeles comes from a mapping of cities in the larger region with over a hundred thousand inhabitants. There were fifteen such cities in 1980, listed and located in map 10. Updating the list to 2010 expands the number to forty, as shown in table 4. The original fifteen are marked with an asterisk.

In addition to *edge cities* and *outer cities*, Lang's *boomburbs* and *edgeless cities,* and my *exopolis* and *off-the-edge cities,* peripheral urbanization and the growing urban-suburban fusion have generated an ever-expanding new vocabulary, almost as if every urban scholar is trying to brand his or her name to the new urban phenomena. Just a partial listing gives us *suburban downtowns, minicities, galactic cities, urban galaxies, postsuburbia, technoburbs, technopoles, disurbs, rururbia, perimeter cities, peripheral centers, urban villages, suburban downtowns, silicon landscapes, nucleations,* even *pepperoni-pizza cities,* to describe the urban blobs in former suburbia.[9]

Particularly interesting—and confusing—is the term *periurbanisation,* spelled with an *s* rather than a *z* to indicate its European, specifically French, origins. Periurbanisation (a slightly abbreviated version of peripheral urbanization) has been identified by the National Institute for Statistics and Economic Studies in France as a distinct urban category describing increasingly dense settlement beyond the former hinterland of (allegedly) compact European cities. As such, it fits the process I am calling regional urbanization, but it is conceptualized in Europe as an even more insidious example of sprawl and unsustainable urban growth. Used in this way, often disregarding where density increases are located, the concept of periurbanisation permits

TABLE 4 Cities with Population Greater Than
100,000 in 2010

*Los Angeles (4,065,585)	Corona (148,597)
*Long Beach (492,682)	Lancaster (145,074)
*Santa Ana (355,662)	Orange (141,634)
*Anaheim (348,467)	*Fullerton (137,624)
*Riverside (300,430)	Thousand Oaks (128,564)
Irvine (212,793)	El Monte (126,308)
*Glendale (207,303)	Simi Valley (125,814)
*San Bernardino (204,483)	Inglewood (118,868)
*Huntington Beach (202,480)	Costa Mesa (116,479)
*Oxnard (197,067)	Downey (113,469)
Fontana (188,498)	West Covina (112,648)
Moreno Valley (186,301)	Norwalk (109,567)
Rancho Cucamonga (177,736)	Victorville (109,441)
Santa Clarita (177,150)	Ventura (108,787)
*Garden Grove (174,715)	Burbank (108,082)
*Ontario (173,188)	South Gate (102,770)
*Pomona (162,255)	Temecula (102,604)
Palmdale (151,346)	Murrieta (100,714)
*Pasadena (150,185)	Mission Viejo (100,242)
*Torrance (149,111)	Rialto (100,022)

* = The fifteen cities that had populations greater than 100,000 in 1980.

observers to avoid recognizing the increasing urbanization of suburbia, the development of large outer cities, the often reduced density in the urban core, the growth of polycentric urban networks, and other indications that the metropolitan model is becoming something else.

In China, however, *periurbanization* is widely used to refer to rapidly growing zones in *extended urban regions* (EURs), where areas formerly classified as rural and agricultural increase in density, shift toward a manufacturing or service economy, and are reclassified as urban. Chinese planners expect at least two hundred million people to be added to these rapidly densifying zones in the near future, a Chinese version of the urbanization of suburbia but seemingly done from scratch as planned new outer cities. For example, twenty miles north of downtown Beijing, relatively near the international airport and the Olympics site, is a $60 million gated city literally called Orange County, or *Ju Jun,* designed, developed, and built by OC architects, developers, interior decorators, and industrial designers, another reflection of regional urbanization and especially the global reach of Southern California's outer cities.[10]

A recent addition to our new vocabulary for the city region is *chengzhongcun*, roughly meaning "village in a city," something between a slum and a new residential complex. These urban villages are located both on the periphery and in the downtown areas and are now often filled with multistory buildings packed together. Relatively unregulated by any form of centralized urban planning, they typically provide cheap accommodation for impoverished migrants from rural areas as well as the huge floating population in the cities; hence their common description as slums. Many are classified as rural even when surrounded by dense urban land use. Many village landowners have become rich landlords unencumbered by outside interference. Government intervention is difficult, especially given the political sensitivities associated with the predominantly poor and transient population. There is no doubt that there will be more discussion and recognition of the *chengzhongcun* as China continues to urbanize.

From the Pearl River Delta to the regional city of Los Angeles, interpreting the growing urban-suburban fusion and the formation of outer cities requires disconnecting from the metropolitan model and its deeply ingrained way of thinking. Rather than seeing regions as continuing suburban sprawl with a few accidental boomburbs sprinkled in, the entire metropolitan region is better viewed as being in-filled to urban densities, in large part by the creation of a polycentric network of cities surrounding the old downtowns.

In most megacity regions, it is not just the area beyond the old hinterland that is becoming increasingly dense. With growing immigration flows, some of the most globalized inner cities are experiencing increased density—and so too are the "inner suburbs," such as the *banlieues* of Paris. Indeed, in many megacity regions, including Los Angeles, population growth and increasing density have been occurring without significant expansion into "rural" agricultural land or wilderness. These are among the many signs that mass suburbanization is being replaced by mass regional urbanization.

The urbanization of suburbia is not a homogeneous process happening everywhere, nor is it easily categorizable. It takes many different forms in different city regions, as well as in different parts of a single urban periphery. The same is true for the inner city, which takes on many different variations, including what some observers call the suburbanization of the city, as densities decline, neatly completing the picture of the city turned inside out and outside in at the same time. These new urban dynamics lead to many questions: Are compact European cities becoming more dispersed? Is there no longer a characteristically European city? Is there any longer or was there ever a typical North American city? Using conventional measurements, is densely populated Los Angeles now the most compact, least sprawling, and hence most sustainable and "smart" American city? How do we define and describe such postmetropolitan city clusters as Orange County and Silicon Valley?

Maintaining a metropolitan mentality and, in particular, continuing to envision the contemporary city as neatly divided into urban and suburban areas, is as absurdly off base to the LA observer as are the claims that urbanization is now postindustrial. Division into urban and suburban areas is close to impossible in Los Angeles. The easiest, laziest, and perhaps most misleading answer to the question of how to separate the urban from the suburban in LA—also probably the one most often used in comparative studies—is to take the peculiarly shaped City of Los Angeles (roughly four million) as urban and the rest of the County of Los Angeles (around six million), with its more than eighty-five municipalities, as suburban. But surely the urban must include Long Beach, with its nearly half a million inhabitants. How can Long Beach be classified as a suburb of Los Angeles? Similarly, how do you deal with post-suburban Orange County? Is it a city? A cluster of cities? A county city? Do we classify it on its own or with Los Angeles County? Can we classify Anaheim and Santa Ana, both containing more than three hundred thousand people, as suburbs? Is Irvine, the largest new town in the United States, a suburb, even though it probably contains more jobs than bedrooms?

And what about such areas surrounded by the City of Los Angeles, such as Beverly Hills, Culver City, San Fernando, and West Hollywood, as well as adjacent, densely populated, unincorporated areas in East Los Angeles and around Watts-Willowbrook, the heart of what was once called South Central, an iconic inner-city ghetto that is typically left out of "urban" Los Angeles? Another problem (which is becoming less so with regional urbanization) is the San Fernando Valley, most of which is administratively included within the City of Los Angeles but has, until recently, contained great swathes of classic American suburbia? For comparative purposes, it is classified as urban, while the more than three dozen edge cities with at least one hundred thousand inhabitants are classified as suburbs.[11]

When Los Angeles appears in comparative studies or even simple comparisons of city size—and similar problems are likely to arise in many other (formerly) metropolitan areas—the total population can range from four million (LA City only), to ten or eleven million (LA County), to fourteen million (LA and Orange Counties), to almost eighteen million (the five-county city region). With such confusion, it may be necessary to eliminate entirely the notion that metropolitan areas can be neatly divided into city and suburbs—and to dismiss the findings of studies that do so as potentially misleading and inaccurate. It may have been possible to do this a few decades ago but not any longer, at least for the largest urbanized areas.

These problems extend to the broader urban studies literature, insofar as writings are conceptually dedicated to either urbanism or suburbanism, as if they were separate and distinct ways of life. It must be recognized that parts of suburbia are now urban or, at least, certainly no longer suburban. Major research projects are needed to study the differentiation of former suburbia: the emergence of many in-between and hybrid settlement types that do not fit into conventional models and are no longer representative of a suburbanization process.

For several reasons, this research should not be based on a distinction between inner (older) and outer (newer) suburban rings. In addition to assuming that city and suburb can be clearly differentiated to define the rings, the use of multiple suburban rings presupposes a monocentric decentralization process, not the in-filling, leap-frogging, polycentric dynamic typical of regional urbanization. Although not all metropolitan areas have experienced advanced forms of regional urbanization, we must abandon the notion that the old model of singular centrality and distinct urban and suburban worlds is as applicable today as it once was.

THE RISE AND FALL OF THE METROPOLIS ERA

What, then, are the most important distinguishing features of regional urbanization? First of all, it must be recognized that metropolitan urbanization represents just one phase in the development of the industrial capitalist city, a phase that may now be coming to an end. Taking definitive shape in the late nineteenth century, the modern metropolis, with centralized urbanization and sprawling suburbanization as its dominant mode of urban growth, emerged from an earlier form, the even more centralized and densely agglomerated (but not suburbanized) competitive industrial capitalist city. Manchester was its primary early exemplar, with nineteenth-century Chicago magnified by the Chicago School in the 1920s into its American quintessence.

Although often assumed to have done so, the Chicago School of Urban Ecology did not theorize the metropolitan city, even though Chicago in the 1920s and 1930s had already become metropolitan. There were no extensive suburbs in the classic Chicago School models, just a vaguely defined "commuter zone." There were a few studies of the relatively wealthy northern suburbs, but they were seen mainly as extensions of the inner city's Gold Coast along the shore of Lake Michigan rather than as part of a mass suburbanization process. Even when University of Chicago urban geographers later identified multiple nuclei, these were mainly either satellite industrial cities, like Gary in nearby Indiana, or intra-urban nodes. The terms *outer city* or *regional city* were, as far as I can tell, never used.

Although some may have thought they were theorizing the contemporary city, the Chicago School of urban ecologists was for the most part theorizing the remainders of the older, slowly fading, highly centralized and competitive industrial capitalist city of the nineteenth century. Indeed, it was Friedrich Engels, observing the geography of Manchester in 1848, who first noticed urban concentricity, well before Ernest Burgess's famed formulation of the concentric zone model. Confusing matters further, the centrality that exists in every urban agglomeration always produces some degree of concentricity, even if inconsequential in its effects.

There is an interesting comparison here to the present era, with its ongoing shift from metropolitan to regional urbanization. Most urban scholars today analyze the twenty-first-century regional capitalist city as if it were a continuation of the twentieth-century metropolitan model. It is no wonder, then, that urban studies today often seems to be in a state of utter confusion, or else self-servingly proclaiming a new urban age without accentuating what is actually new and different. Recognizing the end of the metropolis era, however, does not mean that the modern metropolis has disappeared entirely, but rather that its predominance as the primary urban form of modern society has weakened significantly, and this weakening is likely to continue.

It is also worth noting that regional urbanization, like all social processes, is unevenly developed geographically, advancing farther and faster in some places than in others. Even if one could find a large urban area where there is no explicit evidence at all of regional urbanization—no peripheral urbanization, no domestic out-migration from the urban core, no areas where city and suburb mix—this would not necessarily negate the overall argument, given the notion of geographically uneven development.

When and why the modern metropolis began to take shape probably has to do in part with the earlier agglomeration of factories, workers, and the reserve army of laborers in the densely packed central core of the early industrial capitalist cities. As Engels predicted correctly for Manchester, dense proximity and the intensified social interaction it promoted encouraged working-class consciousness and an active labor movement, creating unstable conditions in the city center and stimulating—typically in association with improvements in mass transit—a selective and growing centrifugal decentralization of population and economic activities that initiated large-scale suburbanization.

Here too there is a contemporary comparison with the agglomeration of the working poor—in the core of Los Angeles, for example—becoming an important generative force for new labor-community coalitions that are helping to reshape the national labor movement. That Los Angeles has become a leading center of the American labor movement and that it also exploded with anger toward the uneven effects of globalization and the New Economy in 1992 are indications that regional urbanization has not been all that successful as a spatial fix for the new capitalism. I will discuss this development in more detail in the next chapter. For now, we return to the metropolitan model.

In the early decades of the twentieth century, the still relatively highly centralized and dense inner core of the emergent modern metropolis continued to grow, annexing territories on its fringe. Sometime in the interwar years, at least in the United States, annexation slowed down and a municipal incorporation movement began to grow in metropolitan suburbia, led mainly by the rapidly expanding middle class, even where working-class suburbanization had begun. As we have seen, Los Angeles never experienced the intense downtown centralization of the nineteenth-century city; rather it grew predominantly in the metropolitan era, as a spread-out collection of suburban, often industrial, nucleations and municipalities.

This dispersed urban settlement was served in the early twentieth century by one of the most advanced and encompassing public transit systems in the world, the Pacific red cars, whose traces were revived in the dense freeway network that replaced them, contributing to further dispersal and decentralization.[12] Over the past forty years, the freeway system facilitated the diffusion of minority populations and the urbanization of suburbia. According to a recent report (subject to some qualification due to its presumed separation of urban and suburban areas), ethnically diverse suburbs, defined as 20–60 percent nonwhite, have been growing much faster in the fifty largest U.S. city regions than either predominantly (more than 80 percent) white or nonwhite

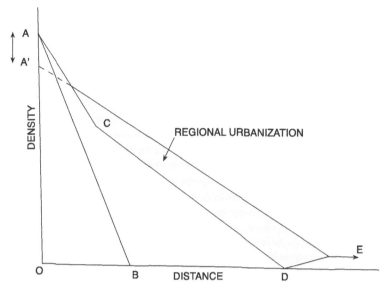

FIGURE 7 Density diagram (prepared by Sean Combs).

suburbs. As one urban expert commented, "The old division in politics used to be city-suburbs. The new division is within the suburbs."[13]

A key summary indicator of the regional urbanization process has been the growing *density convergence* it generates. Not every part of suburbia is being urbanized. Some areas stubbornly remain in a classical low-density suburban mode (for instance, Palos Verdes), while other areas have grown into sizable outer cities, with many variations in between. This differentiation of suburbia into various alternative typologies is likely to accelerate over the next several decades, but a general pattern of changing urban density can be identified.

Figure 7 is a cross section showing this density convergence. The vertical axis measures population density, while the horizontal axis indicates distance from the city center (at O). The early capitalist city had a very steep decline in density from the center (AB). Beyond B was clearly the countryside, where the industrial bourgeoisie, the third new population defining the industrial capitalist city (with the urban proletariat and the reserve army of temporary workers and unemployed), competed with the landed gentry for manor houses, villas, and local socioeconomic status, while commuting to their wealth-generating factories in the crowded city center. Unplanned as such, the earliest industrial capitalist cities tended, when physical features and preindustrial urban forms did not interfere, toward a fairly regular urban morphology, with a concentric zonation of residential land use and the geographical segregation of social status, ethnic identity, and race, as depicted in the "ecological" models of the Chicago School and first glimpsed by Engels in Manchester.

Metropolitan urbanization jumbled but rarely erased completely the earlier spatial regularities. Instead, they were reordered around the urban-suburban dualism. In the metropolitan model, the decline in density around the center was less sharp, and a break (at C on line ACD) marked the start of lower-density, sprawling suburbia. Some city centers grew, as new clusters of corporate headquarters and government bureaucracies developed in expanding central business districts and civic centers. The often skyscrapered refilling of the downtown core typically required removal of at least some of the urban poor from their best central sites, a process that was rationalized in public policy as a search for urban renewal. Struggles over centrality and urban renewal, involving different segments of capital, labor, and the state, were a characteristic feature of metropolitan urbanization in many of the largest cities in the advanced industrial countries, with Los Angeles and Paris providing excellent examples.[14]

The modern metropolis expanded outward through mass suburbanization and the decentralization of many economic activities. Constellations of autonomous municipalities grew around the city in a series of suburban rings, which, at least until the 1970s, grew faster than the central city and increasingly influenced politics, culture, and the national economy. Recovery from war and the Great Depression in the United States was driven as much as anything else by the economic stimulus provided by this mass suburbanization.

Automobile-centered suburban life hungrily expanded consumer demand and pressured governments to provide enormous public funds to sustain the increasingly expensive and expansive infrastructure of sprawling low-density suburbia. At the same time, minorities and the poor were increasingly compacted in the "inner cities," a term that became, for many, synonymous with the crime-infested neighborhoods of the poorest minorities. Significantly, the term *outer cities* was rarely if ever used. The concept in its fullest meaning was almost incomprehensible at the time, when urbanism and suburbanism defined separate and all-encompassing worlds.

The growing gulf between a relatively homogeneous and wealthy suburbia and an increasingly poor and culturally heterogeneous inner city, along with the associated struggles over control of the city center, made the postwar modern metropolis inherently unstable and prone to social unrest. In the field of urban studies, library loads of literature described these contrasting and tensely interconnected urban and suburban worlds. As if this was a permanent condition, the urban core was seen as heterogeneous, exciting, stimulating, dangerous, crime-filled, culturally sophisticated, filled with museums, galleries, and fashionable boutiques but also with crack houses, strip joints, and sleazy bars. In stark contrast was suburbia: homogeneous, middle-class, boring, and monotonous, but healthy, an ideal place for children to grow, with detached single-family houses, nuclear families, lots of bedrooms for breadwinners, two-car garages at least, and acres of green space.

Everything began to change after the urban crises of the 1960s, from Watts in 1965 to Paris in 1968 and so many others across the world. In retrospect, it can be said that these urban crises marked the beginning of the end of metropolitan urbanization and the onset of regional urbanization processes. Returning to the density diagram, regional urbanization is erasing the prominent urban-suburban break as the density gradient (A'E) flattens out. Density convergence, however, affects urban core and periphery very differently. Peripheral urbanization, with its edge cities and boomburbs, was happening outside almost every major city in the world and can reliably be expected to continue in the twenty-first century, filling the shaded area in the density diagram. How regional urbanization will affect the inner city, however, is much less predictable.

In its early stages, densities were reduced in most old downtowns, as many mainly domestic populations (and unionized industrial jobs) moved out. In Los Angeles, an estimated million and a half, mainly poor whites and blacks originally from the southern states, moved out, either to the outer cities or back to their home areas. But in the second half of the twentieth century, more than five million migrants moved in, one of the largest single-city-targeted foreign migration streams in history. This created residential densities in inner-city LA that compare with Manhattan and, by far, the most overcrowded housing in the United States. The line segment A'A is meant to indicate this great variation in peak inner-city densities.

While many large city regions, especially the centers of former European colonial powers such as London, Paris, and Amsterdam, also refilled with immigrant populations, many just experienced an intensive "hollowing out" of their inner-city populations. But even in this hollowing out there were contrasting results. Osaka—once Japan's densest downtown area—and the great automobile manufacturing center of Detroit each lost over six hundred thousand inhabitants, with large numbers moving into thriving suburban areas. Downtown Detroit, however, has remained a disaster zone, while Osaka's large downtown core continues to be a flourishing commercial, entertainment, sports, and office center.[15]

This unpredictability has made downtown planning in an age of regional urbanization a challenging and competitive discipline, especially when planners continue to maintain a metropolitan rather than regional mentality. Faced with declining densities and population totals, many central-city planners panic, thinking that if the heart of the metropolis is in decline, the whole metropolis might be dying. Overreacting to this perceived threat to the health of the region has had many consequences.

Desperate attempts to revive an allegedly "dying" downtown, along with reduced financial resources, have encouraged a pronounced entrepreneurial turn to urban and regional planning. Time and energy, devoted in the past to welfare and antipoverty programs, are now concentrated in city-marketing and city-branding efforts. This, in turn, often leads to extravagant and attention-grabbing megaprojects, such as major athletic events and trade fairs, or seeking a "Bilbao effect" through spectacular buildings from "starchitects" such as Frank Gehry and Santiago Calatrava. When all else fails, downtown planners can turn to several "Shrinking Cities" organizations to help make decline more efficient and bearable.

Downtown redevelopment in Los Angeles—based on the dream of making it like downtown New York or Chicago—has driven LA's politics and planning for nearly a century and thus is not purely a product of regional urbanization. Regional urbanization has, however, reinvigorated the dream. There have been many recent cycles of investment and planning aimed at creating a 24/7 city center appropriate to America's second largest city and one of the great global cities of the world. With each cycle, there were ambitious claims that this redevelopment process had truly begun and would continue. Although a cluster of skyscrapers is now available to symbolize LA on postcards and popular imagery, downtown Los Angeles is nowhere near what the dreaming planners and avid boosters hoped for.

The most recent downtown development effort, centered around the Staples Center basketball and hockey arena and what has been called LA Live—a $2.5 billion entertainment extravaganza—is one of the most successful, expanding residential populations south of the old downtown, but I doubt it will produce a city center comparable to New York or other major world cities. Downtown LA remains the largest node in the city region—and would reach a more impressive size if all the agglomerations along Wilshire Boulevard were added to it as an extended downtown corridor to the sea— but I am convinced that, with continued regional urbanization, downtown LA itself will never reach a level of development commensurate with its population size and density.

EXTENDED REGIONAL URBANIZATION

Continuing the discussion of regional urbanization brings us back to figure 7 and the arrow at the end of the A'E line. The arrow pointing outward indicates that the outer boundary of the regional city is no longer what and where it used to be. The hinterland of the metropolis was usually defined around commuting patterns or newspaper readers or some such indicator of regional or local identity. Regional urbanization, however, has "unbound" the metropolis, blurring its internal boundary between urban and suburban but also expanding its outer boundary to several larger scales in a process of extended regional urbanization, leading to what I described earlier as the urbanization of the world.

The first of these extensions is the polycentric network of agglomerations that makes up the city region or regional city itself.[16] As mentioned, there are probably close to five hundred city regions in the world with over one million inhabitants, at least one hundred in China. The term *megacity region* has been used for these million-plus city regions, although more commonly it refers to those greater than five million. In almost all cases, the city region is larger than the old metropolitan area, although the boundaries of both are difficult to draw when there is no official government recognition. Even when there is a regional government, as with the Greater London Authority, some argue for a larger "functional" boundary that can vary in scale from the M25 Ring Road to virtually all of southern England. Extending another scale upward is a "Greater-Greater London"—what Richard Florida and others call a *megalopolitan region*, which would include all of England and parts of Scotland and Wales and reach a population of around forty million.[17]

This form of extended regional urbanization marks what can be described as a growing scalar compression or fusion between what were formerly called metropolitan and subnational regions. At this enlarged scale, the metropolitan and the regional meld together, creating a new tier of regions for which no name has yet been widely accepted. Some call them urban galaxies or constellations; others use the term *citistate*. Arthur Nelson and Robert Lang, in *Megapolitan America: A New Vision for Understanding Metropolitan Geography* (2011), identify twenty-three of what they call *megapolitan areas,* clustered into ten mostly contiguous *megaregions*. Significantly, these megaregions collectively, the authors claim, are more densely populated than Europe, India, or Japan taken as a whole and have a total population greater than any country except China or India.

Not surprisingly, the densest megapolitan area is Southern California, even though it appears that the vast empty areas of San Bernardino and Riverside Counties were included in the calculation. Nelson and Lang cluster Southern California with the Las Vegas and Phoenix–centered Sun Corridor megapolitan regions in a Southwest megaregion. Alternatively, reminiscent of Jean Gottmann's earlier notion of the San-San corridor, one could expand Southern California to include Tijuana as well as San Diego, adding the adjacent Sierra Pacific and, farther away, the Cascade megapolitan regions to produce a West Coast corridor that would almost match the extended Bos-Wash (Boston to Washington) megalopolis of the East Coast, which can today be extended southward to the Carolinas and Atlanta.

The North American megaregions are relatively small in comparison to the "megaregional galaxies" of East Asia. As previously noted, the United Nations identifies the Pearl River Delta (combining Hong Kong, Shenzhen, Dongguan, and Guangzhou) as the largest in the world, with 120 million people. The Yangtze Delta around Shanghai is close behind, while combining Tokyo-Yokohama with the nearby Kansai region (Osaka-Kyoto-Kobe-Nagoya) creates a Honshu Island megaregional galaxy of one hundred million or more.

Eastern Asian scholars are especially sensitive to the crisis of governance associated with the new megaregions, but governance has become an important issue all over the world. A widespread governance crisis is emerging in large part because political and administrative structures and boundaries have remained rigid and unchanged compared to socioeconomic borders, boundaries, and flows. Stated differently, the new economy, the network society, and regional urbanization have been emerging in administrative and regulatory structures that are in essence anachronistic and poorly adapted to contemporary needs and trends. Furthermore, this disjuncture exists and is creating governance crises at multiple levels, from the global to the local.

Fortunately, a few new forms of regional organization are springing up in an attempt to deal with the demands of expansive and polycentric city regions. In South Africa, the cities of Johannesburg, Pretoria, Vereeniging, and mineral-rich Witwatersrand have been combined into Gauteng, the first officially named "global city region" in the world, now the largest province in the country, with around twelve million people and more than thirty municipalities of over one hundred thousand inhabitants. Gauteng has embarked on a number of potentially innovative programs based on regional integration and identity, but existing authorities—not unexpectedly—have strongly resisted these efforts. Maintaining the initiative, however, is the Gauteng City-Region Observatory, a new think tank specializing in city region research.[18]

More successful in many ways, at least before the crash of 2008, are the EUREGIO program and the European Spatial Development Perspective (now official policy throughout the EU). Starting with the successful Øresundbron connecting Copenhagen in Denmark with Malmö in Sweden, many cross-border regional organizations have been created across Europe where there used to be confrontational forces. Related to these developments, more advanced forms of spatial and regional planning are fostering "innovative regions" and major interconnections among the largest city regions.

An entirely new region has emerged on the eastern flank of what Florida, in "The New Megalopolis," calls the Euro Lowlands, the most populated megapolitan region of Europe without a large megacity such as London or Paris. Uniting around the global financial hub of Luxembourg are the previously combative subregions of Lorraine in France, the Saar basin and Rheinpfalz in Germany, and part of eastern Belgium. This area is variably called La Grande Région or SaarLorLux and provides a financial counterbalance to the Amsterdam-centered Randstad in the Netherlands, which was perhaps the first polycentric city region. Also worth mentioning again is the series of ad hoc regional regulations, without a formal governmental structure, that have been successful in maintaining fairly steady growth in the Silicon Valley region of Northern California.

Some of the most hopeful signs of more adaptive forms of regional governance and planning are coming from China. The most rapid process of urban industrial development in history has been guided by regional policies that began in the coastal ports, fostered rapid growth in the coastal region, were then intentionally expanded to a second region farther inland, reaching into populous Szechuan, and now are trying to extend still farther inland to promote development in the rest of China—including, not yet very successfully, Tibet and Xinjiang. A few years ago, the Chinese government shifted its policy orientation from rapid growth to greater equity, focusing on rebuilding many degraded agricultural areas (for example, by ending taxes on most farm products) and dealing in new ways with the enormous "floating population" in the major cities. The extended urban region, an innovative concept in itself, is increasingly being given administrative powers, and there seems to be widespread awareness in academic and policy circles of the new regional debates and theories around the world.

The regional urbanization process can be extended still further with the merging of megaregional galaxies into continental-size "conurbations," to recycle another old term originating with the early regional thinker Patrick Geddes. Northeast Asia would be the largest, with at least 300 million, followed by Western Europe at around 260 million, and eastern North America at a little more than 200 million. The urbanization of the world, as the furthest extension of regional urbanization, is likely to continue indefinitely as the leading edge of the globalization process.

In line with the globalization discourse, some form of urban industrial capitalism is now covering every square inch of the earth's surface, in the Amazon rainforest, Siberian tundra, deserts, icecaps, and even oceans, kindling a new notion of planetary urbanism that is likely to receive major attention in the next few decades.

THE PERSISTENCE OF A METROPOLITAN MENTALITY

So why is it that more scholars and others are not embracing the notion of an epochal shift in the urbanization process? Why does a metropolitan mentality still persist despite abundant countervailing evidence? One possible reason is that many scholarly careers are based on the old model, and changing paradigms is difficult, if not threatening. Some argue that the accumulated evidence is too parochial, because it refers only to Los Angeles and perhaps a few other cities, or that it is Eurocentric in failing to recognize that developing countries have today by far the largest share of the world's urban population and will undoubtedly increase this share in the future. Why bother with Los Angeles and regional urbanization, one might ask, in a "planet of slums" on the edge of environmental disaster? Don't stay in the developed North, they say. Go South, young urbanists!

Then there are the nostalgic historicists who lament recent urban trends, seeing in them a different break point: the destruction of the (allegedly) vibrant "historic" city, usually idealized as a semiutopia. The regional city (and you can read LA here) is accordingly described as "city lite," comparable to lite beer in missing the strength and stimulating flavor of the original. Branching off this critique is the growing horde of antipostmodernists, who take particular delight in dismissing Los Angeles as the fountainhead of regressive postmodern urbanism. A dramatic urban change has occurred, but it is entirely for the worse and LA is its apotheosis. A subset of this group, especially on the far left, see only continuity, the same old capitalism, now in a neoliberal guise, using regional urbanization and the New Regionalism in which it is embedded as little more than fodder for capitalist developers seeking a competitive edge in consumer markets.

There is no reasonable response to such skepticism beyond what I have written here. I can only repeat my conviction that learning from Los Angeles can help us better understand urbanization processes happening all over the world. I must make it clear, however, that I am not saying that every city is destined to be like Los Angeles, or that we can project what has happened in LA directly onto all other urban regions. Every trend or tendency identified in Los Angeles will be channeled through unique and differentiating local circumstances in other city regions. Some of what has been discovered in LA is uniquely local and is not likely to spread to other places, but the general trends discussed in the previous chapter, I suggest, will be played out to greatly varying degrees in all the five hundred or so megacity regions of the world.

I would add that maintaining a metropolitan mentality can have negative planning, policy, and political consequences. Such an approach will typically overemphasize the importance of the old downtown center, for example, sucking up resources that could be spent on more urgent antipoverty projects. Planners also typically overlook the vital need for coordinated regional planning and policy. Regional urbanization is almost everywhere accompanied by a worsening crisis of governance, as new processes flow through unyielding political and administrative structures. Without new forms of specifically regional regulation, from the global to the local scales, the already massive social, economic, and spatial inequalities and injustices, as well as advancing environmental degradation, can only get worse. *Thinking regionally* will certainly not solve all problems, but it is an effective start.

As I was finishing *My Los Angeles,* an article appeared in the *Los Angeles Times* that dramatically illustrates the persistence of a metropolitan mentality and the potential confusion and planning problems it engenders.[19] Reporting on a new book by Elizabeth Kneebone and Alan Berube, researchers at the Brookings Institution (a leading commentator on the state of

America's cities and suburbs), the article announced that, for the first time ever, more poor people in the United States live in suburbs than in central cities. This announcement reminded me of a not unrelated claim by the United Nations Habitat Agency that, as of 2007, more people in the world live in cities than in rural or nonurban areas. In both of these threshold breakers, perfectly in keeping with expanding regional urbanization, there are major terminological problems.

The *Times* article is riddled with a confusing metropolitan vocabulary. It is noted that "poverty shifted to the suburbs earlier in Los Angeles than nationwide," but the defining distinction between city and suburb is characteristically blurred. Were the municipalities of Compton, Carson, and Inglewood, as well as the unincorporated barrio of East Los Angeles, classified as suburban? Irvine is described as one of the fastest growing cities in the country but is used to illustrate suburban poverty in Orange County. The Brookings study defined the suburbs as outside not just the City of Los Angeles but also Long Beach and Santa Ana, using the defining centers of the Metropolitan Statistical Area—an improvement over using just LA City. Without wondering if it made a statistical or interpretive difference, however, the authors also noted that a major portion of the City of LA consisted of the once classic suburbia of the San Fernando Valley. While Irvine and Anaheim were considered suburbs of Santa Ana, smaller centers such as Delano and Bakersfield were considered to be cities surrounded by some of the state's highest suburban poverty rates.

I have not read the Kneebone-Berube book, but the article reports that the authors call for special *regional* programs sponsored by the federal government to address the new problems of poverty. If this involves better forms of regional governance and intrametropolitan planning rather than just different programs for different areas of the country, it deserves strong support. Only some degree of regional coordination and cooperation, sustained by a new regional (and not metropolitan) consciousness, can deal with the intensifying problems of geographically uneven development in what was once suburbia.

NOTES

1. See "Urban Restructuring: Process and Action," a special issue of *Critical Planning* 16 (2009). The issue contains a symposium on "Urban Restructuring and the Crisis," with commentary by Neil Brenner, John Friedmann, Margit Meyer, Allen Scott, and Edward Soja.

2. Although not yet used widely today, the term *regional city* is an old one. The first reference I can find is by Benton Mackaye, pioneer of the Appalachian Trail and one of the early organic regionalists, who, with Clarence Stein and Lewis Mumford, formed the Regional Planning Association of America. See Mackaye, *The New Exploration: A Philosophy of Regional Planning* (Champaign: University of Illinois Press, 1991 [1928]).

3. Robert E. Lang has been particularly prolific in creating new terms. See *Edgeless Cities* (Washington, DC: Brookings Institution Press, 2003); Robert E. Lang and P. A. Simmons, "Boomburbs: The Emergence of Fast-Growing Cities in the U.S.," in *Redefining Cities and Suburbs: Evidence from Census 2000,* ed. B. Katz and R. E. Lang (Washington, DC: Brookings Institution Press, 2001), 51–62. See also Arthur C. Wilson and R. E. Lang, *Megaregions of America: A New Vision for Understanding Metropolitan Geography* (Chicago and Washington, DC: American Planning Association, 2011).

4. This terminological explosion is captured well in P. J. Taylor and R. E. Lang, "*The Shock of the New:* 100 Concepts Describing Recent Urban Change," *Environment and Planning A* (2004): 951–58. There is a list of fifty "names given to new metropolitan forms" and fifty "names given to new intercity relations," with each entry accompanied by a bibliographic reference. Several interesting interpretations are given for this unprecedented expansion, but missing is the idea that it signals the emergence of an entirely new form of urbanization that is fundamentally regional and no longer metropolitan.

5. One of the first and best books to describe this urban-suburban fusion in the United States is Paul Knox, *Metroburbia* (New Brunswick, NJ: Rutgers University Press, 2008).

6. Again, it is important to remember that this is a *regional* definition of density. New York City is much more densely populated than the City of Los Angeles, although perhaps not to the degree usually imagined. There are now a few areas of the City of Los Angeles that are as dense as all but a few census tracts in Manhattan.

7. G. Breckenfeld, "Downtown Has Fled to the Suburbs," *Fortune* (1972): 80–87, 158, 162. An even earlier premonition comes from the well-known urban designer Kevin Lynch, "The Dispersed Sheet, Urban Galaxy, and the Multinucleated Net," in *The Changing American Countryside,* ed. E. N. Castle (Lawrence: University Press of Kansas, 1961), 39–62.

8. Joel Garreau, *Edge City: Life on the New Frontier* (New York: Anchor, 1991), 3.

9. Taylor and Lang, "*The Shock of the New,*" provides the original references for nearly all of these terms. Also relevant here is Knox, *Metroburbia.*

10. Elizabeth Rosenthal, "North of Beijing, California Dreams Come True," *New York Times,* February 3, 2003. Despite the growth of these dense outer suburbs, the central cities in China remain dominant.

11. The rapidly urbanizing San Fernando Valley was the site of an unsuccessful secession movement in 2002 aimed at splitting off a third of the City of Los Angeles as an autonomous incorporated city. The Valley portion of LA City has also been

the site of numerous name changes for local community areas, nearly all related to land values and perceived prestige. The old political-administrative structure and boundaries still are highly resistant to change but have loosened up a bit in recent years.

12. The best and most detailed geohistorical description of transportation development and planning in Los Angeles, including the Bus Riders Union discussed in the next chapter, is Mark Garrett, "The Struggles for Transit Justice: Race, Space, and Social Equity" (PhD diss., UCLA, 2006).

13. Haya El Nasser, "Suburbanites Live in Diverse Areas," *USA Today*, July 20, 2012. The subtitle states: "Such neighborhoods take on political value in this election year," suggesting this might help in the re-election of President Obama.

14. This volatile metropolitan model did not fit well into existing liberal urban theories, which tended to see built-in tendencies toward balanced equilibrium rather than crisis and unrest. Brewed in the urban crises of the 1960s, a new field of Marxist urban studies, focused on crisis formation, produced highly insightful analyses of the unstable postwar metropolis, with its conflict-filled and increasingly poor inner cities and fragmented suburban worlds. Neo-Marxist urban analysis, after a brief period of heavy influence in such fields as urban and regional planning, was much less insightful with regard to the urban restructuring process and the metropolitan-to-regional shift. Its influence has lessened, but certainly not disappeared, in recent years.

15. I was privileged to be shown around Osaka by Kenkichi Nagao, who also led the translation into Japanese of my book, *Postmodern Geographies*. Kenkichi, an economic geographer, visited the Department of Geography at UCLA several times over the years.

16. The term *city region* is much more widely used than *regional city,* largely because it seems a more innocent and noncommittal combination of terms, *region* simply meaning the hinterland of a city. Putting *regional* first, as in *regional city,* however, suggests some regional causality—that is, the city has been significantly regionalized. I expect *regional city* to be used much more widely in the years ahead, as regional causality is more widely understood.

17. Richard Florida, "The New Megalopolis," *Newsweek,* July 3–10, 2006.

18. *Gauteng* is a Sesotho word, also linked to Afrikaans, meaning "place of gold." It was formed specifically as a global city region in 1994 and, through the more recent formation of the Gauteng City-Region Observatory, has become a research center and think tank for conceptualizing city regions more generally and investigating their use in planning and governance.

19. Emily Alpert, "Poverty's New Address Is in Suburbs," *Los Angeles Times,* May 20, 2013. The subtitle notes that the number of poor living in suburbs is now higher than in urban areas, although the percentage remains greater in cities.

EIGHT

Seeking Spatial Justice in
Los Angeles

Accompanying the rise of Los Angeles as the densest urbanized area in the
country, its move from WASPish homogeneity to perhaps the most culturally heterogeneous city in the world, and its shift from exemplary model of
the modern metropolis to forerunner of regional urbanization has been the
transformation of Los Angeles from a notoriously antilabor environment to
the leading edge of the American labor movement. Just as much a part of
urban restructuring, postmodern urbanism, the postmetropolitan transition, and the unfolding force of regional urbanization has been a reverberat-
ing political activism that has shaped the flow of research on LA and, at the
same time, been shaped by it.

It is no coincidence that LA in 1992 had what were almost surely the highest levels of economic inequality and social polarization in the United States,
which at the time had the widest income gap of any industrialized country.
It is perhaps not surprising that the city region with the worst inequalities
generated the most vigorous social movements against inequality and injustice. Coalition building in Los Angeles was also distinguished by its awareness of the politics of space and place and, as I argued In *Seeking Spatial
Justice* (app. 1, source 8A), by its critical spatial consciousness—its ability to
translate spatial theory into active political practice.[1]

The justice movement in Los Angeles took a spatial turn earlier than other
city regions, taking the lead in such "spatial struggles" as those involving the
"right to the city" and the fight again racism and other forms of discrimination based on residence, the focus of the environmental justice movement. In
Seeking Spatial Justice and this chapter, justice is seen as fundamentally spatial or geographical. In this sense, spatial justice is not an alternative to social
justice but a formative aspect of it—that is, social justice or injustice is

219

expressed in specific geographies, while at the same time it is itself shaped by the geographies in which it is embedded. In this way, the social and the spatial are seen as mutually formative, which is a key component of the new spatial consciousness and what I described earlier as the socio-spatial dialectic.

The search for increasing spatial justice can take many forms. A primary goal is fair geographical distribution of society's resources, especially with regard to level of need. The carless poor, for example, have greater need for public transit than the rich. Other priorities include establishing fair political representation as shaped by electoral districting, maintaining the openness of public space, resisting purposeful territorial segregation (as in apartheid) or colonial domination, breaking through spatial barriers based on gender, race, or sexual preference, and on a larger scale, reducing regional and international inequalities in income and well-being. Although one can find something spatial about the efforts of every social movement, not all, in my view at least, represent struggles for specifically spatial justice.

ORIGINS AND DEVELOPMENT OF THE JUSTICE MOVEMENT IN LOS ANGELES

As discussed in the first chapter, the starting point for both the academic and activist streams of development in LA is the same. It all began with a call by one of the earliest labor-community alliances, the Coalition to Stop Plant Closings (CSPC). Although not particularly successful in its aims to curb the deindustrialization process and resist the tactics of highly mobile capital, the CSPC triggered both a remarkable expansion of academic research on urban restructuring as well as the emergence of some of the most successful alliances of labor union locals, community-based organizations, and supportive university activists found anywhere in the country.

The resurgence of labor-community coalition building has its roots in the early development of *community unionism,* inspired in large part by the United Farm Workers' (UFW) campaigns to achieve justice for immigrant workers in California in the 1960s and 1970s. UFW activities tied the labor movement more closely to the wider immigrant, mainly Latino/a community as a whole and, more directly, to local neighborhood and community groups and their priorities. Struggles over wages, workplace conditions, and threatened factory closures were extended to include demands for better housing, schools, social services, and other *residential rights* to justice and equality. New labor-community coalitions, often assisted by university-based activism and research, began to take the lead in promoting a regional justice movement of unusual strength and persistence.

The union-community link worked effectively in both directions. Community support gave added strength to the labor movement and increased its sensitivity to the local and regional geographies in which work and workers' lives took place. At the same time, ties to local unions and workers' issues bolstered community development efforts and fostered new strategies for achieving what would come to be described as *development with justice.* As place-based knowledge and strategic action became increasingly important, civil society in Los Angeles changed significantly. What was once a relatively "placeless" urban world, where local communities rarely impinged on people's lives, has today become a hive of place-based community organizations and locationally strategic grassroots activism.

These local and regional achievements are even more remarkable given the deteriorating economic conditions, huge job losses, and declining union power that have plagued most of the country over the past four decades. While union membership declined nationally, however, it grew in California and expanded even faster in Los Angeles, with a major jump occurring between 1999 and 2002, reflecting the unionization of in-home care givers and other largely minority occupations, including what was in 1999 one of the largest one-year increases in union membership in U.S. urban history.

How did this transformation take place? Why did it happen in Los Angeles, of all places? What are the distinctive features of the new labor-community coalitions that have emerged? Four arguments respond to these questions:

1. The recent resurgence of labor-community coalition building in Los Angeles represents a local response to the especially intensive and polarizing effects of globalization and economic restructuring in the Los Angeles metropolitan region.

2. The uprising and riots of 1992 marked a turning point for labor and the working poor in Los Angeles, stimulating a growing recognition that government was unlikely to respond effectively and that new place-based grassroots methods and strategies were needed in the struggles for greater social and economic justice.

3. A heightened awareness of the politics of space and the potential strategic importance of seeking spatial justice and democratic rights to the city distinguishes these movements from their counterparts in other metropolitan regions.

4. The relatively higher spatial consciousness of the local movements and the emergence of specifically spatial strategies of political activism derive in large part from linkages between activist groups and university students and faculties involved in urban planning and geography.

What was happening through the 1980s era of Reaganomics and Thatcherism was not just a cementing together of labor-community-university linkages in Los Angeles but also a major shift in activist strategies and objectives. Whereas at first the struggles were defensive ones, against deindustrialization and its effects on local communities, the emerging new wave of efforts sought justice and basic human rights for everyone but especially for all workers. This generated a broader and more provocative activist agenda, opening up the justice struggle to questions of education and health, public services, immigrants' rights, affordable housing, and financial access.

Justice for Janitors

The leading edge of these new developments was the Justice for Janitors Movement (J4J). Founded in Denver in 1985, J4J began organizing in Los Angeles in 1988, led by Local 399 of the Service Employees International Union (SEIU), which would continue to be at the forefront of coalition building in LA. Research had shown that janitors in downtown LA were receiving lower wages and were much less unionized than those working in other major U.S. cities. Most were Latino, part of the massive agglomeration of the working poor. Few were union members, many were without documents, and nearly all were forced to work at subpoverty wages. A strike seemed appropriate, but who would organize it?

The answer was a labor-community-university coalition called Justice for Janitors, bringing the search for justice to the fore in local activist politics. Justice more than freedom, liberty, or equality had become the organizational metaphor of choice, capturing more crosscutting support in terms of class, race, gender, and ethnicity than its alternatives. The big bang of the justice movement took place on June 15, 1990, in Century City, once a movie lot but then an early edge city filled with law offices and tall buildings. This date has come to be celebrated around the world as International Justice Day.

The choice of Century City was significant. In 1967, the Century Plaza Hotel housed President Lyndon Johnson as thousands of demonstrators protested outside against the Vietnam War and were met with violence by the Los Angeles Police Department. Century City was the largest cluster of high-rise buildings outside downtown and was an established and well-known battleground (later to become the headquarters of the Fox Corporation, parent of ultraconservative Fox News). The J4J coalition had learned from the Coalition to Stop Plant Closures to be especially sensitive to location and the local commitment of whomever they were protesting against. Striking against footloose Fordist industries in old industrial neighborhoods was futile. Supporting those who clean large buildings at sites that had unusually strong local roots and could not simply be packed up and moved to another location was likely to be much more productive.

The 1990 strike represented a new mode of activism, more like a Situationist happening than a nonviolent demonstration or strike. Four hundred or more janitors, with red T-shirts and strike caps, sang and danced along the streets, always aware of the LAPD presence on foot and horseback and attuned as well to the location of the media and those invisible lines of public/private transgression on the streets and sidewalks that, if crossed, would induce immediate police action. At an appropriate time and place, the lines were crossed, the police reacted violently, the violence against defenseless janitors was filmed and shown on the nightly news, popular sympathy and support for the janitors grew, and eventually the LAPD was blamed for starting the riot and forced to pay $3.5 million in damages to Local 399 of the SEIU.

A new contract was signed, with an increase in wages and health benefits, but in this age of globalization, another step was needed. The provision of janitorial services in Los Angeles and major cities around the world was dominated by a multinational corporation, then called International Services Solutions, based in Copenhagen, Denmark. As office managers in LA were not directly responsible for the contract, the janitors had to go to Copenhagen, which they did—quite successfully.

Justice for Janitors was not just a local development. The protest in Century City lit a spark that would generate a wide variety of workers' justice movements in the United States and around the world.[2] One offshoot from J4J, led in part by experienced organizers from Los Angeles, was Justice for Cleaners in the financial district of London, known as the City, where the term *janitor* is rarely used. The J4J experience in Los Angeles was captured in *Bread and Roses* (2000), a bilingual film by well-known British director Ken Loach (see app. 2, video 4).

So the struggle for justice was in the air in Los Angeles when the city exploded in 1992. It is no surprise that the events have become known as the Justice Riots. There is no doubt that this search for justice, with its commanding banners proclaiming "No Justice—No Peace," was accompanied by destructive fires, uncontrolled violence, and widespread looting, but it surpassed the Watts Riots in many other ways. The concept *Latino* came to the forefront to encompass much more than Mexican American or Chicano/a. The mainly Mexican East Los Angeles barrio was relatively quiet in 1992, as the focus of attention, for the LAPD especially, shifted to areas such as Pico-Union and other Salvadoran and Nicaraguan neighborhoods more attuned to social uprisings and protest movements.

It is significant that more Latinos than African Americans were arrested in 1992, and many were immediately deported despite police promises not to become an immigration authority. It is also very likely that the majority of the looters, which included members of nearly every race and class, were Central American immigrants taking advantage of the anarchic conditions to obtain food and baby diapers, as well as TV sets and other luxury items. Radical women of color—Latino, Black, and Asian—became prominent leaders, as the justice movement received a powerful stimulus from the events.

In part, the emergence of radical women of color was related to the abandonment of politics by many radical Anglo men, who were convinced that no government effort, even on the scale of the postwar Marshall Plan, could solve the deepening problems of poverty, inequality, and injustice in post-riot Los Angeles. At the same time, nowhere else in the country were local activists so avid to return to grassroots organizing and innovative coalition building. In what had become one of the world's most culturally and economically heterogeneous cities, coalition building was necessarily multicultural, multilingual, and powerfully shaped by the huge agglomeration of immigrant working poor who had occupied the urban core of Los Angeles, another major factor in the emergence into leadership positions of radical women of color.

The Living Wage Campaign

The burgeoning justice movement turned first to organizing for *a living wage*, a key focus for workers' justice as well as immigrants' rights, especially in an area with an unusually high rate of poverty mixed with a high cost of living and ignorance of minimum wage laws, especially for undocumented workers. Following the lessons learned by J4J and the plant closure coalition, the struggle for a living wage, which began in eastern cities, took on greater force in Los Angeles, clearly focused on locally rooted activities and employment clusters. The first and main target was probably the least footloose of all activities, local government. Assisted by a veteran activist on the city council, the City of Los Angeles passed a Living Wage Ordinance covering all city workers in 1987.

From this point, the movement snowballed. Two years later, the ordinance was extended to county workers, and in 2001 an even stronger ordinance affecting private businesses that received grants from the city was passed in Santa Monica after a campaign led by María Elena Durazo, then head of Local 11 of the Hotel Employees Restaurant Employees Union, and by Santa Monicans Allied for Responsible Tourism, an offshoot of an even larger coalition that would gain international renown, the Los Angeles Alliance for a New Economy (LAANE), led by Madeline Janis, then called Madeline Janis-Aparicio. The workers' justice campaign would grow beyond local government to affect all locally rooted sectors, firms, and activities that hired large numbers of immigrant workers: tourism, office development, hotels, restaurants, home care, and the garment industry.

Two achievements of the workers' justice movement deserve particular attention. In 1999, after more than ten years of struggle, SEIU Local 434B won the right to represent 75,000 home care workers in Los Angeles County. This was the largest number of new union members mobilized in one year since 1941, when workers at Ford Motor Company's River Rouge plant near Dearborn, Michigan, the definitive symbol of assembly-line mass production and the largest integrated factory in the world at the time, joined the United Auto Workers. The transfer of power from industrial to service unions was never more evident.

The second achievement involved Justice for Janitors, which spearheaded a national movement of more than one hundred thousand janitors seeking a new contract for increased wages and benefits. On April 7, 2000, janitors affiliated with SEIU marched down Wilshire Boulevard from downtown LA through Beverly Hills to Century City again, receiving one of the most amazing demonstrations of public support in U.S. labor history. The city attorney and soon-to-be mayor led the parade, followed by Jesse Jackson and dozens of elected officials, ministers, priests, and rabbis; en route people leaned out of windows to lend support, and those on the street cheered, some with raised fists. Several bystanders in Beverly Hills ran into the street to offer cash to the janitors. Celebrations of the new contract, which was signed a few weeks after the parade, included an odd picture: amid dancing and water spritzing stood a country supervisor holding a mop, the then state assembly leader and future mayor wielding a broom, and a prominent developer and downtown building owner with a striker's hat.[3]

A SPATIAL TURN IN THE JUSTICE MOVEMENT

Sometime in the 1990s, the justice movement took a pronounced spatial turn. Although Justice for Janitors and some of the earlier organizations, including the Coalition to Stop Plant Closures, seemed to understand the politics of space and place and the injustices embedded in the new intrametropolitan geography, three coalitions in particular began to add explicitly spatial strategies to their repertoire as the movement advanced. Not all the leaders of these justice struggles would agree with me, but I believe it can be argued that this new spatial consciousness played an important role in the most significant and innovative of their achievements.

The Bus Riders Union and the Labor/Community
Strategy Center

A remarkable moment in American urban history occurred in October 1996, in a courtroom in downtown Los Angeles. A class action lawsuit brought against the Los Angeles Metropolitan Transit Authority (MTA) by a coalition of grassroots organizations on behalf of those dependent on public transit for their basic needs was resolved in an unprecedented and momentous consent decree. It was decided that, for at least the next ten years, past decades of discrimination against the transit-dependent urban poor—those who could not afford a car—would be remedied by making MTA give its highest budget priority to improving the quality of bus service and guaranteeing equitable access to all forms of public mass transit.

According to the consent decree that was declared in the case of *Labor/ Community Strategy Center et al. v. Los Angeles County Metropolitan Transit Authority,* known as the Bus Riders Union decision, not only was MTA required to purchase a specific number of new environment-friendly buses, but they would also have to reduce overcrowding, freeze fare structures, enhance bus security, reduce bus stop crime, and provide special services to facilitate access to jobs, education, and health centers. If followed to the letter, this would soak up almost the entire operating budget of the MTA, making it impossible to continue with ambitious plans to build an extensive fixed rail network—a priority in keeping with the perceived view of Los Angeles as the only major world city of its size without a metro or subway.

The Bus Riders Union case was a direct attack on discriminatory practices, and for a while it seemed to revive the civil rights movement, stimulating comparisons to the famous *Brown v. Board of Education* case in 1954, which ordered racial desegregation of schools. Here too, it was deemed that the rights of a particular segment of the population were being trampled by the existence of two separate but unequal systems in the provision of a vital public service, in this case public mass transit. One system, with a disproportionate share of investment and finance, served the wealthy, while another, much less well funded, served the decidedly more urgent needs of the poor.

As much as it was a civil rights decision, the consent decree was also a stirring expression of the environmental justice movement, which had begun much earlier in LA with the Los Angeles City Energy Recovery (LANCER) project. The LANCER project revolved around a proposal to locate an incinerator and the new jobs it required in South Central LA, then predominantly African American. When it was seen to be part of a larger scheme to locate hazardous and polluting facilities in poor neighborhoods, an unlikely coalition of local residents, liberal Westside environmental activists, and university researchers came together to stop the project.[4] The Bus Riders Union case was seen as involving environmental (or transit) justice; it also enhanced the search for spatial justice by combating all forms of discrimination based on place of residence and affirming the view that where one lived could have negative repercussions on important aspects of daily life as well as personal health.

Nothing quite like this had ever happened with regard to public transit services in any major American city, although several other cities brought similar cases without success. Giving such priority to the needs of the inner city and largely minority working poor was a stunning reversal of the conventional workings of urban government and planning in the United States, as service provision almost always favored wealthier residents, even in the name of alleviating poverty. It also ran against the grain of American politics at the time, with its neoconservative ascendancy, detrimental welfare reform, and weakening civil rights and antipoverty efforts. There were very few examples anywhere in the country of successful grassroots social movements affecting urban planning and governance at such a scale of financial commitment. In essence, the consent decree resulted in the transfer of billions of dollars from a plan that disproportionately favored the wealthy to one that worked more to the benefit of the poor.

The two key organizations behind the successful class action lawsuit were the Bus Riders Union itself and the lead plaintiffs in the case, the Labor/Community Strategy Center (L/CSC), which initiated the court action and spearheaded the creation of the larger coalition. The Bus Riders Union/Sindicato de Pasajeros (BRU) is not a traditional labor union but rather an assertively multiracial and antiracist mass organization of the transit-dependent aimed at improving the public transportation system and the lives of the more than four hundred thousand predominantly minority and female working poor of Los Angeles. It forms a branch of the L/CSC or Strategy Center, an activist organization founded in 1989 and described on its web page as "an antiracist, anticorporate, and anti-imperialist think tank/act tank focusing on theory-driven practice." It aims at generating "mass campaigns of the working class and oppressed nationalities, in particular black and Latino workers and communities." The Strategy Center runs a National School for Strategic Organizing and publishes *AhoraNow,* a bilingual political magazine edited by Lian Hurst Mann, an architectural critic and theorist and cofounder of the Strategy Center.

After the consent decree was announced, the victorious BRU and Strategy Center organizers proclaimed their achievements in deservedly epochal language. Eric Mann, cofounder of the Strategy Center, spoke of "driving the bus of history," producing "billions for buses" in an ongoing struggle for justice at the "intersection of mass transit, civil rights, and the environment," creating "a new vision for urban transportation" and "a new theory of urban insurgency in an age of transnational capitalism."[5] Hollywood noticed the significance of the decision too. Activist and Academy Award–winning cinematographer and director Haskell Wexler spent three years with the Bus Riders Union and produced a feature-length film detailing its visionary efforts, adding to his earlier works on labor issues (*Matewan,* 1987), the Vietnam War, torture in Brazil, and the uprising in Chiapas, Mexico. While rooted in the local milieu, the victory took on a global significance, enhanced by the international ambitions of its leaders. (See app. 2, video 5.)

Many factors figured into the stunning court decision in 1996. In part, it reflected the recognition that any investment in alternative forms of mass transit (such as fixed rail or subway construction) that compromised vital bus services, especially for the inner-city poor, was discriminatory and unjust. In specific legal terms, such investment violated Title VI of the Civil Rights Act of 1964, the generative act that defined and propelled the civil rights movement. The transit needs of the poor and racial minorities were never entirely ignored by the transportation planners, but it was argued that they were systematically subordinated to the needs and expectations of those living well above the poverty line. A massive redistribution of resources and a major shift in public policy were deemed necessary to redress decades of systematic geographical (spatial) and racial discrimination.

This entrenched discrimination in meeting the mass transit needs of the poor was rooted in a larger pattern of discriminatory investment that had shaped the geography and built environment of Los Angeles and probably all other major metropolitan areas throughout the twentieth century. I refer here to the pronounced investment gap between the building and maintenance of roads and highways on the one hand, and the construction of all other means of mass public transit on the other. The outcome almost everywhere of this socially and spatially discriminatory process was an unjust metropolitan transit geography, which favored the wealthier population in (urbanizing) suburbia, who owned multiple cars, over the massive agglomeration of the immigrant working poor in the inner core of the urban region, who were urgently dependent on public transit.

Economic restructuring, which increased poverty and social polarization, and the rise of the so-called New Economy had worsened the problems of the transit-dependent poor and minority households concentrated in the inner city. Nearly every low-wage worker held multiple jobs, and in most cases these jobs—as domestics, gardeners, cleaners, nannies, and home-care specialists—were multilocational, requiring travel to many sites scattered around the city. The simple hub-and-spoke spatial structure of the proposed and partially built fixed rail system could never serve the inner-city working poor as effectively as the dense mesh of a flexible bus network.

The court case was characterized by a clash between contrasting views of equity and justice. The MTA felt it was committed to transit justice, but its concept of equity was quite different from the BRU's. As a county authority strongly influenced by the generally conservative, predominantly white and suburban board of supervisors, the MTA defined equity primarily in administrative and rigidly territorial terms. If every supervisorial district had equally efficient mass transit and served in some way the needs of the poor, the system was considered to be equitable. The very thought of giving additional attention to the special transit needs of the poor was out of the question.

This territorial district view of equity and transit justice was rooted in a "flat" geographical perspective that ignored the markedly uneven geography of transit need. It was acceptable that special attention needed to be given to the downtown core of the city region and such key activity locations as the international airport and the twin ports of Los Angeles–Long Beach, but to give special attention to the neighborhoods of the immigrant working poor was not only intolerable but unconstitutional.

A constitutional principle of nondiscrimination guaranteed some degree of transit justice, but for the U.S. Congress, nondiscrimination was ensured mainly by not favoring one territorial district or constituency over another in the distribution of benefits (with the disguised exception of pork-barrel allocations for the most influential politicians). It could have been argued that the special attention being asked for by the Bus Riders Union was unconstitutional, but this would open up the possibility of arguing that subsidizing suburbanization was also unconstitutional, so constitutionality was not a central issue in the BRU case.

The MTA used mountains of data to argue that every segment of its planned transit system would carry large if not majority numbers of minorities and poor people. If a few segments, such as the light-rail Metrolink system that served the expansive San Fernando Valley or the Blue Line link to Pasadena, carried mainly white suburban passengers, this was only fair in this something-for-everyone logic. How could there be claims of racial and spatial discrimination?

The coalition entered the battle with a very different strategic perspective. They argued, with abundant incriminating data displayed on excellent maps, that there was a long historical record of discrimination through disproportional investments and attention to mass transit facilities that served the relatively wealthy, while those who were most transit dependent in their everyday lives and who were densely clustered in what was defined as the inner city, remained seriously and systematically underserved. At one point it was shown that each Metrolink rail trip was subsidized at a rate of more than twenty-one dollars, compared to a little over one dollar per bus trip. They made clear that when the needs of the transit-dependent poor are given priority, a very different view of justice and discrimination emerges, one that calls for significant changes in public policies and planning practices.

The court deliberations revealed the deeply embedded biases in urban transportation planning that shaped not just the actions of the MTA but practically every planning agency in the country. The bias was not just a matter of overemphasizing simplistic cost/benefit analyses, but of intrinsically privileging the nonpoor automobile driver, and thus actively discriminating against those residents who had little choice other than to use public transit for journeys to work, school, health services, shopping, and entertainment.

This car-centered ideology seemed rational to the majority of professional planners. Aiming to provide the best possible service for the population as a whole, they focused attention on the majority of riders and their needs, a seemingly admirable strategy. In metropolitan regions of the world that, like Los Angeles, are not served by widely used metro rail/subway systems, most travel is done by automobile. This usually means that the individualized transit sector outweighs the public or mass transit sector in levels of investment both in absolute and per capita terms, especially when public costs for street and freeway construction and maintenance, as well automobile prices, insurance, and so on, are measured in.

When well-intentioned transportation planners approach mass transit issues on these terms, especially when making the choice between rail and bus, the bus loses out almost every time. Even if fixed rail systems, such as BART or any of the more recently built systems, never reach the overly optimistic goals of their promoters in substituting for private automobile trips, thousands of car trips will nonetheless be avoided. Buses also take riders out of their cars, but they continue to keep street traffic gridlocked and contribute more pollutants to the air unless extraordinary investments are made. When most people use cars, or when this is perceived to be the case by transportation planners, rail investment seems more attractive than improving bus transit. And for the most part, the urge to become more like New York, or London, or Paris intensifies this bias and adds to the pressure to make rail investment appear both efficient and equitable.

Once the specific and immediate needs of the transit-dependent poor are clearly recognized, however, everything changes. Los Angeles, once considered the most suburban of cities, provided an especially visible expression of transit injustice in the 1990s, with its massive agglomeration of immigrant working poor in the dense corona surrounding the city center. With many of the transit-dependent holding multiple jobs and with each form of employment typically requiring movement between multiple locations, flexible, multi-nodal, densely meshed bus networks are nearly always preferable, and urgently so, to fixed rail systems, whether light or heavy, above or under ground.

As was shown for Los Angeles and can probably be demonstrated in almost every U.S. city, transit discrimination or transit injustice has prevailed as normal practice, almost entirely unconstrained and unquestioned, for at least the past eighty years, or since the beginning of the age of Fordism. Maintaining these automobile-driven discriminatory practices does not require evil people intentionally making racially biased decisions, just well-trained experts following conventional procedures to make decisions and plans that almost always favor the wealthier and more powerful segments of urban society. That this ideology-bound system of transit discrimination was successfully challenged and judged to require enormous and immediate remedial action was among the most extraordinary accomplishments of the case of *Labor/Community Strategy Center et al. v. Los Angeles County Metropolitan Transit Authority.*

The significance of the decision, however, would not go unnoticed by local and federal authorities. For all its local roots, the BRU victory had implications that extended well beyond the Los Angeles region. If allowed to expand to its potential limits as a legal precedent, it could have led to radical changes in urban life throughout the country. Imagine the possibilities. Any plan by any public authority, whether for mass transit or the location of schools and fire stations, or the closure of hospital emergency rooms, could be subjected to a social and spatial "justice test" to determine whether the distributional pattern proposed was fair and equitable for all areas and communities affected, with fairness based on the different needs of the rich and the poor as well as majority and minority populations. Similar legal tests could potentially be applied to tax policies, electoral districting, school-building programs, the health effects of air and water pollution, siting of toxic facilities—practically every planning and policy decision influencing urban life. If the plan failed the test, the courts would throw it out.

Not surprisingly, the consent decree triggered vigorous reactions. The MTA and other major planning authorities, reinforced by conservative as well as some liberal political voices, mobilized in a determined effort to reverse or sabotage the decision. Legal appeals were made (and rejected). Hints of a "red scare," similar to that which destroyed public housing efforts in Los Angeles in the 1950s, were floated in the local media. When they did not take hold, there were more direct personal attacks. Web pages multiplied to focus the raging criticism, including one listing the salaries over the past several years received by the leading figures in the L/CSC, bemoaning their lack of "true" progressive credentials because of their relatively high incomes.

Reactions were not confined to Los Angeles. The radical potential of the BRU decision and consent decree was not lost on Washington and the Bush administration, especially in the wake of the Bush-Cheney regime's infusion of presidential power into the judicial system over the 2000 presidential election. The federal effort to block the potential spread of the legal precedent came to a head in 2001. In the case of *Alexander v. Sandoval,* based on a challenge to the federal Department of Transportation (DOT) raised in Alabama over driving license exams given only in English, the U.S. Supreme Court effectively blocked further legal application of the BRU precedent. In a 5–4 decision, it ruled that intent to discriminate had to be proved, drawing on earlier decisions that seriously weakened the entire civil rights movement, then went further to proclaim that private parties cannot sue the DOT or any other federal agency based on disparate action claims—that is, on the basis of alleged discriminatory practices. There were other efforts to limit the impact of cases such as the BRU based on the need to show intent, but none went as far as *Alexander v. Sandoval* in protecting public authorities from antidiscrimination lawsuits.

The Sandoval decision built a thick legal barrier around attempts to extend the BRU victory beyond its immediate local impact, although efforts continue to encourage the spread of the BRU's organizing and strategic model to other cities. The local impact, however, has been impressive. According to the BRU website, more than $2.5 billion was redistributed to serve bus riders in the ten-year period 1996–2006. The largest clean-fuel fleet in the country was created, replacing more than 1,800 diesel buses. At least a million annual bus service hours were added, more than 800 "green," unionized jobs were created, bus ridership increased by 12 percent, and many rapid bus lanes were added to major surface streets. There are probably no other metropolitan areas in the country where bus services have improved more significantly over the past fifteen years.

In the face of so many antagonistic forces, little could be done to extend the consent decree after its termination in 2006. The BRU and Strategy Center, however, have remained active forces in the environmental, transit, and spatial justice movements. On May 1, 2006, they played an important role in organizing the "Great American Boycott," or in Spanish *El Gran Paro*

Estadounidense (the Great American Strike), when perhaps as many as two million people marched peacefully for immigrant rights and against the rising national tide of anti-immigrant feeling. The strategic coalition has, if anything, broadened and intensified its efforts in protesting environmental racism, police mistreatment of minorities, new plans for rail construction, proposed bus fare increases, and larger issues such as the war in Iraq.

As indicated on its current website, the Strategy Center and its allied groups have promoted extensions of the BRU model to other cities, such as Atlanta, protested vigorously against recent regressive shifts in MTA policy, and expanded its publication and multimedia programs. In 2009, it published the *Clean Air Economic Justice Plan,* which presented a new bus-centered model for urban transportation, environmental justice, and economic development that would build on federal funds from the Obama government's economic stimulus package. After creating a national alliance of Transit Riders for Public Transit, the Strategy Center/BRU staged a mass rally on July 25, 2012, to continue its protest against the MTA for cutting thousands of miles of bus service and to appeal to President Obama to reverse the new Federal Surface Transit Act, which violates his commitment to environmental justice by maintaining the 80–20 split in highway versus public transit investment. It also demanded action on the Federal Transit Administration's finding that the Los Angeles MTA has the worst record in the country for violating civil rights. There is probably no more important struggle over environmental and transit justice going on in the United States today than that being waged in Los Angeles.

The Los Angeles Alliance for a New Economy

The Los Angeles Alliance for a New Economy (LAANE), a flexible collection of more than a hundred organizations, has become a kind of regional watchdog for Los Angeles, extending its positive influence and support to dozens of places in Los Angeles County and beyond. In any discussion of the major achievements in labor-community-university coalition building, especially with regard to the development of specifically spatial strategies of social action, LAANE deserves to take center stage. It played a key role in the Living Wage campaign and has been a primary force in the networking of grassroots organizations since 1990. More than other coalitions, it draws strategically upon university-based research and researchers and has served to bring into the public realm innovative ideas about urban restructuring, the

New Economy, the dynamics of regional development, the widening divide between rich and poor, and the spatiality of injustice.

LAANE was founded in 1993 under the leadership of Madeline Janis-Aparicio (now Madeline Janis), a lawyer and former executive director of CARECEN, the Central American Resource Center. It started out as the Tourism Industry Development Council, an organization that grew directly from the first project organized by the newly established UCLA Community Scholars Program (CSP). The CSP, led by Gilda Haas, Allan Heskin, and Jacqueline Leavitt from Urban Planning and Kent Wong from the Labor Center, brought together experienced activists from various community groups and labor unions to attend classes, meet with students, and work with them in joint projects. The first of these projects, conducted in the academic year 1991–92, was aimed at the local tourism industry, at a time when huge investments were planned for expanding the downtown Convention Center and related facilities.

The CSP team sought strategies to promote greater economic benefits for low-wage workers and their communities in an industry notorious for its weak positive spillover effects and exploitative working conditions. The final report, called *Accidental Tourism,* argued that, without special intervention, the normal workings of public and private decision making favor results that discriminate against the poor and minorities, an outcome that was likely to occur again if downtown tourist development went ahead as originally planned.

Like so many campaigns aimed at worker and community justice, one of the primary intentions and effects of the CSP study was to raise public awareness about the location of investment and its positive and negative impacts on surrounding communities. As with MTA plans for a "world-class" fixed rail system and the motivations behind the LANCER incinerator project, public officials assumed that the mere addition of jobs and improved social services would be enough to satisfy urban residents. The particular social and spatial distribution of benefits remained out of sight and out of mind. While the language of *Accidental Tourism* was not overtly spatial, its underlying message and the interaction between the community scholars and the urban planning students were informed by a sensitivity to the spatiality of justice and injustice, especially for the working poor trying to survive in the New Economy.

Some important benefits for workers made their way into the contract for the Convention Center, initiating what would develop into LAANE's hallmark achievement: the creation and expanded use of negotiated community benefits agreements (CBAs). LAANE's offshoot, the Growth with Justice coalition, later succeeded in promoting agreements with local governments and private developers to attach benefits for workers and minority communities to all new development plans in every sector of the local economy. In another important breakthrough, agreements were reached to make new developments produce a community impact assessment, examining potential spillover effects of the development on jobs, traffic, and local quality of life.

Significantly, the landmark CBA for what is called LA Live was negotiated jointly in 2001 by LAANE and Strategic Actions for a Just Economy (SAJE), teaming Madeline Janis with "insurgent planner" and SAJE founder and former director Gilda Haas. The agreement was part of SAJE's Figueroa Corridor Coalition for Economic Justice campaign and was worked out in conjunction with the huge Staples Center development project in the downtown area. It included provisions for living wage jobs, affordable housing, local hiring, and green space.

LAANE and SAJE have contributed as much as any organization to the unusually productive interaction between the university and the wider community and to filtering strategic spatial and regional thinking into local activism. LAANE has shown an acute awareness of the geography of worker injustices as well as the necessity to organize on a regional scale. Avoiding the mistakes and failed strategies of the plant closures coalition in the early 1980s, LAANE focused its attention on employers who were rooted in the region and could not easily relocate when pressured by community or labor groups. As with the Living Wage campaign, local government was an obvious starting point.

Selecting strategic sites for protest and demonstration was vital. Once the local government base was ensured, strategic action was extended to the major industrial clusters of Los Angeles, such as entertainment and the garment industries, and the essential infrastructure of the regional tourism economy, almost by definition locally rooted. Little Tokyo and the major office blocks of downtown and Century City, the international airport, the Hollywood Redevelopment Project, dry wall construction workers and tortilla makers, large hotel chains (especially near the coastal beaches), the booming new developments in Playa Vista and Universal Studios, home care workers and day laborers, nannies and gardeners—all became targets. At all times and places, serving the needs of the immigrant working poor was central.

Probably more than anywhere else in the country, the notion that businesses receiving any public subsidy have an obligation to the communities their activities affect entered into public awareness and public policy. The goal was not to stop development, but rather to guarantee development with justice for workers and communities, with day care and local hiring, parks and worker centers, health benefits and living wages—in short, to ensure democratic rights to the city and to the resources generated by and in the city and region. While not evident in all LAANE's projects, a critical spatial awareness informed many of its practices, promoted and sustained by an extraordinary flow of hired student researchers and activists from urban planning at UCLA—as many as forty over the past fifteen years, with several rising to executive and managerial roles.

At the heart of LAANE's work has been the promotion of more effective CBAs, the hallmark of LAANE's persistent campaign for development with justice or, as it proclaims in its current website, "Building a City of Justice." Drawing on the successful Living Wage campaign and other victories related to jobs with justice, LAANE pioneered the CBA strategy in the late 1990s with an innovative agreement associated with the redevelopment of Hollywood Boulevard. Ever since, CBAs have multiplied throughout the City and County of Los Angeles and have been spreading to many cities across the country, including Denver, Milwaukee, Seattle, Pittsburgh, New Haven, Phoenix, and Atlanta.

Although the basic idea of the CBA is relatively straightforward, its spread represents a radical innovation in local economic development planning, participatory governance, the labor movement, and the struggle over residential rights to urban resources. The CBA is a legally binding document negotiated by a defined labor-community coalition and a developer, usually but not necessarily supported financially by the local government or redevelopment agency. In return for public subsidies, greater ease in meeting land use and other local regulations, and the added advantage of dealing with a formally defined and government-recognized community coalition, the developer negotiates an agreement to provide benefits that typically include quality jobs, local hiring, affordable housing, environmental mitigations, and various community services.

In another arena of activism extending its influence well beyond the boundaries of Los Angeles, LAANE has been the leader of what has come to be known as the *Battle for Inglewood*, a struggle against the world's largest retail corporation and renowned fountainhead of workers injustices,

Wal-Mart. The retail giant Wal-Mart has become a prominent target for justice struggles of many different kinds locally, nationally, and around the world, filling bookshelves with such unsubtle titles as *How Wal-Mart Is Destroying America (and the World)*.

Perhaps not surprisingly, this LA story is effectively illustrated in a film/DVD, significantly titled *Wal-Mart: The High Cost of Low Price* (see app. 2, video 6). Telling the stories of people and communities across the country who are affected by the insidious labor policies and union-busting tactics of the world's largest retail corporation, with five thousand stores and 1.5 million employees around the world, the film reaches its crescendo of optimistic deliverance with the story of the Battle for Inglewood, a successful effort to fight Wal-Mart's "invasion of urban America" that would stimulate many dozens of similar victories. After the Inglewood story, a long list of small town and big city victories against Wal-Mart scrolls across the screen at the film's ending.

In addition to being a vital part of the larger anti-Wal-Mart struggle, the Battle for Inglewood illustrates the continued expansion of labor-community-university coalition building in Los Angeles. Inglewood is an independent municipality located near Los Angeles International Airport and reputedly one of the largest majority African American cities in the country. Its population is a little more than 115,000, with just about as many Latino residents as African Americans today, and with more than 20 percent of the population living below the poverty level. Within its boundaries are Hollywood Park Race Track and the Forum, formerly the main arena for the Los Angeles Lakers professional basketball team, before its move to the Staples Center in the heart of downtown Los Angeles.

In the early 2000s, Wal-Mart, with its traditional base in small-town America, was developing an urban strategy aimed at relatively poor but densely populated urban communities, with special emphasis on California, where other big-box retail chains such as Costco had captured a lion's share of the market. Inglewood, for many reasons, was an especially attractive target for entering the second-largest urban market in the country.

In March 2002, LAANE, through its development monitoring program and association with the United Food and Commercial Workers Union, discovered that Wal-Mart had purchased, through an intermediary developer, an option on a site near the Forum that was located in a sixty-acre area thought to be one of the largest pieces of undeveloped land in the entire county. Almost immediately, LAANE began organizing to resist this "invasion," spurred further a month later when Wal-Mart announced its plans to build forty big-box supercenters in California, including a flagship store in Inglewood. Early organizing efforts contributed to the city council's passage of an ordinance banning big-box stores. In reaction, Wal-Mart brought out its biggest guns to threaten legal action against the city while gathering signatures for a referendum to, in their view, let the people decide. In December, the city council rescinded the ordinance, and the Battle for Inglewood began in full force.

The first major offensive in the battle came in August 2003, when an unusual ballot initiative was submitted, backed by the (submissive) Citizens Committee to Welcome Wal-Mart to Inglewood. If passed, the initiative would not just allow Wal-Mart to build a superstore on the sixty-acre lot; it would give them the equivalent of extraterritorial rights to a virtual fiefdom on the land. Wal-Mart was allowed, indeed invited, to do whatever they wanted with the site, without government, judicial, or community oversight. Stunned by this presumptive strike, LAANE, with assistance from Clergy and Laity United for Economic Justice (CLUE), local religious leaders, and grocery workers, began strategic coalition-building efforts in earnest, leading to the creation of a new organization, the Coalition for a Better Inglewood (CBI).

In addition to organizing help, LAANE contributed in two other vital areas, promoting extensive analytical research as well as effective public relations and media linkages.[6] The ballot initiative was scheduled to be voted upon in April 2004. Early polls showed roughly 60 percent in favor, as Wal-Mart waged a media blitz on the people of Inglewood. CBI efforts were weakened by what would turn out to be a lengthy countywide strike against the two leading retail grocery giants in the Los Angeles region, propelled in part by efforts to control if not lower wages in the face of potential Wal-Mart superstore competition. Wal-Mart's campaign emphasized its traditional arguments that its low prices were serving the urgent needs of the relatively poor, that it achieved these low prices by keeping labor and other costs low, and that its stores created vitally needed jobs and raised local tax revenues. Was it not the democratic way to let the people decide whether they wanted a store to be built?

Wal-Mart clearly underestimated the power of the resurgent coalitions of Los Angeles. Through targeted university research, counterarguments were developed to show that wages at Wal-Mart were so low that its workers had to rely on state welfare benefits such as food stamps to survive. A report chaired by Representative George Miller (D-Cal) estimated that the low wages were subsidized by California taxpayers to the tune of nearly fifty million dollars. Researchers challenged the way Wal-Mart estimated its net effect on jobs and tax revenues as giving insufficient attention to spillover effects on surrounding areas in terms of lost jobs and revenues, especially with respect to smaller retail stores forced to close because of the insurmountable competition. A long list of labor grievances and lawsuits was also marshaled against the corporation, as were stories of Wal-Mart closing stores soon after subsidies ran out and its creation of a specialized executive cadre of union busters.

On April 6, 2004, a month after the grocery strike ended, the people of Inglewood rejected the initiative by 61–39 percent, but this was not the end of the battle. In July 2006, a superstore ordinance similar to one enacted in the City of Los Angeles two years earlier was passed by the Inglewood City Council requiring the completion of a full economic impact report before approval could be considered. Wal-Mart was not entirely stopped in its plans to expand in California, but there is little doubt that its ambitions were significantly thwarted by the surprising power of local grassroots coalitions. The Battle for Inglewood played an important role in globalizing what had been happening in Los Angeles and, at the local scale, in bringing together many different streams and strategies of coalition building. There was no overt mention of spatial or territorial justice, nor were there any explicit claims about the right to the city, but I do not think it would be stretching things too far to say that these concepts and their related strategies were involved in a significant way.

Building a National Coalition on the Right to the City

The most recent institutional extension from successful coalition building in Los Angeles has been the creation of a new national alliance built on an idea developed more than forty years ago in Paris by the renowned urban theorist and spatial philosopher Henri Lefebvre. Observing how the dense agglomeration of the French working class in the center of Paris was being dispersed by politics and policies that moved most of them into high-rise "inner suburbs" called *banlieues,* Lefebvre argued that the working-class population had to rise up and take greater control over the production of urban space. As they became increasingly aware that the geographies in which they lived were being shaped by powerful corporate and state forces, the people must demand their right to the city, *le droit à la ville.*

The idea became a rallying cry of the May 1968 uprising in Paris and was used to mobilize student and worker support. When the uprising failed to meet its objectives, Lefebvre's ideas were buried and largely forgotten for decades, only to be revived in the past two decades, especially after the first English translation in 1991 of his arguably most important work, *La production de l'espace (The Production of Space)*, originally published in 1974. In recent years, as part of a general revival of interest in Lefebvre and urban and spatial issues, the notion of organizing over the right to the city has attracted widespread attention around the world.

A hint of what was to come appeared in 1998 with the European Charter for the Safeguarding of Human Rights in the City. By 2012, more than 350 European cities had approved a related charter specifically focusing on "the right to the city" as a concrete version of universal human rights. The first and only North American city to take the idea seriously was, appropriately enough, Montreal. The National Film Board of Canada produced a film called *Le droit à la ville* in 1972, with Lefebvre leading the discussion (in French) throughout. In 2006, as "groundwork for a new understanding of citizenship and the city," the city of Montreal enacted the Montreal Charter of Rights and Responsibilities (Charte montréalaise des droits et responsabilités). Activist groups using the name Right to the City are today based in Concordia and McGill Universities.[7]

In a separate development, the revival of the right to the city as an organizing principle and focus for strategic activism in the United States reached a significant political threshold in January 2007 with the inaugural meeting of a national coalition that would be called the Right to the City Alliance (RTTC). The meeting took place at the Japanese American Cultural Center in Little Tokyo, downtown Los Angeles. Three objectives were made clear: 1) to begin the process of building collective capacity for local urban struggles so as to become a national movement around the right to the city; 2) to provide a frame and structure to set the stage for regional organizing and for connecting intellectuals to the work being done; 3) to build a national network/alliance that will allow organizations to learn from one another, create national debate on issues affecting urban communities, and help coordinate an expanding national program. Framing the discussion was the broader ambition of asserting a new vision of democracy that would build upon a contemporary understanding of the dynamics of urban and regional development and change.

Addressing gentrification and displacement was at the core of the action programs discussed. A discussion led by a representative from the Miami

Workers Center identified a series of urban restructuring processes that had intensified the problems associated with gentrification over the past thirty years, including the decline in federal support for urban programs, privatization and massive outsourcing of public services, deindustrialization, inflated real estate and housing markets, the increasing gap between rich and poor, and the criminalization of poverty. This "New Gentrification" was seen as the strategic mobilizing focus for the right to the city movement, at least in its early stages. It also tied in well with the growing academic literature on urban restructuring.

New theoretical approaches were also discussed, particularly with regard to the rise of neoliberalism and the uneven effects of globalization and the New Economy. Particular attention was given to the need for regional organizing, especially the creation of regional networks that would extend beyond core urban areas into the periphery, creating something like an extended right to the city region. Also introduced were Henri Lefebvre's original ideas about the colonization of urban space by capital and the culture of consumption, reflected in the cogent words of René Poitevin from NYU: "Right to the city is the response of oppressed communities to the attempt by market forces to reshape the city as if these communities don't matter, as if they don't have every right to be here, and to shape the city in ways that meet their needs and their visions."[8]

At the core of the approach outlined by the Alliance was the strategic objective of creating lasting and effective ties *between separate social movements* and activist struggles based on a shared experience of the injustice and oppression inherent in the social production of urban space. The formation of regional networks around the right to the city concept provided a new and potentially more effective mobilizing and unifying force in fighting all forms of discrimination.

The Right to the City Alliance has become a vital part of what is rapidly becoming a global movement of unusual proportions. Spurring this globalization has been the World Charter of the Rights to the City, which appeared in 2004 in conjunction with the Social Forum of the Americas held in Quito and the World Urban Forum in Barcelona, as well as an ongoing series of UNESCO conferences and publications that have inspired hundreds of European cities to join the RTTC movement. Attempting to draw together the global justice, environmental justice, and human rights movements, the Charter begins by recognizing that the city "is a rich and diversified cultural space that belongs to all its inhabitants," and that everyone "has a Right to the City free of discrimination based on gender, age, health status, income, nationality, ethnicity, migratory condition, or political, religious, or sexual orientation, and to preserve cultural memory and identity."[9]

Citizens are defined to include not just permanent inhabitants but also those "in transit." The "Principles of the Right to the City" include democratic management, full exercise of citizenship and use of economic and cultural resources, equality and nondiscrimination, special protection for vulnerable persons and groups, and economic solidarity and progressive policies. The Charter also recognizes that the Right to the City is not confined to the formal city, thus relating it to regional urbanization and its global extensions: "Urban territories and their rural surroundings are also spaces and locations of the exercise and fulfillment of collective rights as a way of assuring equitable, universal, just, democratic, and sustainable distribution and enjoyment of the resources, wealth, services, goods, and opportunities that cities offer."[10]

The Charter and most of the growing literature on the RTTC refer to Lefebvre's original idea, but there is usually little critical evaluation of the concept. In many cases, the notion seems to be little more than a slightly different way of speaking about human rights in general or merely a generic reference to the need for more democratic forms of planning and public policy. For the most part, Lefebvre's radical approach to urban spatial causality is reduced to softer liberal egalitarianism or normative platitudes about urban justice. One major exception has been the geographer-planner Mark Purcell, a UCLA graduate.

In *Recapturing Democracy*, Purcell presents an insightful reevaluation of Lefebvre's ideas, surveying the recent literature and cautioning against reductionist interpretations of the call for a radical urban metamorphosis, including Lefebvre's often implied narrowing of the struggle to include only the working class as agents of change. The right to the city is seen not just as a right to appropriation, participation, and difference, but more broadly as a *right to space*—the right to inhabit space, wherever one chooses to dwell. In stretching the concept to a larger regional and global scale, Purcell quotes Brenner: "Urban social movements . . . do not merely occur within urban space but strive to transform the socioterritorial organization of capitalism itself on multiple geographical scales. The 'right to the city' . . . thereby expands into a broader 'right to space' both within and beyond the urban scale. Even as processes of global capitalist restructuring radically reorganize the supraurban scalar hierarchies in which cities are embedded, cities remain strategic arenas for sociopolitical struggles which, in turn, have major ramifications for the supraurban geographies of capitalism."[11]

Purcell also argues against orthodox Marxist perspectives, insisting that there are openings in the concept of RTTC to multiple agents and targets, thus widening the scope of political action to include discriminatory and unjust geographies of many kinds, relating to gender, race, sexuality, environmental conditions, and other forms of oppression. This links up with the political philosopher Iris Marion Young's more pluralistic five-sided concept of injustice as oppression, in which class struggle per se focuses primarily around economic exploitation at the workplace and place of residence, while other structures of social advantage and hierarchical power define broader fields of social action related to cultural and political domination and other axes of discrimination not directly or exclusively related to class.[12]

Combining Purcell and Young opens up new possibilities in the converging movements for spatial justice and the democratic right to urban space. The monolithic and focused forms of class struggle inherent in Lefebvre's and Harvey's approaches are expanded and opened up to meet the multifaceted and multiscalar demands for justice in the contemporary world. Most important for the challenges of seeking specifically spatial justice is the implied necessity of building diverse coalitions and networked social movements that extend beyond the narrow and often essentialist channels of the past. In today's world, separate movements to support labor, fight racism, patriarchy, or cultural domination, or achieve peace, respond to global warming, or promote local community development are less likely than ever before to be successful on their own. Crosscutting alliances and coalitions are essential.

In an insightful turn of phrase, Purcell calls the right to the city, especially in the sense of a right to occupy and inhabit space, an organizational and mobilizing "linchpin," suggesting that it forms an integrative umbrella for coalition building, a kind of connective tissue or "glue" that can help to *unite diverse and particularized struggles into larger and more powerful movements.* The new spatial consciousness and its expression in the search for spatial justice provide just such an integrative umbrella. We all experience in one way or another the negative effects of unjust geographies. This makes struggles over space and the right to the city a potentially powerful source of shared identity, determination, and effectiveness in changing the world for the better.

It is not yet possible to evaluate the full impact of the RTTC movement, but it is certainly tempting to make connections between its formation and the development of the Arab Spring and Occupy movements, finding here good examples of how academic theories are taken up by activists and used to advance their objectives.

NOTES

1. Thanks to its editor, Bob Caterrall, the journal *CITY* devoted a large part of two issues to A Forum on Seeking Spatial Justice, with fifteen brief commentaries from academics as well as activists, along with my reactions. See *CITY* 14, no. 6 (2010): 597–635; and *CITY* 15, no. 1 (2011): 64–102. The full list of comments are given in appendix 1, under source 8A.

2. Harold Meyerson, "The Red Sea: How the Janitors Won Their Strike," *L.A. Weekly*, April 28, 2000. For more on Justice for Janitors, see C. Erickson, C. Fisk, R. Milkman, D. Mitchell, and K. Wong, "Justice for Janitors in Los Angeles: Lessons from Three Rounds of Negotiation," *British Journal of Industrial Relations* 40 (2002): 543–67; and Lydia Savage, "Justice for Janitors: Scales of Organizing and Representing Workers," *Antipode* 38 (2006): 648–67.

3. Nancy Cleeland, "Justice for Janitors: Janitors Victory Galvanizes Workers across the Nation," *Los Angeles Times*, April 25, 2000.

4. For more on the LANCER project and other developments in the environmental and related movements in Los Angeles, see Robert Gottlieb, *Reinventing Los Angeles: Nature and Community in the Global City* (Cambridge, MA: MIT Press, 2007); and R. Gottlieb, M. Villianatos, R. Freer, and P. Dreir, *The Next Los Angeles: The Struggle for a Livable City* (Berkeley and Los Angeles: University of California Press, 2005). Gottlieb, a journalist turned academic, taught for many years in Urban Planning at UCLA before moving to an endowed chair at Occidental College.

5. Eric Mann (with the Planning Committee of the Bus Riders Union), *A New Vision for Urban Transportation: The Bus Riders Union Makes History at the Intersection of Mass Transit, Civil Rights, and the Environment* (Los Angeles: Labor/ Community Strategy Center, 1966).

6. A series of courses, ranging from undergraduate honors seminars to Community Scholars projects, were held in the UCLA Urban Planning Department, leading to a variety of reports, such as *Researching Wal-Mart: A Guide to an Annotated Bibliography* and *Wal-Mart and Wal-Martization: Challenges for Labor and Urban Planning*, both mentored by Jackie Leavitt, and *The Price We Pay for Wal-Mart*, published by the ILWU Educational Committee with the assistance of Goetz Wolff and three urban planning graduate students. The latter report included detailed comparisons between Wal-Mart and Costco, a more progressive and efficient big-box retailer.

7. It is interesting to note that the city charter in Montreal emerged in part to guide the formation of a new regional organization of the metropolis, which later fell apart due to linguistic and other differences. In addition to being advanced by

the two university-based activist groups, the right to the city idea has become part of a growing citizens movement that linked to (and partially absorbed) an Occupy Montreal group in 2012. My thanks to Catherine Bella and Alexis Sornin of the Canadian Centre for Architecture in Montreal, where I spent a productive six weeks finishing the first draft of this book in July and August 2012.

8. The quote is taken from *Right to the City: Notes from the Inaugural Convening,* 2007, available from Right to the City, 152 W. Thirty-Second Street, Los Angeles, CA 9007. See also www.righttothecity.org. Some eastern voices ignore this initial meeting. David Harvey, for example, in his recent book *Rebel Cities: From the Right to the City to the Urban Revolution* (New York: Verso, 2012), claims the Alliance started in Atlanta in June 2007, when "all manner of social movements came together at the US Social Forum . . . and decided to form a national Right to the City Alliance," adding, incorrectly, that "they did so without for the most part knowing Lefebvre's name."

9. Habitat International Coalition, *World Charter for the Right to the City* (Paris: UNESCO, 2005).

10. Ibid.

11. Mark Purcell, *Recapturing Democracy: Neoliberalization and the Struggle for Alternative Urban Futures* (New York: Routledge 2008), 102. See also Purcell, "Excavating Lefebvre: The Right to the City and Its Urban Politics of the Inhabitant," *Geojournal* 58 (2002): 99–108.

12. Iris Marion Young, *Justice and the Politics of Difference* (Princeton, NJ: Princeton University Press, 1990). Young also has important observations on "democratic regionalism" in *Inclusion and Democracy* (New York: Oxford University Press, 2000).

NINE

Occupy Los Angeles

A VERY CONTEMPORARY CONCLUSION

Every chapter of *My Los Angeles* has been shaped by an assertive spatial perspective that builds on the notion that the material geographies which we produce and in which we live have a significant effect on our lives and our histories. Particularly powerful in this geographical effect is what can roughly be described as *urban spatial causality,* the explanatory force that derives from the stimulus of urban agglomeration, from the way urban life is spatially organized.

Examples of the force that emanates from urban agglomeration have been central to understanding the urban restructuring process and the rise of regional urbanization in Los Angeles. The clustering of industrial firms—in aerospace and entertainment, as well as in jewelry and furniture manufacturing—has been an essential impetus in the development of the regional economy, while the huge agglomeration of the working poor in the core of Los Angeles has been an important generative force in the resurgence of successful and diverse labor-community coalitions, as well as in sustaining an expanding New Economy. The social production of urban space does not just create a material background or environment for social processes to unfold; it also serves as an active and influential force in itself, shaping social life and societal development.[1]

In this brief conclusion, I take the idea of urban spatial causality and agglomeration effects further into the immediate present and the imminent future, to explore how such contemporary movements as those associated with the Arab Spring and Occupy Wall Street feed off the positive stimulus of urban agglomeration and the geopolitical consciousness associated with it. The spatial organization of the city region in this sense is both a manifestation of the unjust effects of neoliberal globalization and the New Economy of "flexible capitalism" and an activating force for new spatially informed social movements aimed at (although not always successfully) changing the world for the better.

While earlier roots can be found for what has been called the Arab Spring, and it is probably too early to measure its actual achievements, the organized uprising in Tahrir Square in Cairo and its diffusion around the world can be seen as a representative starting point for a new politics shaped by agglomeration effects and struggles over the right to the city, even if not explicitly expressed as such. By now, many have noted the repeated significance of dense public gatherings in spaces such as Tahrir Square (now called Freedom Square), Puerta del Sol in Madrid, and Syntagma Square in Athens in stimulating strategically emancipatory processes. Most sympathetic outsiders observing these and subsequent events have tended to emphasize the expanded role of social media and social networking, and there is no doubt that new technologies played an important part in mobilizing and informing participants and spreading the word. But little would have happened without the stimulating ideas and strategies—the creative buzz—generated by the concentrated clustering of people and protesters in urban public spaces.

It is difficult to find hard proof for this argument, and it probably would never have been seriously proposed were it not for the findings of geographical economists and others about agglomeration effects and what they now call "Jane Jacobs externalities." Giving such explanatory power to urban spatiality is uncommon and remains uncomfortable for most scholars unaccustomed to geographical causality of any kind. Although there is no doubt that the stimulus of urban agglomeration exists and that it may be a primary factor in economic development, technological innovation, cultural creativity, and perhaps even the origin and development of urban social movements, we still know very little about it. Are big agglomerations, for example, always more generative than smaller ones? Can agglomerations be too big or too small to have any effect? What makes one agglomeration more generative than another? Considering present trends, is a regional network of agglomerations more or less innovative than one large central city? Is regional urbanization (or, for that matter, the Internet) increasing or diminishing innovative agglomeration effects? What is the role of face-to-face interaction in an age of instant electronic communication?

There are still many who are unwilling to accept any form of urban spatial causality. After all, there is little in the literature to conclusively support such claims, and surely we must avoid simplistic environmental or geographic determinism. Much of this discomfort and fear arises, however, from a traditional physical and externalized view of urban space—space seen only as material form and patterning. The spatial perspective behind an understanding of urban spatial causality starts with the recognition that urban space, like all the geographies in which we live, is *socially produced*. It represents a kind of "second nature" that is as much an integral part of human societies as kinship relations or politics. If this socialized geography is unjust and inequitable, with some groups suffering much more than others from its spatial structures of advantage and disadvantage, we must organize to change the geography we have socially created (or which has been created for us by powerful others). This is the basic principle behind the search for socio-spatial justice.

This need to change the unjust geographies in which we live was associated not only with the concept of the right to the city that arose in Paris in 1968; it was also apparent in the related cry, "Changer la ville pour changer la vie" (Change the city to change life). I see this spirit behind the momentum of the Arab Spring and nearly everything about the Occupy movement, which started with Occupy Wall Street but has spread to major cities almost everywhere, most often sparked by dense gatherings in public spaces, from Zuccotti Park in Manhattan to City Hall Lawn in Los Angeles.

The list of generative public spaces of protest goes well beyond the sites mentioned, to include Paternoster Square and the lawn in front of Saint Paul's Cathedral (as well as the Stock Exchange) in London, Saint Andrews Square in Edinburgh, Congress Square and the Stock Exchange in Ljubljana, Alexanderplatz and the Brandenburg Gate in Berlin, Schlossplatz in Stuttgart, and Narinkkatori Square in Helsinki. It is not just that "space matters" in these developments but that spatial agglomeration and clustering—the compulsion of proximity, as Harvey Molotch and Dierdre Boden describe it—become in themselves a generative force for new ideas, strategies, and potentially transformative social action.[2]

OCCUPY WALL STREET

The social movement sparked by Occupy Wall Street was in part the brainchild of the Estonian "mystical anarchist" Kalle Lasn, Canadian founder and editor-in-chief of the radical magazine *Adbusters*. Lasn proclaimed in June 2011 that "America needs its own Tahrir." Soon after, he registered the website OccupyWallStreet.org. One other possible name he thought of was AcampadaWallStreet.org, to honor the Acampadasol or 15-M movement in Madrid, where on May 15, 2011, many thousands of demonstrators *(indignados)* gathered in Puerta del Sol, the city's central and best-known square, to protest imposed austerity and the New Economy. Lasn's continuing campaign to "kill capitalism" through new tactics has contributed to Occupy's commitment to "horizontal" democracy and leaderlessness.[3]

To understand the Occupy movement, one must have some grasp of the meaning of *horizontality*—and to do this requires a look back at developments in Argentina after the breakdown of its neoliberal government in 2001. *Horizontalidad* was a vital part of the new social movements that arose from the crisis of neoliberalism with the aim of creating a radically autonomous, antihierarchical, and highly participatory democracy free from institutional and other constraints. Argentina in the late 1990s expressed an extreme form of neoliberal politics and policy, with a shrinking government sector and heavy dependence on global markets. In a national microcosm and harbinger of the worldwide crash of 2008, Argentinian neoliberalism disintegrated in 2001. Into this opening flowed a number of innovative popular movements seeking to move as far as possible from the remembered clutches of the neoliberal state and market.

At the vanguard of these movements was a resurgence of social anarchism that built upon earlier notions of *autogestion,* self-management, and absolute democracy. Leading the way were new movements in postneoliberal Argentina, including such organizations as the Unemployed Workers Movement, the Piqueteros (who practiced direct action to interrupt the production and circulation of commodities), and *asambleas barriales,* neighborhood assemblies that formed the main base for decision-making without centralized authority. The participating middle classes also created new movements, such as *empresas recuperadas,* takeovers of bankrupted factories that promoted worker self-management and engendered a new sense of confederalism. In a way, these developments reflected renewed experiments with left libertarianism, just as the later Tea Party movement in the United States, with a much more conservative civil society, found inspiration in right-wing libertarian concepts.

The Argentinian case has been written up in detail by the lawyer-journalist Marina Sitrin.[4] While many ignore these Argentinian roots, the spirit of horizontal democracy and autonomous self-management, the vital role of general assemblies, and deep suspicion of all forms of centralized authority have infiltrated the Occupy movement all over the world. Horizontal democracy helps to keep the aims and objectives of the movement open ended, keeping all possibilities alive. Specific political or policy goals and agendas tend to be avoided.

These ideas and inclinations have marked the Occupy movement from the start, and some argue they also influenced the events in Tahrir Square and elsewhere in the Arab world, as well as the still ongoing 15-M Indignados movement in Spain and the Greek resistance to imposed austerity. It can be argued that just as the destruction of neoliberal capitalism in Argentina inspired new social and spatial movements, the Great Crash of 2008 led to experimental movements of a different kind. Particularly important for our story here is the emphasis on socio-spatial equality and justice of the movements, symbolized by and focused on the growing chasm between the super-rich 1 percent and the rest, and the strategic importance of social gatherings in strategically located public spaces.

After the limits of neoliberal capitalism were brutally revealed in 2008, there could be no better place to start a social movement than Wall Street. The spaces behind the formidable financial walls of southern Manhattan were so heavily guarded, however, that the movement had to shift to alternative strategic sites. Occupy Wall Street began its occupation in Zuccotti Park on September 17, 2011. The park, named after a chairman of the company that now owns it and recently redubbed Liberty Square (it is adjacent to Liberty Plaza) was and is a very special space. It was created in 1968 adjacent to a giant building owned by U.S. Steel, as the corporation reacted to the Fordist deindustrialization of the 1960s by shifting its assets to urban real estate. The skyscraping height of One Liberty Plaza was based on a negotiated zoning variance that created the park.

The building and park were severely damaged in the September 11 attacks and reopened in 2006. Not only was the site almost equidistant from Ground Zero, the New York Stock Exchange, and the New York Federal Reserve, but it was a remarkably contradictory invention called a privately owned public space, or POPS. As part of the POPS agreement, the park had to stay open twenty-four hours and therefore served a vital purpose for the Occupiers. On November 15, the police closed the park (illegally?), but the movement continued to stir. Protesters attempted to reoccupy the park on New Year's Eve but were violently repelled by police, with nearly seventy arrested. Later, at least ten thousand would march to an even more central and symbolic site, Times Square, as the movement diffused to other spaces.

Occupy Wall Street stimulated similar protests around the world, nearly all focused in a local public space and interconnected via social networking media. In total, 951 cities erupted in 82 countries, from Oakland to Santiago de Chile, from Madrid to Johannesburg, from Rome to Hong Kong, to mention some of the largest and most vigorous demonstrations. Not surprisingly, it also reached deep into Southern California.

OCCUPY LA-OC

The Occupy movement in the Los Angeles urban region has been, as one might expect, both polycentric and clearly centered. Today, for example, there are Occupy movements in Long Beach, the San Fernando Valley, South Gate, Pico Rivera, Ontario, and Riverside, in addition to such focused groups as Occupy the Hood, Occupy Skid Row, Occupy Rose Parade, Occupy Fights Off Foreclosures, Occupy LAUSD (United School District), and Occupy the Military Industrial Complex. A vigorous Occupy Orange County network has developed with (sequentially) active foci in Santa Ana, Irvine, Huntington Beach, and Fullerton. For the most part, however, Occupy LA has been centered in the public space in front of iconic City Hall, adjacent to the second-largest cluster of government employment in the United States after Washington, D.C. (see figure 8).

Here is a brief chronology of Occupy Los Angeles:

October 1, 2011—Occupation of lawn at Los Angeles City Hall begins. Occupy LA's leaderless general assembly (GA) begins meeting amid encampment of tents.

October 5, 2011—LA City Council passes resolution supporting Occupy objectives (see below); LA mayor gives ponchos to Occupiers.

October 15, 2011—Global Day of Action, commemorating events in Spain. Rallies take place in nearly one thousand cities around the world.

November 17, 2011—Day of Action marks two-month anniversary of Occupy Wall Street movement. In New York City, thirty thousand march in the streets. In Los Angeles, labor union members march in solidarity, as a break-off wing of Occupy members, upset by union

OCCUPY

LOS ANGELES

People of Los Angeles,
we will occupy our city
for the 99% of the world.
We will not be silent.

October 1, 2011

LA City Hall
200 N Spring Street

Bring tents, sleeping bags,
food, supplies, friends.

http://on.fb.me/q1Jzpz
#occupyla

FIGURE 8 Occupy LA flier (from Occupy LA website).

support, organize a countermarch to Bank of America tower. Thirty are arrested.

November 19, 2011—Students from the University California at Davis pepper-sprayed by campus police. The action against nonviolent student protesters on campus garners media attention and evokes public outrage.

November 29, 2011—1,350 LAPD officers raid and drive off Occupy LA, arresting 292 in one of the last and least violent police actions against the Occupy movement. Occupy LA branches off in many directions, as it increases ties with Occupy OC.

May 1, 2012—Occupy resurfaces downtown, organizes "four winds" demonstration (marches from north, south, east, and west), and holds general assembly in Pershing Square, traditional site for May Day demonstrations in the past.

July 12–13, 2012—Occupy-related chalk artists brutally stopped by police at monthly ArtWalk downtown. Occupy LA files complaints against LAPD for injuries to protesting chalkers.

July 24, 2012—Occupy LA joins Occupy Orange County for joint protest against the fatal shooting of unarmed Manuel Angel Diaz by Anaheim police on July 21. Members of Occupy LA and Occupy OC train protestors in nonviolent protest at Stoddard Park in Anaheim. Occupy takes up protest location in front of Disneyland on July 28.

Since the August 2012 protest by chalk artists at the monthly ArtWalk, there has been little major activity directly under the Occupy LA banner. Smaller groups that link themselves to Occupy continue to protest home foreclosures, and there was some participation in assisting storm relief after Superstorm Sandy in October 2012. Importantly, however, Occupy LA continues to hold general assembly meetings, maintains a lively website (www .occupylosangeles.org), and tries to develop and keep alive ties with other branches of the Occupy movement nationally as well as locally.

Although Occupy efforts in New York and Oakland (described in a *New York Times Magazine* article on July 29, 2012, as the "last refuge of radical America" and the "capital of anti-capitalism") received the most media attention, Occupy LA has many distinctive features that help us understand more about the local and global expressions of the Occupy movement. For example, Occupy LA was the largest encampment after the closure of Zuccotti Park, with at least 485 tents regularly in City Hall Park. The occupation also lasted longer than almost any other (fifty-six days) and, in contrast to Oakland and elsewhere, the police were relatively nonviolent in evicting the occupiers from the park.

In many ways, Occupy LA was also more successful than any other occupation in getting its demands and goals understood and accepted locally, in large part due to the heritage of its innovative labor-community coalition building. Occupy LA did not have to "float alone" without a strong and progressive civil society to fall back on.

An Exceptionally Supportive Local Power Base

What distinguished Occupy LA from the Occupy movement in most other cities and regions was the solid foundation of powerful and innovative labor-community coalitions, along with close ties between the diverse communities of LA and at least some parts of the region's universities. In other words, Occupy LA has had an exceptionally supportive local power base from the start.[5] Nowhere else, at least among the larger occupations, was there greater and more open public support from unions and local government. Unionized teachers joined students and parents in Occupy LA's protest against the LA

Unified School District's cuts in services, while SEIU and other labor unions marched with Occupy LA on May Day 2012 to celebrate the workers' justice movement. However, a few protesters, probably not familiar with the foundation of grassroots coalitions in LA or else entirely absorbed by the leaderless philosophy of horizontal democracy, saw unions as part of the problem and broke away from the union-led march to move instead to the Bank of America office building.

But nothing anywhere compared with the Los Angeles City Council's remarkable resolution expressing its support for Occupy LA. The resolution was made public on October 5, a rainy day on which the mayor gave out one hundred ponchos and the City Council president told the protesters in front of City Hall, "Stay as long as you need, we're here to support you." A week later, the resolution passed unanimously. The resolution effectively summarized the demands and goals of Occupy LA and lots more.[6] Here is a sampling of the City Council resolution:

> WHEREAS, Angelenos, like citizens across the United States, are reeling from a continuing economic crisis that threatens our fiscal stability and quality of life
>
> WHEREAS, "Occupy Los Angeles" is fueled by Angelenos . . . in solidarity with and support for the national movement started by the "Occupy Wall Street" protests . . . 17 days ago
>
> WHEREAS, on Saturday, October 1st, 2011, "Occupy Los Angeles" started a peaceful protest on the Lawn of Los Angeles City Hall . . . and demonstrators are working to secure permits to continue the protest
>
> WHEREAS, the "Occupy" demonstrations are a rapidly growing movement with the shared goal of urging U.S. citizens to peaceably assemble and occupy public space in order to create a shared dialogue by which to address the problems and generate solutions for economically distressed Americans
>
> WHEREAS, today corporations hold undue influence and power in our country, and the key to this power is . . . the Supreme Court's recent 5–4 ruling in *Citizens United v. the Federal Election Commission* [which] rolled back legal restrictions on corporate spending in the electoral process, consequently influencing the selection of candidates, the outcome of elections, and policy decisions—threatening the voices of the people
>
> WHEREAS, . . . over 25 million Americans who seek work are unemployed; more than 50 million Americans are forced to live without health insurance; and, even using our current poverty measure that is widely

recognized to be inadequate and outdated, more than 1 in 5 children are growing up poor

WHEREAS, . . . income inequality in the United States is the highest in the world among any advanced industrial nation, with wide-spread inequities in health outcomes by income, race, and gender

WHEREAS, over the past 30 years, both the average and the median wage in America has remained almost stagnant . . . and almost all the gains to the economy have accrued to the very top income earners—largely the top 1%, who now control 40% of the wealth in the United States

WHEREAS, the top 1 percent of Americans own half of the country's stocks, bonds, and mutual funds; and the 400 richest Americans at the top control more than the 180 million Americans at the bottom

WHEREAS, one of the largest problems causing our economy to continue to flounder is the foreclosure crisis, with some banks continuing the use of flawed, and in some cases fraudulent, procedures to flood the market. . . . California has been particularly hard-hit. . . . 1 in 5 foreclosures are in California . . . [a total of] 1.2 million since 2008 . . . [with] property tax losses estimated at $4 billion

WHEREAS, on March 5, 2010, the Los Angeles City Council unanimously passed the Responsible Banking measure . . . which would create a Responsible Banking program . . . scoring financial institutions . . . along a "Community Reinvestment Score" that measures the institution's Los Angeles investments in an objective and data-driven manner

NOW, THEREFORE, BE IT RESOLVED, with concurrence of the Mayor, that by the adoption of the Resolution, the City of Los Angeles hereby stands in SUPPORT for the continuation of the peaceful and vibrant exercise in First Amendment Rights carried out by Occupy Los Angeles.

Weak indications of local support for Occupy Orange County were initially expressed in Santa Ana, the county seat, but were quickly withdrawn. Much stronger support came from the City Council of Irvine. When the occupation there was disbanded, the movement shifted to Huntington Beach (hardcore punk and surfing capital of Southern California) and later to Fullerton, where the city council, after 130 days of local occupation, passed two of three proposed resolutions, the first involving local community investment by banks and the second protecting university students from predatory lending. The third resolution, which did not carry, was the most ambitious, calling for a rejection of the concept of corporate/union personhood and opposition to the Citizens United Supreme Court decision, a focal point for the Occupy movement across the country.[7]

Occupy OC would join with Occupy LA in a new grouping called #Occupy Together. The Occupy OC website (www.occupy-oc.org/declaration/) included the following declaration:

#Occupy Together—Declaration of Occupation

As we gather together in solidarity to express a feeling of mass injustice, we must not lose sight of what brought us together. We write so that all people who feel wronged by the corporate forces of the world can know that we are your allies. As one people, united, we acknowledge the reality: that the future of the human race requires the cooperation of its members; that our system must protect our rights, and upon corruption of that system, it is up to the individuals to protect their own rights, and those of their neighbors; that a democratic government derives its just power from the people, but corporations do not seek consent to extract wealth from the people and the Earth; and that no true democracy is attainable when the process is determined by economic power. We come to you at a time when corporations, which place profit over people, self-interest over justice, and oppression over equality, run our governments. We have peaceably assembled here, as is our right, to let these facts be known.

- They have taken our houses through an illegal foreclosure process, despite not having the original mortgage.
- They have taken bailouts from taxpayers with impunity, and continue to give executives exorbitant bonuses.
- They have perpetuated inequality and discrimination in the workplace based on age, the color of one's skin, sex, gender identity and sexual orientation.
- They have poisoned the food supply through negligence, and undermined the farming system through monopolization.
- They have profited off of the torture, confinement, and cruel treatment of countless animals, and actively hide these practices.
- They have continuously sought to strip employees of the right to negotiate for better pay and safer working conditions.
- They have held students hostage with tens of thousands of dollars of debt on education, which is itself a human right.
- They have consistently outsourced labor and used that outsourcing as leverage to cut workers' healthcare and pay.
- They have influenced the courts to achieve the same rights as people, with none of the culpability or responsibility.
- They have spent millions of dollars on legal teams that look for ways to get them out of contracts in regards to health insurance.

- They have sold our privacy as a commodity.
- They have used the military and police force to prevent freedom of the press.
- They have deliberately declined to recall faulty products endangering lives in pursuit of profit.
- They determine economic policy, despite the catastrophic failures their policies have produced and continue to produce.
- They have donated large sums of money to politicians, who are responsible for regulating them.
- They continue to block alternate forms of energy to keep us dependent on oil.
- They continue to block generic forms of medicine that could save people's lives or provide relief in order to protect investments that have already turned a substantial profit.
- They have purposely covered up oil spills, accidents, faulty bookkeeping, and inactive ingredients in pursuit of profit.
- They purposefully keep people misinformed and fearful through their control of the media.
- They have accepted private contracts to murder prisoners even when presented with serious doubts about their guilt.
- They have perpetuated colonialism at home and abroad.
- They have participated in the torture and murder of innocent civilians overseas.
- They continue to create weapons of mass destruction in order to receive government contracts.

To the people of the world: We, the Los Angeles General Assembly occupying City Hall Park in Downtown Los Angeles urge you to assert your power. Exercise your right to peaceably assemble; occupy public space; create a process to address the problems we face, and generate solutions accessible to everyone. To all communities that take action and form groups in the spirit of direct democracy, we offer support, documentation, and all of the resources at our disposal.

In few places have the demands of the Occupy movement been made so explicit and detailed. In some ways, this has pushed the local movement to the limits of horizontal democracy and agendaless strategies while harnessing the power of local particularities. Another example of this localization has been the active participation of graffiti artists and muralists.

FIGURE 9 *Solidarity with Tahrir Square,* graffiti-mural by Mear One. Aerosol paint on brick wall. Photograph by Stefano Bloch.

Supportive Connections with Local Muralists and Graffiti Artists

Still another distinctive feature of Occupy LA has been its unusually productive linkage to the vigorous local movement of graffiti writers and muralists, especially in the strategic occupations of downtown. Graffiti artists and muralists have been instrumental in popularizing the Occupy movement through the creation of new murals ranging from signs announcing Occupy LA to pictures of freedom fighters in Tahrir Square (see figures 9 and 10).

Graffiti writers have traditionally focused on downtown, writing on freeway walls and the closed shutters of the business district after its occupants disappeared in the evenings. Downtown has also traditionally been a basing point for "All City" bombing missions, coordinated actions aimed at expressing the geographic extent and power of the local graffiti movement, as powerful and expressive as any in the country. Graffiti artists helped Occupy members popularize the movement with original murals, pieces of public art, and hand-painted signs. Graffiti writers have also been important in helping to organize and lead break-out movements focusing on banks and other institutions downtown.

FIGURE 10 *New World Order,* graffiti-mural by Mear One. Aerosol paint on brick wall. Photograph by Stefano Bloch.

In addition to being familiar with downtown LA as a location for wall bombing, many graffiti writers are employed as bike messengers downtown. One well-known crew (DTLA, or Downtown LA) has worked to connect graffiti artists with Occupy members through the rapidly growing bikers movement in LA. Graffiti bike riders are highly politicized, organizing sanctioned and unsanctioned midnight bike rides through downtown in addition to hanging around graffiti yards such as Belmont (a "safe" showplace site for graffiti artists) and under the bridges to the Museum of Contemporary Art and the Grand Avenue axis. Recently, graffiti writers and bike riders Cache and Eye One have been instrumental in organizing, respectively, the very popular CicLAvia monthly bike ride through nine miles of closed city streets and the Midnight Drag Race through the Second Street Tunnel in downtown (see figure 11).

Mear One, an internationally known graffiti artist, recently returned from a world tour to publicize his work as well as the Occupy movement. In a recent interview with Stefano Bloch, a former graffiti artist himself and now a Mellon Scholar at Brown University, Mear One proclaimed, "I am taking the Occupy message to the streets in the form of enlightening political murals that speak to the 99% everywhere."

A recent Mear One graffiti-mural in London features the Rothschilds, Morgans, and other wizards of Wall Street and the financial City of London playing monopoly on the backs of the working class. Behind them is the

FIGURE 11 *CycleLAVia,* mural for CicLAvia by Cache and Eye One. Photo by Stefano Bloch.

truncated and cyclopic pyramid that appears on U.S. currency and is the Freemasons' symbol. Behind that is a polluted world of smoke-belching nuclear reactors; to the right, a woman and child seeking protection; to the left, a protester carrying a sign saying "THE NEW WORLD ORDER IS THE ENEMY OF HUMANITY" (fig. 12).

In May 2013, Mear One joined with Ben Slow, a member of Occupy from London, to produce a new mural in Silver Lake. In an interview with Bloch, Slow stated, "Occupy has splintered and become disorganized, so I bring my political statements back to the streets. This is what Occupy is all about. Collaborating with people from other places and reaching people through street art and murals."

Occupy LA has become a window on the remarkable history of graffiti writing and mural artistry in Los Angeles. The mural movement began in the interwar years with a controversial work by David Alfaro Siqueiros, *América Tropical,* which depicts a Mexican peasant chained to a post capped by an American eagle and near an armed U.S. soldier. As noted earlier, it first appeared on a wall visible from Olvera Street in downtown LA, was white-washed about a week later for being too radical, became a target for restoration in 1969 as part of the Chicano movement, and after more than a decade of indecision and political critique, was opened to the public in October 2012 under the aegis of the Getty Foundation. Siqueiros, a Mexican Communist

FIGURE 12 *The New World Order Is the Enemy of Humanity*, graffiti-mural by Mear One on Brick Lane in the Shoreditch area of East London. Photograph by Mear One.

Party member, was deported soon after finishing the mural. He later relocated to New York, where he became internationally known as the first to use spray paint in his art and the originator of the familiar bulbous graffiti writing. Some say he taught drip painting to Jackson Pollack.

Until the late 1990s, the mural movement in LA and the closely allied graffiti writing were highly politicized, mainly in regard to Chicano/a identity and protest. Over the last fifteen years or so, the movement, the murals, and the graffiti art have become less specifically Chicano/a and more generically political. This broader politicization led to the connection with Occupy LA.[8]

An understanding of the graffiti-muralist movement is necessary to make sense of recent battles between the police and Occupy chalk artists, called "chalktivists" by the media. On July 12, 2012, during the monthly ArtWalk downtown, police and Occupy protesters clashed on the corner of Fifth Street and Spring, near Skid Row, site of the largest concentration of homeless people in the United States. Police had dispersed chalking protesters before, and on this day they were unusually determined not to allow chalk protests. Chalking, said an LAPD captain, is "vandalism," not a protected form of speech. More than fifteen protesters were arrested and four police officers were injured in the confrontation.

To some extent, police equate the chalktivists with "illegal" graffiti writers, an idea reinforced by Occupy members chanting "Whose streets? Our streets," echoing the take-back-the-streets slogans of the graffiti movement. A special document, "Chalkupy the World," was produced and sent around the world to stimulate commitment and community. The next monthly ArtWalk, in August 2012, was again charged with tension between police and Occupy members, including some chalkers from Oakland, but major confrontations were avoided. Peaceful celebrations centered in Pershing Square.

It was clear, however, that the downtown chalkers' movement had become an integral part of Occupy LA. Even though Occupiers have no immediate plans to fill LA's public spaces en masse as they did in 2011, graffiti writers continue to take the Occupy aesthetic and message to the walls, making it clear that Occupy has become an indelible part of the urban landscape.

A FINAL POINT

Looking back on all that has been said in this chapter, several summary conclusions about the particularities of the Los Angeles experience suggest themselves. I emphasize the "particular" not to oppose it to the general trend-setting features of LA's move through urban restructuring to regional urbanization, for I think the particular and the general feed into each other. Learning from LA requires an appreciation of both its particular and its generalizable features.

Over the thirty years before the crash of 2008, Los Angeles emerged from its archly conservative past as one of the most liberal and progressive city regions in the United States, challenging if not shattering long-standing stereotypes. Powerful forces of resistance arose from new labor-community coalitions that shielded the region from some of the worst effects of neoconservative attacks on the welfare state, civil liberties, and the New Deal tradition that devastated workers and the poor in much of the rest of the country. The major exception had to do with political and economic polarization, as the gap between rich and poor widened as much if not more than in any other urban region over this period, mainly reflecting the leading role played by LA in the development of the New Economy. Unfortunately, the cries of concern over these worsening inequalities were hardly heard outside LA.

Always a field of opposites, from utopian and dystopian visions to its combination of intensified deindustrialization and reindustrialization, LA saw new tensions arising from its liberal ascendance and deepening socioeconomic inequalities, leading to what can be considered the first major explosion of a new era of urban politics in the Justice Riots of 1992. While blurred by media misinterpretations and political spin-doctoring, the events of 1992 in Los Angeles were generated not so much by the same old race-related upheavals or class-generated protests of the past as by more eclectic expressions of anger and frustration over the injustices of the New Economy, the uneven impact of globalization, and the distorted geographies they had produced—described earlier as a shift from a long period of crisis-generated restructuring to the onset of restructuring-generated crises.

For many reasons, including a persistent bias against seeing Los Angeles as a center for progressive if not radical politics, the lessons of 1992—signaling that the concentration of wealth in a small minority (1 percent?) while growing poverty and homelessness prevailed elsewhere was not tolerable—were not felt to any significant degree outside LA. When such radically innovative events as the Bus Riders Union consent decree of 1996 threatened to spread elsewhere, the biased U.S. Supreme Court was marshaled to prevent any equity-oriented legal precedent from diffusing to the rest of the country. In some ways, one could say that the Justice Riots were the only major expression, in the United States at least, of discontent with rising income inequality—now alleged to be the greatest in U.S. history—until Occupy Wall Street and its successors.

That it took nearly four years after the crash of 2008 for something resembling a social movement to arise over the widening wealth gap, even with the exposure of neoliberal capitalism's fraudulent ideology and corrupted policies, tells a sad tale of political quiescence in America and much of the rest of the industrial world. Although they have accelerated in the past decade, the downward trend in average wages and other signals of economic decline in the United States have been evident for at least thirty years. While the political vacuum right of center has been filled by the media-generated and extremist national movement of Tea Party supporters, many inspired by conservative forms of libertarian anarchism, there was no equivalent growth on the extreme left of center, where the noisiest sounds seem to be coming from a very small cadre of violence-prone (left libertarian) anarchists.

The Occupy movement entered this vacuum with its own soft brand of anarchism defined around a notion of horizontal democracy, with all forms of authority and leadership under suspicion. Growing out of fears of co-optation and some misunderstandings of the distinctive features of local social movements, vigorous City Council support and strong union participation in Occupy LA, there were some vehement negative responses. A small minority of activists noted that City Council members over the years have received millions of dollars in corporate "donations' and worried that "pushy" local unions were trying to control the Occupy movement. The pairing of unions with corporate interests in the Citizens United decision was also a factor. These strong local supporters, it was argued, are part of the problem, not the solution. Little was done accordingly to build upon these special local opportunities.

Exposed here is one of the most intense internal divisions and political challenges in the Occupy movement as it tries to survive after spreading around the world: how pure and constant should the desire to avoid all forms of leadership and authority be? Should everything that flows from the top down be rejected? Does this commitment to horizontality make it impossible to develop and fight for specific demands and goals? Related here are such questions as how absolute must claims of antiglobalization and, indeed, anticapitalism be? Is nothing short of total revolution acceptable?

The politicized youth of the Internet generation, familiar with the anarchic claims of the "network society," are committed to no constraints on freedoms of speech and expression and, similarly, no interference from centralized authority, be it corporations, government, or unions. This may be acceptable policy for the movement as a whole—a rejection of top-down or hierarchical expressions of support in favor of maximizing horizontal or lateral connections—but are there occasionally special conditions that make for exceptions to the rule?

The Los Angeles experience with the Occupy movement does not provide unequivocal answers to these questions, but it presents a point of view that needs to be recognized by all movement participants and supporters. Occupy LA has been somewhat different from other Occupy movements, including Occupy Wall Street. It has lasted longer than most at its original site, has received unusually strong support from the local political culture, and despite strong commitments to horizontal democracy, has been more programmatic and explicit in its goals and demands. I think it will also be more effective in its impact on contemporary urban and national politics.

Questions about leadership and commitment to horizontality, related struggles over local democracy and sociospatial justice, the need to address increasing socioeconomic inequality and other oppressive effects of globalization and the New Economy are not just issues for the Occupy movement; they need to become the focal points for politics and policy formation and for the organization of grassroots social movements throughout the country. Here again there is an opportunity to learn from LA. To do so, however, requires that the persistent biases against Los Angeles be set aside to allow for a serious appreciation of both the unique and general characteristics of the Los Angeles experience with urban restructuring and regional urbanization. I will be pleased if *My Los Angeles* contributes to this process.

NOTES

1. As Jane Jacobs once noted, this generative force of urban agglomeration arises not because people are smarter in cities but rather due to the creative stimulus of intensified social interaction brought about by the combination of proximity and density. Jacobs has been the fundamental reference for nearly all contemporary studies on urbanization economies and the generative effects of cities, from Nobel-prize-winning economists to Richard Florida's popular writings on creative cities.

2. Dierdre Boden and Harvey Molotch, "The Compulsion of Proximity," in *Now/Here: Space, Time, and Modernity,* ed. R. Friedland and D. Boden (Berkeley and Los Angeles: University of California Press, 1994), 257–86. They also provide a

vivid sociological description of the spatial stimulus of agglomeration: the thickness of copresent social interaction.

3. Lasn's most recent work is *Meme Wars: The Creative Destruction of Neoclassical Economics* (London: Penguin, 2013), a call to economics students in particular to rise up and protest against conservative and neoliberal teachers and teachings.

4. First published in 2005 in Spanish as *Horizontalidad* and then in English as *Horizontalism: Voices of Popular Power in Argentina* (Oakland, CA, and Edinburgh: AK Press, 2006). A more recent work by Sitrin is *Everyday Revolutions: Horizontalism and Autonomy in Argentina* (London: Zed Press, 2012).

5. I was reminded of the importance and strength of these supportive coalitions when I lectured on seeking spatial justice at Harvard's Graduate School of Design a few years ago. After I spoke about the innovative community benefit agreements pioneered by LAANE and Madeline Janis, a local activist jumped up to say that the CBAs in his city had failed miserably. How he described this failure was revealing. Without a strong and vigilant foundation of local coalitions, developers could create local "coalitions" of their own and negotiate easy terms while progressive action groups complained fruitlessly from outside.

6. For a copy of the resolution, see the *Public Intelligence* webpage for October 6, 2011, available at http://publicintelligence.net/los-angeles-city-council-resolution-in-support-of-occupy-la/.

7. For more on the Fullerton occupation, see Samantha Schaefer and Lou Ponsi, "Occupy O.C. Protesters Set Up in Fullerton," *Orange County Register*, January 11, 2012.

8. For an excellent and vividly illustrated history and geography of the graffiti and muralist movement in LA, see Stefano Bloch, "The Changing Face of Wall Space: Graffiti-Murals in the Context of Neighborhood Change in Los Angeles" (PhD diss., University of Minnesota, 2012).

Source Texts by the Author

Texts referred to and drawn most heavily upon are numbered by chapter.
Translations, reprints, and major revisions are listed below the numbered references.

CHAPTER 1

1A (with Rebecca Morales and Goetz Wolff): "Urban Restructuring: An Analysis of Social and Spatial Change in Los Angeles," *Economic Geography* 59 (1983): 195–230.

French translation: "La Restructuration de la région de Los Angeles: Vers une rethéorisation de l'urbain," trans. B. Planque, *Revue d'Economie Régionale et Urbaine* 4 (1985): 727–40.

New version (with Allan Heskin and Marco Cenzatti): "Los Angeles nel caleidoscopio della restrutturazione," *Urbanistica* 80 (1985): 55–60; and "Los Angeles through the Kaleidoscope of Urban Restructuring" (Los Angeles: Graduate School of Architecture and Urban Planning, UCLA, Special Publication, 1984).

Reprint: "Industrial Restructuring: An Analysis of Social and Spatial Change in Los Angeles," in *International Capitalism and Industrial Restructuring*, ed. R. Peet (London: Allen and Unwin, 1987).

Reprint: "Urban Restructuring in Los Angeles," in *Atop the Urban Hierarchy*, ed. Robert Beauregard (Totowa, NJ: Rowman and Littlefield, 1988).

Reprint: "Urban Restructuring: An Analysis of Social and Spatial Change in Los Angeles" (with Rebecca Morales and Goetz Wolff), in *Regional Dynamics*, ed. Kingsley E. Haynes et al., Modern Classics in Regional Science Series (Cheltenham: Edward Elgar Publishing, 1997).

1B: "It All Comes Together in Los Angeles," in *Postmodern Geographies: The Reassertion of Space in Critical Social Theory* (London: Verso, 1989), 190–221.

German translation: "In L.A. kommt alles zusammen—Die Dekonstruktion und Rekonstitution von Modernität," trans. A. Schroeder and H.-P. Rodenberg, in *Die neue Metropole: Los Angeles-London,* ed. Bernd-Peter Lange and Hans-Peter Rodenberg (Hamburg and Berlin: Argument Verlag, 1994), 7–32

1C: "Economic Restructuring and the Internationalization of the Los Angeles Region," in *The Capitalist City,* ed. M. P. Smith and J. Feagin (Oxford: Basil Blackwell, 1987), 178–98.

German translation: "Ökonomische Restrukturierung und Internationalisierung der Region Los Angeles," in *Das neue Gesicht der Städte,* ed. Renate Borst, Stefan Krätke, Margit Mayer, Roland Roth, and Fritz Schmoll (Basel, Boston, and Berlin: Birkhäuser Verlag, 1990), 170–87.

Reprint: Selections from "Economic Restructuring and the Internationalization of the Los Angeles Region" (1987), in *Human Societies: A Reader,* ed. Anthony Giddens (Cambridge: Polity Press, 1992), 301–5.

CHAPTER 2

2A (with Allen Scott): Editorial essay, "Los Angeles: Capital of the Late Twentieth Century," *Environment and Planning D: Society and Space* 4 (1986): 249–54.

2B: "Taking Los Angeles Apart: Some Fragments of a Critical Human Geography," *Environment and Planning D: Society and Space* 4 (1986): 255–72.

2C: "Taking Los Angeles Apart: Towards a Postmodern Geography," in *Postmodern Geographies: The Reassertion of Space in Critical Social Theory* (London: Verso, 1989), 222–48.

Reprint (with some additional material): "Taking Los Angeles Apart: Towards a Postmodern Geography," in *The Post-Modern Reader,* ed. Christopher Jencks (New York: St. Martin's Press/London: Academy Editions, 1992), 277–98.

German translation: "Los Angeles, eine nach aussen gekehrte Stadt: Die Entwicklung der postmodern Metropole in den USA," in *Rom-Madrid-Athen: Die neue Rolle der städtischen Peripherie,* ed. V. Kreibich, B. Krella, U. von Petz, P. Potz, Dortmunder Beiträge zur Raumplanung 62 (Dortmund: IRPUD, 1993), 213–28.

"Postmodern Geographies: Taking Los Angeles Apart" (adapted from chapters 1 and 9 of *Postmodern Geographies*), in *Now/Here: Space, Time and Modernity,* ed. R. Friedland and D. Boden (Berkeley and Los Angeles: University of California Press, 1994), 127–62.

Portuguese translation: "O desenvolvimento metropolitano pós-moderno nos E.U.A.: Virando Los Angeles pelo avesso," in *Territorio: Globalização e Fragmentação,* ed. M. Santos, M. A. de Souza, and M. L. Silveira (São Paulo: Editora Hucitec, 1994), 154–68.

Reprint: "Taking Los Angeles Apart: Towards a Postmodern Geography," in *The Cities Reader,* ed. R. T. Legates and F. Stout, 2d ed. (London and New York: Routledge, 1999), 180–92. Also in subsequent editions.

2D: "Heterotopologies: A Remembrance of Other Spaces in the Citadel-LA," *Strategies: A Journal of Theory, Culture and Politics* 3 (1990): 6–39.

CHAPTER 3

3A: "Inside Exopolis: Scenes From Orange County," in *Variations on a Theme Park: The New American City and the End of Public Space,* ed. M. Sorkin (New York: Hill and Wang, 1992), 94–122.

3B: "Inside Exopolis: Everyday Life in the Postmodern World," in *Thirdspace: Journeys to Los Angeles and Other Real-and-Imagined Places* (Oxford: Blackwell, 1996), 237–79.

CHAPTER 4

4A: "The Stimulus of a Little Confusion: A Contemporary Comparison of Amsterdam and Los Angeles," in *Texts of a Special Lecture* (Amsterdam: Centrum voor Grootstedilijyk Onderzoek [Center for Metropolitan Studies], 1991.

Reprint: "The Stimulus of a Little Confusion: A Contemporary Comparison of Amsterdam and Los Angeles," in *After Modernism: Global Restructuring and the Changing Boundaries of City Life,* ed. M. P. Smith (New Brunswick, NJ, and London: Transaction Publishers, 1992), 17–38.

Reprint: "The Stimulus of a Little Confusion: A Contemporary Comparison of Amsterdam and Los Angeles," in *Understanding Amsterdam: Essays on Economic Vitality, City Life, and Urban Form,* ed. L. Deben, W. Heinemejer, and D. van de Vaart (Amsterdam: Het Spinhuis, 1993), 69–91.

Reprint: "The Stimulus of a Little Confusion," in *Strangely Familiar: Narratives of Architecture in the City,* ed. I. Borden, J. Kerr, A. Pivaro, and J. Rendell (London and New York: Routledge, 1996), 27–31. Excerpts with new photographs.

German translation: "Anregung für ein wenig Verwirrung: Ein zeitgenössischer Vergleich von Amsterdam und Los Angeles," in *Capitales Fatales:*

Urbanisierung und Politik in den Finanzmetropolen Frankfurt und Zürich, ed. H. Hitz, R. Keil, U. Lehrer, K. Ronneberger, C. Schmid, and R. Wolff (Zürich: Rotpunk, 1995), 160–75.

Reprint: "On Spuistraat: The Contested Streetscape in Amsterdam," in *The Unknown City: Contesting Architecture and Social Space,* ed. Iain Borden, Joe Kerr, and Jane Rendell (Cambridge, MA, and London: MIT Press, 2001), 280–95. With added illustrations.

New version: "The Centrum Reminds Me . . .," in *Cultural Heritage and the Future of the Historic Inner City of Amsterdam,* ed. Leon Deben, Willem Salet, and Marie-Therese van Thoor (Amsterdam: Aksant Academic Publishers, 2004), 23–34.

Reprint: "The Stimulus of a Little Confusion: A Contemporary Comparison of Amsterdam and Los Angeles" in *Global Cities Reader,* ed. Neil Brenner and Roger Keil (London and New York: Routledge, 2006), 179–86.

4B: "Poles Apart: New York and Los Angeles," in *Dual City: The Restructuring of New York,* ed. J. Mollenkopf and M. Castells (New York: Russell Sage Foundation, 1991), 361–76.

4C: "Sprawl Is No Longer What It Used to Be," in *Post Ex Sub Dis: Urban Fragmentations and Constructions,* ed. Ghent Urban Studies Team (GUST) (Rotterdam: 010 Publishers, 2002), 76–88.

CHAPTER 5

5A: "Postmodern Urbanization: The Six Restructurings of Los Angeles," in *Postmodern Cities and Spaces,* ed. Sophie Watson and Kathy Gibson (Oxford and Cambridge, MA: Blackwell, 1995), 125–37.

German translation: "Postmoderne Urbanisierung," in *Mythos Metropole,* ed. G. Fuchs, B. Moltman, and W. Prigge (Frankfurt: Suhrkamp Verlage, 1995), 143–64.

5B: "Los Angeles 1965–1992: From Crises-Generated Restructuring to Restructuring-Generated Crises," in *The City: Los Angeles and Urban Theory at the End of the Twentieth Century,* ed. Allen Scott and Edward Soja (Berkeley and Los Angeles: University of California Press, 1996).

Reprint: "Los Angeles 1965–1992: From Crisis-Generated Restructuring to Restructuring-Generated Crisis," in *Imported: A Reading Seminar,* ed. Rainer Ganahl (New York: Semiotext(e), 1998), 281–316.

Italian translation with photos: "Los Angeles as a Postmodern Metropolis," in *Los Angeles,* ed. Lorenzo Spagnoli (Rome: Laterza, 1997), 45–61.

Also of interest: Edward Soja and Allen Scott, "Introduction to Los Angeles: Metropolis and Region," in *The City: Los Angeles and Urban Theory at the End of the Twentieth Century,* ed. Allen Scott and Edward Soja (Berkeley and Los Angeles: University of California Press, 1996), 1–21.

5C: "Six Discourses on the Postmetropolis," in *Imagining Cities,* ed. Sallie Westwood and John Williams (London and New York: Routledge, 1997), 19–30.

Reprint with Spanish translation: "Six Discourses on the Postmetropolis," *Cartas Urbanas* 5 (April 1999): 6–20.

5D: "Six Discourses on the Postmetropolis," part 2, in *Postmetropolis: Critical Studies of Cities and Regions* (Oxford: Blackwell, 2000), 145–348.

Also of interest: "Exploring the Postmetropolis" and "Afterword," in *Postmodern Geographical Practice,* ed. Claudio Minca (Oxford: Blackwell Publishers, 2001).

New version: "Fractal Los Angeles: The Restructured Geographies of the Postmetropolis," in *Stadt und Region: Dynamik von Lebenwelten,* ed. Alois Mayr, Manfred Meurer, and Joachim Vogt (Leipzig, 2001), 255–60.

Reprint: "Six Discourses on the Postmetropolis," in *The Blackwell City Reader,* ed. Gary Bridge and Sophie Watson (Oxford and Malden, MA: Blackwell Publishing, 2002), 188–96.

Also of interest: "Urban Tensions: Globalization, Economic Restructuring, and the Postmetropolitan Transition," in *Global Tensions: Challenges and Opportunities in the World Economy,* ed. Lourdes Beneria and Savitri Bisnath (New York and London: Routledge, 2003), 275–90.

Spanish tranlsation: "Seis discursos sobre la postmetropolis," in *Lo urbano en 20 autores contemporáneos,* ed. Angel Martín Ramos (Barcelona: Edicions UPC, 2004), 91–98.

Reprint: "Six Discourses on the Postmetropolis," excerpts in *The Blackwell City Reader,* ed. Gary Bridge and Sophie Watson, 2d ed. (Oxford and Chichester: Wiley-Blackwell, 2010), 374–81.

Dutch translation: "Digitale gemeenschappen: Simcities en de hyperrealiteit van het dagelijkse leven," *Andere Sinema* (Antwerp) 148 (Nov.–Dec. 1998): 17–28 (Dutch translation, by Tom Paulus, of "Digital Communities: Simcities and the Hyperreality of Everyday Life," paper presented and distributed online at Symposium on Transarchitectures: Visions of Digital Community, Getty Research Institute, Getty Center, Los Angeles, June 1998, available at www.members.labridge.com/lacn/trans /soja2.html).

5E: "Postmetropolitan Psychasthenia: A Spatioanalysis," in *Urban Politics Now: Re-Imagining Democracy in the Neoliberal City*, ed. BAVO (Rotterdam: NAi Publishers, 2007), 78–93.

CHAPTER 6

6A: *Postmodern Geographies: The Reassertion of Space in Critical Social Theory* (London: Verso, 1989).

6B: *Thirdspace: Journeys to Los Angeles and Other Real-and-Imagined Places* (Oxford: Blackwell, 1996).

German translation (selections): "Thirdspace: Die Erweiterung des geographischen Blicks," in *Kulturgeographie: aktuelle Ansätze und Entwicklungen,* ed. Hans Gebhardt, Paul Reuber, and Gunter Wolkesdorfer (Berlin and Heidelberg: Spektrum Akademische Verlag, 2003), 269–88.

Also of interest: "Thirdspace: Towards a New Consciousness of Space and Spatiality," in *Communicating in the Third Space,* ed. Karen Ilkas and Gerhard Wagner (New York and London: Routledge, 2009), 49–61.

6C: *Postmetropolis: Critical Studies of Cities and Regions* (Oxford: Blackwell, 2000).

Also of interest: "Writing the City Spatially," in *City* 7, no. 3 (November 2003): 269–80.

Also of interest: "Borders Unbound: Globalization, Regionalism, and the Postmetropolitan Transition," in *B/ordering Space,* ed. Olivier Kramsch, Henk van Houtum, and Wolfgang Zierhofer (Aldershot: Ashgate, 2005), 33–46.

Also of interest: "Vom 'Zeitgeist' zum 'Raumgeist': New Twists on the Spatial Turn," in *Spatial Turn: Das Raumparadigma in den Kultur- und Sozialwissenschaften,* ed. Jörg Döring and Tristan Thielemann (Bielefeld: Transcript Verlag, 2008), 241–62.

Also of interest: "Taking Space Personally," in *The Spatial Turn: Interdisciplinary Perspectives,* ed. Barney Warf and Santa Arias (New York and London: Routledge, 2008), 11–34.

Also of interest: "Resistance after the Spatial Turn," in *What Is Radical Politics Today?,* ed. Jonathan Pugh (Basingstoke: Palgrave Macmillan, 2009), 69–74.

6D: "The Socio-Spatial Dialectic," *Annals of the Association of American Geographers* 70 (1980): 207–25.

French translation: *Notes de recherche,* Centre d'Economie Régionale, Aix-en-Provence, 1982.

Japanese translation: "The Socio-Spatial Dialectic," in *Horizons in Socio-Spatial Studies: Reading Neo-Classics in Human Geography,* ed. Masahiro Kato, Toshio Mizuuchi et al. (Osaka City University, 1996), 46–64.

Reprint: "The Socio-Spatial Dialectic," in *Reading Human Geography,* ed. Trevor Barnes and Derek Gregory (London: Arnold, 1997), 244–55.

6E (with Miguel Kanai): "The Urbanization of the World," in *The Endless City,* ed. Ricky Burdett and Dayan Sudjic (New York and London: Phaidon, 2008), 54–69.

CHAPTER 7

7A: "Regional Urbanization and the End of the Metropolis Era," in *The New Blackwell Companion to the City,* ed. Gary Bridge and Sophie Watson (Oxford and Chichester: Wiley-Blackwell, 2011), 679–89.

Also of interest: (with Allen J. Scott, John Agnew, and Michael Storper), "Global City-Regions," in *Global City-Regions: Trends, Theory, Policy,* ed. A. J. Scott (Oxford and New York: Oxford University Press, 2001), 11–30.

Also of interest: "Regional Planning and Development Theories," in *International Encyclopedia of Human Geography,* ed. Rob Kitchin and Nigel Thrift (New York: Elsevier, 2009), 259–70.

7B: "From Metropolitan to Regional Urbanization," in *Companion to Urban Design,* ed. Tridip Banerjee and Anastasia Loukaitou-Sideris (London and New York: Routledge, 2011), 552–61.

Interview: Renia Ehrenfurt, "The New Regionalism: A Conversation with Edward Soja," *Critical Planning* 9 (Summer 2002): 5–12.

Pamphlet: "Regional Urbanization and the Future of Megacities," in *Towards the Megacities Solution,* ed. M. Visser, T. Jengenell, S. S. Stedebouw, and Architectural Management (Amsterdam: Megacities Foundation, 2008).

"Regional Urbanization and the Future of Megacities" (extended version), in *Megacities: Exploring a Sustainable Future,* ed. S. Buijs, W. Tan, and D. Tunas (Rotterdam: OIO Publishers, 2010), 56–75.

Reprint: "Regional Urbanization and the End of the Metropolis Era," in *Global Visions: Risks and Opportunities for the Urban Planet,* ed. A. Gonzalez Brun, B. L. Low, J. Rosemann, and J. Widodo (Singapore: Centre for Advanced Studies in Architecture, National University of Singapore/International Forum on Urbanism, 2011).

CHAPTER 8

8A: *Seeking Spatial Justice* (Minneapolis: University of Minnesota Press, 2010).

"Lessons in Spatial Justice," *hunch* 1 [Berlage Institute, inaugural issue] (1999): 98–107.

"The City and Spatial Justice," *Justice Spatial/Spatial Justice* 1 (2009): 31–38.

"Spatializing the Urban, Part I," *City* 14, no. 6 (2010): 629–35. Responses to Forum on Seeking Spatial Justice, Part I, composed of the following commentaries, with Soja response, pp. 625–35.

> Andrea Gibbons and Celine Kuklowsky, "Introduction," 597–600.
> Martin Woessner, "A New Ontology for the Era of the New Economy: On Edward W. Soja's *Seeking Spatial Justice,*" 601–3.
> David Cunningham, "Rights, Politics, and Strategy: A Response to *Seeking Spatial Justice,*" 604–6.
> Kurt Iveson, *Seeking Spatial Justice:* Some Reflections from Sydney, 607–11.
> Jon Liss, "In Virginia . . . Desperately *Seeking Spatial Justice,*" 612–15.
> Jane Wills, "Academic Agents for Change," 616–18.
> Andrea Gibbons, "Bridging Theory and Practice," 619–21.
> Andrew Davey, "Confronting the Geographies of Enmity," 622–24.

"Spatializing the Urban, Part II," *City* 15, no. 1 (2011): 96–102. Responses to Forum on Seeking Spatial Justice, Part II, composed of the following commentaries, with Soja response. pp. 87–102.

> Andrea Gibbons, "Introduction," 64–65.
> Nuria Benach, "The Spatial Turn in Action," 66–68.
> Abel Albet, "Spatial Justice: Where/When It All Comes Together," 69–72.
> Marcello Lopes de Souza, "The Words and the Things," 73–77.
> Peter Hall, "Great Title, Wrong Book," 78–80.
> Eduardo Menieta, "The Spatial Metaphorics of Justice: On Edward W. Soja," 81–84.
> Fran Tonkiss, "Spatial Causes, Social Effects: A Response to Soja," 85–86.
> Gilda Haas, "Mapping (In)justice," 87–95.

Complementary Video Sources

The video sources here are meant to provide a visual accompaniment to the text. Nearly all can be viewed free online; some are available for purchase as DVDs.

CHAPTER 2

1. "The Postmodern City—Bonaventure Hotel," interview with Edward Soja, extracted from BBC–Open University Sociology Department video "Los Angeles: City of the Future." Available on YouTube.
2. "Los Angeles: City of the Future," produced by the BBC for the Open University course on urban sociology, 1990. Available in four parts on YouTube.

CHAPTER 3

3. VH1 TV News Special: *Orange County: America's Hip Factory,* written by Mike Goudreau, produced by Lucas Traub, first appeared March 12, 2002, available online with subscription, www.imdb.com/title/tt0838207/ combined.

CHAPTER 8

4. *Bread and Roses,* 2000, directed by Ken Loach, feature film in English and Spanish. Free online at www.ovguide.com/bread-and-roses-9202a8c 0400064. Available on DVD through Lionsgate (US).

5. *Bus Riders Union,* 2000, a film by director and cinematographer Haskell Wexler. Free online at www.thestrategycenter.org/.../nlov-5-bus-riders-union-documentary. DVD available through IMDbPro and the Labor/Community Strategy Center.

6. *Wal-Mart: The High Cost of Low Price* (2005), a documentary film produced and directed by Robert Greenwald, available on YouTube.

INDEX

Italic page references indicate illustrations.

Mear One, ix, *259, 260*, 260–261, *262*
megacity regions. *See* megaregions
megaregions, 119, 181–182, 189, 211–213, 217n
Mellon Foundation, x
metroburbia, 23, 198, 217n
metropolarities, 158–162
metropolis era, 53, 54
metropolis unbound, 9, 186
metropolitan model, 54
Metropolitan Transit Authority (MTA), 226–234
Miami, 30, 198, 241–242
Milkman, Ruth, 56n
Mission Viejo, 99–100, 152, *277 (video 2)*
Molecule Man. See Borofsky, Jonathan
Mollenkopf, John, 122–123, 125, 138n
Monterey Park, 78–79, 148, 169n
Montreal, ix, x, 241, 246n
Moore, Charles, 94
Morales, Rebecca, ix, 33, 56n
Moreno Valley, 64, 72, 152–153, 169n
Muller, Peter, 199
muralists, 258–263

neoliberalism, 41
New Economy, 17, 51–55, 119, 124, 143–145, 163–164, 184, 195, 206, 229, 247–248, 250, 264
New Left Review, 16, 81
New Regionalism, 141–146, 189–190, 215
New World. See Otterness, Tom
New York City, 3, 4, 7, 9, 10, 11, 20–21, 28, 32, 42, 43, 47, 133, 160, 161, 162, 167n, 184, 196, 200, 252; compared with LA, 122–127, 134, 146, 162, 209, 210, 217n, 231; density in, 11, 21, 25n, 29, 127–133, 199, 217n
Nixon, Richard, 63; and Nixon Library, 92–93
Northwestern University, 33
Norton Air Force Base, 65 83n, 154

Oakland, 10, 144, 188, 254, 263
Occupy movement, 23, 162, 247–266; chalktivists, 254, 263; horizontality, 250–251, 265; Occupy LA and OC, 23, 252–266; Occupy Wall Street, 247, 249–252

off-the-edge cities, 64, 149–155
Orange County, 2, 9, 18, 19, 32, 44, 63, 71, 85–110, 144, 146, 151, 152, 153, 169n, 200, 201, 203, *277 (video 2)*; bankruptcy, 106–107, 169n; Occupy, 252–266; Performing Arts Center, 98–99; punk music in, 90, *277 (video 3)*
Osaka, 187, 209–210, 218n; Kansai region, 212
Otterness, Tom, 74, *77*, 84n
outer cities. *See* regional urbanization

Palmdale, 72, 146, 151, 153–154
Palos Verdes Estates, 156
Palos Verdes Peninsula, 47, 155–158, 207
Parker, Dorothy, 7
Pastor, Manuel, Jr., 192n
Pearl River Delta (China), 182, 212
Pereira, William, 93–94
peripheral urbanization. *See* regional urbanization
periurbanisation, 200–201
Philadelphia, 9
Phoenix, 17, 198, 212, 237
Pico-Union, 79
Plains of Id, 15,
plant closings, *46*
Point Mugu Naval Air Missile Center, 66
Port Hueneme Naval Construction Battalion Center, 66
Port of Los Angeles–Long Beach, 7, 34, 118–119, 155, 230
post-Fordism, 21, 32
postindustrialism, 17, 185; misleading in LA, 31, 32, 91, 124
Postmetropolis, 141, 167n, 176, 178–179
postmetropolis. *See* postmetropolitan transition
postmetropolitan transition, 140–170, 197
postmodern critical perspective, 18, 140, 167n
Postmodern Geographies, ix, 44, 174–176, 218n
postmodern urbanization, 20, 22, 61–62, 68–71, 79–83, 85–110, 197
Preziosi, Donald, 83
Prison, Industrial Complex, 73
privately owned public space (POPS), 251

Thatcher, Margaret, 41, 68, 222
Thirdspace, ix, 176–178
Tokyo, 119, 212
tourist industry, 235
Toy Town, 76, 150–151
trading blocs, 183
Turner, Eugene, ix, *5, 6, 8, 10,* 168n

UCLA Institute for Industrial Research, 56n, 235
UCLA Urban Planning Department, 16, 30, 33, 57n, 192n, 235, 245n
undocumented immigrants, 47
unionization, 44, 220–240
United Farm Workers, 35, 220–221
urbanization of suburbia, 7, 29, 72, 91, 186–188, 206–208, 215–216. *See also* regional urbanization
urbanization of the world, 180–183, 214
urbanized area, 10, 198–199
urban panopticon, 73
urban restructuring, 6–7, 17, 18, 20–21, 27–58, 119, 195–197, 216n; Soja, Morales, and Wolff (1983) on, 33–51; as spatial fix, 51–55
urban spatial causality, 247–248

Vanity of the BonFIRES, 20, 125
Variations on a Theme Park, 86
Venice, 7
Ventura County, 10, 66, 71, 151, 152

Vernon, 78
view from above, versus from below, 121–122

Wallerstein, Immanuel, 142
Wall Street, 20, 119, 124, 126, 260. *See also under* Occupy movement
Wal-Mart, 23, 57n; Battle for Inglewood, 238–240, *278 (video 6)*
Walt Disney Concert Hall, 74
War of 1846–48, 1, 32, 87
Washington, D.C., 4, 9, 10, 73, 126, 200
Watts, 7, 57n, 79, 203; riots, 5, 16, 27, 42, 55, 57n, 147, 179, 195
Webber, Melvin, 29, 56n
Westwood, 49
Whiteson, Leon, 93–94
Wilson, William Julius, 56n, 160, 169n
Wolfe, Tom, 125
Wolff, Goetz, ix, 33–34, 235n
Wong, Kent, 56n, 235
working poor, 18, 31, 196, 231–232, 247
World Charter of the Rights to the City, 242–244, 246n

Yorba Linda, 92–93
Young, Iris Marion, 244, 246n
yuppies, 159

Zardini, Mirko, x
Zuccotti Park, 249, 251